Commoditization and the Strategic Response

To Sally, Thomas and Libby – lights of my life

Commoditization and the Strategic Response

ANDREW HOLMES

GOWER

Published by
Gower Publishing Limited
Gower House
Croft Road
Aldershot
Hampshire
GU11 3HR
England

Gower Publishing Company
Suite 420
101 Cherry Street
Burlington
VT 05401-4405
USA

Andrew Holmes has asserted his moral right under the Copyright, Designs and Patents Act, 1988, to be identified as the author of this work.

British Library Cataloguing in Publication Data
Holmes, Andrew
    Commoditization and the strategic response
    1. Creative ability in business 2. Product management
    I. Title
    658.4'063

    ISBN-13: 9780566087431

Library of Congress Cataloguing-in-Publication Data
Holmes, Andrew, 1965–
    Commoditization and the strategic response / by Andrew Holmes.
        p. cm.
    Includes bibliographical references and index.
    ISBN 978-0-566-08743-1
    1. Commercial products. 2. Consumption (Economics) 3. Management. I. Title.
    HF1040.7.H65 2008
    338'.02--dc22

                                                                    2007034353

Printed and bound in Great Britain by TJ International Ltd, Padstow, Cornwall.

Contents

List of Figures

List of Tables

Acknowledgements

Capturing the essence of what commoditization means for businesses and individuals has not been simple and would not have been possible without the input, advice and help of a wide range of people including academics, business leaders and opinion makers. I would like to thank the following people who gave their opinions freely during the course of writing this book: Jonathan Norman at Gower who received the idea with real enthusiasm; David Lindop of PricewaterhouseCoopers who shared some of his experiences of commoditization; Richard Burton of Infinite Ideas who took a keen interest in the book as it emerged, reading the manuscript and providing valuable feedback; Caroline Lucas MEP who sent me some useful papers regarding the EU and the IT industry; Fiona Czerniawska of the Management Consultancy Association who gave me plenty to think about in the early conception of the idea and took the trouble to read the near completed manuscript; Tom Schember and Tom Christopoul of Global Resources Professionals who shared their views and perceptions of what commoditization means and how to respond; Richard Donkin of the *Financial Times* who was kind enough to include my views in one of his columns; Graham Guest of the CPD Foundation, who recognized the significance of commoditization on Continuing Professional Development; Dale Reeson of National Express Corporation, who was willing to share her personal insights on how commoditization affects major businesses; Nick Birks of HM Revenue and Customs, who not only provided me with the opportunity to discuss how commoditization impacts the tax base with the HMRC Board, but provided some invaluable input into the book, and Professor David Ashton of Cardiff Business School who confirmed my suspicions about the commoditization of white collar work and pointed me in the direction of his research on Global Corporate Strategy and the Future of Skills.

And, lastly, I would like to thank Sally, Tom and Libby who always give me time to write amongst our busy schedule of work, domesticity, homework and timeout. It can be difficult to drag me away from my desk at times, especially when deadlines are looming, so I just hope that I give them enough time too. Rest assured they tell me when I don't!

Using This Book

Like most books, this one is designed to be read from start to finish and guides you through the process of commoditization, its impacts and how best to respond. However, if you are like most readers, you may wish to only focus on those parts which you feel are the most relevant to you or your organization. So in order to help you determine which chapters to focus on, I offer you the following suggestions:

- If you are primarily interested in understanding the underlying dynamics of commoditization and how it impacts industries and white collar work, then I would recommend that you focus on Part I, but do read Chapter 1 first as this sets the scene.
- If you are attempting to navigate the impacts of commoditization on organizations and are concerned with building an effective response, the best place to start is Chapter 3 (again having read Chapter 1 beforehand). Once you have read Chapter 3, you can then move onto Chapter 6 which will give you a clear indication of the impacts before moving onto Chapter 8 which addresses some of the strategic responses you may wish to consider and Chapter 9 which illustrates how other organizations have chosen to respond.
- If you are mainly concerned about how commoditization could affect you and your working life, I would direct you to Chapter 5 followed by Chapter 7 and then Chapter 10. If you are feeling particularly brave then I would also read Chapter 11, which will give you an idea of where the commoditization of work could lead.

However you decide to navigate your way through the book, I hope you will find it thought provoking and challenging and more importantly an incentive to both review how commoditization could be affecting you now (or may do in the future) and to develop an effective response.

Also by Andrew Holmes

Business

Failsafe IS Project Delivery

Smart Things to Know About Technology Management

The IT Value Stack – A Boardroom Guide to IT Leadership (contributor)

The Chameleon Consultant: Culturally Intelligent Consulting

Cultural Intelligence – An Introduction (contributor)

ExpressExec Risk Management

Smart Things to Know About Risk Management

ExpressExec Lifelong Learning

Smart Things to Know About Lifelong Learning

Non-fiction

Pass Your Exams: Study Skills for Success

How Much?! A Miscellany of Money Madness

Humour

Pains on Trains: A Commuter's Guide to the 50 Most Irritating Travel Companions

Pains in the Office: 50 People You Absolutely, Definitely Must Avoid at Work

Pains in Public: The 50 People Most Likely to Drive You Completely Nuts

Preface

The business environment is constantly evolving as companies of every shape and size attempt to capture market share, expand their operations by seeking out new opportunities and find new ways to add value for their customers and shareholders. This process does not work in a vacuum as each and every one of them has to survive in a competitive environment which is becoming more globalized and increasingly cut-throat. Globalization, of course, has its supporters and its detractors, but whatever point of view you may hold, the stark reality of trying to compete in a market that is forever seeking out products and services at the lowest price is one that an increasing number of companies have to contend with. But it is not just the raw costs of products and services that matter, it's also the expertise and experience that go into creating and delivering them. With rising levels of education and particularly the influx of highly qualified graduates from China and India the opportunity to achieve elevated levels of product and service quality at lower cost is fast becoming a reality. Whereas the West struggles to entice its youth into pursuing engineering and science based degrees, India and China are finding it much easier. This helps to create an environment in which labour can be exported to countries where it is both cheaper and smarter; a critical wake-up call for every organization and white-collar worker, not just those at the bottom of the service economy.

But it's not just about labour; the choices we all have to purchase goods and services from wherever we want, often at the touch of a button, increases the competitive edge required to survive. With the world as the shop window, the opportunity to seek out more responsive product and service providers at an acceptable price is forcing businesses to remove unnecessary costs from their supply chains, review their core capabilities and offload activities which can be executed at a lower cost. We are now at the beginning of a wave of commoditization which few of us are prepared for. The parallel with the downsizing of white-collar workers in the 1990s is profound. Assuming commoditization can only happen to the lower educated, or the lesser skilled is as naïve as it was in the 1990s, when many middle managers couldn't believe that it was they who were in the firing line.

Commoditization in its various forms has always been with us. We have witnessed the commoditization of the railways, telecommunications and more recently information technology and to a significant extent, the airline industry, but now it's affecting a broader spectrum of businesses and especially white-collar work. White-collar work is increasingly becoming a commodity, and businesses which have been used to outsourcing and offshoring their manufacturing activities are now shifting white-collar work to locations where the workforce can produce high quality outputs for a fraction of the price. At the same time, companies are waking up to the power of the emerging economies of the East, such as India and China, who are fast catching up and will soon be overtaking the Western economies which have dominated the global economy for the last 250 years.

This book is about the nature of commoditization; how it evolves, how it affects industries, companies and workers and how to respond to it. In it I hope to widen your understanding of what commoditization means for organizations and individuals alike and through this provide the basis for charting a course that either seeks to exploit it or one which attempts to avoid it. Drawing on a wide variety of sources, I will attempt to describe the impacts, issues, risks and opportunities associated with the commoditized zone. I do not profess to have all the answers, as opinions and courses of actions are always down to the individual. What I do hope is that you will find this interesting and thought provoking and a useful guide as you navigate your own and your company's future in an increasingly complex and competitive world. Commoditization is coming, and your response will determine whether or not you and the company you work for, or perhaps own, become commoditized in the process.

Andrew Holmes

1 *Commoditization – Coming to a Company Near You*

When everything is the same and supply is plentiful, said Greer, clients have too many choices and no basis on which to make the right choice. And when this happens, you're a commodity.[1]

Whilst on one of my many trips to Houston, I picked up a copy of the *Wall Street Journal* and came across a five-page advert from IBM. The advert itself was the usual combination of headline grabbing comments and grandiose statements which demonstrated IBM's leadership in the area of innovation. But it wasn't this that caught my eye; what did was a single word on one of the pages – commoditized. The advert was presenting the reader with the challenge of what made them special and, more importantly, how they could retain this unique position in light of the competition posed by the Internet. In particular, it asked whether or not it, whatever it was, could be commoditized. This was certainly the first time I had seen the word appear in an advert of this nature and it was significant in that it was specifically mentioned as a business issue. Digging a little deeper, I started to uncover other references to commoditization. An article in the *Harvard Business Review* discussed the coming commoditization of process; conversations with commentators on the management consultancy industry mentioned the commoditization of consulting activities and I even saw mention of the commoditization of the legal profession. With this and the many other flurries of commentaries, I started to wonder if this was the start of something significant. It was.

We have of course lived with commoditization for a long time and certainly if we look back over the last 200–300 years it should be clear to anyone that commoditization is a natural business process which started long ago on the production lines of the factories of Northern England, played its part in the broadening out of the rail and telecommunications industries and more recently has had a profound effect on both the information technology (IT) and airline industries. However, the significance of the *Wall Street Journal* advertisement and the many other commentaries and articles I read is down to two reasons. First, it is about how quickly commoditization is now sweeping across the corporate world, in sectors and functions which we had previously thought were safe from it. And second, it is the depth and breadth to which commoditization is now penetrating; no longer the preserve of the blue-collar worker it is beginning to spread into white-collar work that is usually considered immune to the negative impacts of commoditization, particularly as it requires the application of intellect, skill and expertise which, unlike blue-collar work, is generally harder to automate. Like so many processes that play out in the business world, it may have started quite slowly and in quite limited areas, but it is speeding up and extending its reach. The tipping point is upon us.

Shifting gear

Commoditization is no longer just about machinery, computers and plant. Nor is it about the odd industry or two. It is beginning to be about people, human capital, skills and expertise and it is spreading into those industries that have previously held up their margins and kept out the competition. Two obvious and quite simple examples spring to mind; the first is project management and the second is software development and maintenance.

About ten years ago, I was a project manager in a government agency working on various IT projects for the business. Being a project manager was special; there was some kudos attached to the title, as the skills, knowledge and expertise were quite limited and restricted to a relatively small number of specialists. Project managers could earn decent salaries and could expect to do so well into the future. But things have changed since then. Project managers, although still critical to the average corporation are more common, cost less, and the kudos attached to the title has diminished considerably. In fact most project managers prefer to be called programme managers these days because of the status that programme managers have over project managers. Why has this happened? There are a few reasons. First, the number of qualified project managers has increased significantly – no wonder when the demand for their skills has grown as organizational complexity and the need for effective change has increased. The basics of supply and demand have meant that project managers can now be hired more cheaply than in the past. Second, professional bodies, academics and practioners alike have strived to improve the quality and repeatability of the underlying processes of project management, thereby opening them up to the forces of commoditization. The introduction of detailed standards, processes and a proliferation of courses which train people to the same level all help to demystify the art of project management and lower the bar to entry. In essence it has allowed much of the tacit knowledge of experienced project managers to be distilled and codified so that it can become explicit and reusable. Finally, the increasing use of technology, aided and abetted by this codification, has reduced some of the toil and intellectual horse power required to execute the project management processes. Some argue that it releases the project manager to do more value-added work and concentrate on leadership and direction. Others believe that it has dumbed down the project manager, or has at least allowed the process of project management to be undertaken by someone who is less qualified, more junior and ultimately cheaper to employ.

A similar argument can be applied to software development and maintenance, which has also seen dramatic shifts in the profitability of the industry and the incomes of those employed within it. Back in the 1950s software development and IT in general were in their infancy. The sheer complexity and associated costs of building systems were major inhibitors to their use. However, as waves of innovation continued to yield major advances in technology, organizations started to harness IT to good effect to the point where it is now ubiquitous and according to some commentators at least, no longer matters. Over the intervening 50–60 years, the process of building and maintaining technology systems has been simplified and codified. And although there are still plenty of problems associated with building complex enterprise-wide applications, there are many examples of package-based solutions which are capable of addressing the needs of any business. As software systems became more widespread the number of people involved with the profession increased and while there were limited or no standards in place, those who were in software could command high salaries, especially if they happened to have knowledge of the latest technology, software language or operating system. Over time as standards were developed, methods for the creation of software systems were designed and promulgated and technologies were stabilised and became more reliable, the need for highly paid specialists reduced. The only blip on this otherwise smooth path towards commoditization was Year 2000 and the global panic that ensued, but the effects of this were short lived. Ironically, Year 2000 served to accelerate the commoditization of IT as it gave the Indian software companies the platform from which were able to take on a much broader role in the industry (see Chapter 4).

There are plenty of similarities to the changes we have witnessed in project management, but there are also at least four additional factors that have accelerated the commoditization of the software professional. The first is the increasingly held belief that IT no longer matters because it is so much part of the fabric of the average organization that it is no longer capable of generating strategic advantage. The second is the rise of highly educated software engineers further east and especially in India. This has allowed companies to develop systems to similar or higher levels of quality but at a fraction of the cost. Heinrich von Pierer of Siemens summed this up incredibly well when he said: 'For the same money it takes to hire 2000 German software developers, I can get 12 000 in China'.[2] This process is commonly known as labour arbitrage and is a subject we will come back to in Part I. The third is the dominance of a small number of software platforms and applications that have allowed organizations to standardize their use of IT and eliminate the need for bespoke systems. And, finally, the ongoing maintenance of software has been pushed out to lower cost providers because it is no longer perceived to be core to the business. The impact has been to depress the income of the software engineering professional and reduce the margins of those providing IT services, mainly through increased competition and the availability of cheap labour.

Simple examples perhaps but they begin to illustrate the forces and factors which are helping to bring commoditization onto the agenda of a wide range of organizations, both large and small. Of course, if it was just about the commoditization of certain types of resources, then maybe organizations wouldn't need to worry. But there are other things to consider which are also helping to drive commoditization deep into the heart of the corporation. Some of the factors which are bearing down include:

- The intellectual competition coming from Asia, and especially India and China who now produce some four million graduates every year. What makes this number even more daunting is the fact that between 30 and 50 per cent of these graduates are unemployed in their home countries, which leaves a vast number of intelligent workers to be mopped up by the global economy.
- Western economies are aging fast and have to adjust to the realities of longer working lives with a less productive workforce. This represents a major issue for employers, who have to deal with the problem of motivating middle aged employees who are feeling increasingly disaffected and rejected (both by their employers, who have failed to live up to the promise of lifetime employment which offered progression and challenging careers; and by the state itself, which is no longer capable of providing for them in their old age). This is something that a recent *Harvard Business Review* article termed middlescence.[2] The article claims that this is a major issue confronting large numbers of organizations and according to its authors, organizations which fail to deal with the issues that middlescence presents are sitting on a time-bomb that will continue to tick louder and louder as the baby boomers, on whom today's organizations were built, retire in droves. Given that 50 per cent of the working population can be considered middlescent, this is something that isn't going away. In another recent book, *The Living*

Dead,[3] David Bolchover outlines the sheer waste that exists in the typical organization; staff who are bored, unproductive, surfing the net and doing very little in the way of work all contribute to the sense of futility that many workers feel in their working lives. Ironically the lack of productivity, motivation and innovation that is associated with middlescence and the living dead provides a healthy breeding ground for the further commoditization of work. Organizations will have no choice but to seek out more productive, innovative and effective employees, principally overseas, in order to insulate themselves from the impact of a disaffected and unproductive workforce.

- Just as the number of smart graduates increases in the East, the number declines in the West. Fewer students are pursuing science and engineering degrees which is making it much harder for companies to innovate. There seems to be a misconception that creative degrees will be the engine of growth for the future economy; creative does not automatically equate to innovative. This makes it difficult for corporations to escape the commoditization trap and sets them on a path to obsolescence. There is also a noticeable dumbing down in education levels which is exacerbating the problem. But that is not the whole story, because the number of jobs which genuinely require graduate level capabilities is declining due to the impacts of technology and process driven change (see next points).

- Technology continues to disrupt the status quo, opening up new opportunities to competitors and facilitating the shift of labour to low cost economies. This is especially true of the Internet which is making it much easier to compete on cost, which increasingly matters in a globalized market. As well as opening up new competition, technology continues to eliminate high paying jobs as business processes are subsumed into enterprise-wide and package-based applications.

- Work continues to be codified and systematized in order to increase the efficiency of core business processes so that organizations can reduce their overheads and focus their capital on innovation and on maintaining or reducing the costs of their goods and services. Achieving a balance is not easy, but the majority of organizations will have little choice but to maintain a focus on cost containment in order to compete. When the balance is wrong it can set the organization onto a downward spiral of cost cutting and lower performance which can result in its ultimate failure. The fundamental problem with competing on cost is that there is always someone else who is willing to cut their costs even further than you.

- There is a growing imbalance between the number of graduates and the jobs that require graduate level skills and capabilities. In the past it was possible for graduates to walk into well paid jobs and expect a career which allowed them to apply their new found expertise and also offered them long-term progression. However, because the number of graduates has been growing faster than graduate level jobs there is now a glut of degree holders. According to the US Labor Department's Bureau of Labor statistics there are 2.6 graduate job seekers for every graduate level job.[4] Having people with graduate level kills working in jobs which do not require these skills fuels the turn-up and tune-off approach which they adopt to dealing with the 7–10 hours they spend in the office – the living dead as mentioned above. And although not in the middlescent zone just yet, it won't be long before a whole new tranche of demotivated employees enters that difficult mid-career period.

- A whole generation has been brought up in a world where goods and services can be obtained cheaply. Unless we are dealing with luxury goods, no one wants to pay more than they have to for the products and services they buy. The availability of cheap goods and services has been significantly enhanced by the Internet, where prices can be readily assessed and where it is possible for one product/service to be compared to another, with the lower cost provider usually winning out; and by the influx of well educated immigrants who are willing to work for lower incomes. However, there are downsides to this focus on cost. First, it forces organizations to concentrate on their costs and overheads to the detriment of everything else. Not a bad thing perhaps, but when this begins to affect peoples' incomes and employability it starts to create issues. Second, it makes it harder for them to innovate and build the products and services on which their future depends. And finally it starts them onto the race to the bottom, where the death spiral of cost reduction leaves the organization hollowed out and bereft of the talent it needs to survive in a commoditized world.

These and many other factors work together to create an environment in which the commoditization of products, services and people is possible. Commoditization may not be new for some, but for many it is a new reality that needs to be understood and responded to. There is little point in hoping that it will not happen to your business or to you as an individual because hope is not a strategy.

The commoditized zone

Commoditization is a very real threat to every organization and it is comparatively straightforward to identify the early warning signs, which include:

* increasing competition
* prevalence of me-too products and services
* a belief that all suppliers are fundamentally the same
* the decreasing desire on the customer's part to look at new options or features
* an increasing preference for customers to select on the basis of price and little else
* a reluctance for customers to pay for anything they consider unnecessary
* increasing pressures on margins.

Strong brands might help to insulate the organization from some of the worst impacts, but as we have seen in the past with organizations such as IBM, even the strongest and most dominant organizations come under threat from time to time. Even for those organizations which operate within a safe sector, such as energy for example, commoditization is still an issue they have to address, especially in terms of their non-core activities. At its extreme, commoditization leaves the leaders of corporations with a very simple and stark choice: do we allow ourselves to become commoditized and hence do our best to survive, or do we do our best to avoid it? Of course for some, the former may be the only choice open to them and for many it will probably be a mix of both. Naturally, there is a strategic choice involved as some organizations can be considered to be driving commoditization. In doing so they are gaining first mover advantage. Take easyEverything, which has a range of companies under its umbrella which are initiating a wave of commoditization in a number of sectors, most notably easyJet, but also cinemas, car hire, cruise liners and hotel accommodation. As the zone of commoditization continues to expand, organizations must do everything they can to ensure they can compete without either destroying the value they offer to their customers or going out of business because their underlying costs are just too high to compete with the leaner more efficient companies which are emerging from India, China, South America and Asia. These companies are able to lower their prices without destroying their business.

Of course commoditization is not just about organizations; it is also about people, especially because the success of any business depends on having staff with the right mix of skills, attitudes and behaviours. We have been hearing for a long time now about the war for talent and how this is going to affect the viability of corporations everywhere. More recently, and as some of the points made above allude to, we have had our attention diverted to the impacts of the impending loss of the Boomer Generation. All this is fine, but the war for talent only really affects a comparatively small number of employees with the experience and expertise which is currently in demand and the Boomer Generation won't all be retiring tomorrow; in fact the last boomers won't be hanging up their boots for another 18 years and perhaps longer given that so few of them have saved enough to retire with a comfortable income. If we look back only a few years the war for talent was a huge issue until downsizing hit the corporate world and the combined impacts of September 11 terrorist attacks and the bursting of the tech bubble ensured that the war for talent was placed firmly on the back burner. But the war for talent is not a static phenomenon because the skills required in the workplace continually shift. Whilst IT and especially knowledge of legacy applications was in high demand in the last few years of the last century, the emergence of highly skilled Indian IT experts has essentially commoditized IT to the point where staff and consultancies alike can no longer command the six figure salaries they got used to. No more war for talent here then – despite all the doom-laden projections claiming that there were not enough software engineers to cope with the anticipated demand for technology solutions. If you look across the wider economy, it seems that the war for talent is shifting to a war for low grade operational staff. Such people are either required to serve others in the increasingly service oriented economy or act as glorified machine minders. An extreme view perhaps, but the impact of technology is dumbing down the world of work to the point where the glut of graduates both here and the emerging economies will wind up in jobs which will barely test their skills. This hollowing out is something that Charles Handy discussed in his book the *Empty Raincoat* as far back as 1994.[5] His metaphor was the doughnut in which the essential core of the organization, which contained all of the necessary jobs and employees, is surrounded by an open and flexible space which is filled by contractors, consultants and, these days, outsourcers. Coming back to the war for talent, it is clear that Handy's model provides another lens through which this can be viewed. The talent war, as far as it exists, is raged at the core of the doughnut, not necessarily beyond it.

Commoditization is therefore a significant threat to the traditional career. The requirement to reinvent yourself many times over during your working life, long a mantra of the management guru, is becoming a reality for many. Reinvention may mean job changes for those seeking challenge and opportunity outside a single organization or it might mean adapting to the changing organizational setting for those who remain within a single company over their working life – although this is becoming increasingly unlikely. Whatever form it might take, it is a skill that few genuinely have. Ensuring that skills, expertise, attitudes and behaviours remain in synch with the local and global economies is vital for the future employee. With China and India churning out vast numbers of intelligent graduates who are willing to work (at least for the time being) for a fraction of what it costs to employ a Western equivalent, the current wave of outsourcing and offshoring is unlikely to slow anytime soon. What is significant is that the current and future waves of both outsourcing and offshoring will be focused on white-collar work. Manufacturing has been declining in the West for so long now that there is little left to offshore, which makes white-collar work the next and most obvious target.

But before organizations and individuals throw up their arms in despair, it is important to note that commoditization is not all bad and if approached in the right way the organization and the individual can succeed. What is clear is that there is a choice involved and that the choice is about responding to the threats and opportunities which commoditization represents. The purpose of this book therefore is to explore what commoditization means in practice. In doing so I will address the nature of commoditization, how it impacts organizations and individual employees and how to respond. The book is structured into four parts:

- Part I is designed to bring reader's up to a level of awareness at which they understand why commoditization is so significant. It discusses the nature of commodities and the process through which products, services and increasingly work become commoditized and draws upon both historical and recent examples of commoditization.
- Part II addresses the impacts of commoditization and focuses on how commoditization affects the competitiveness of organizations and how work, and white-collar work in particular, is changing as a result.
- Part III covers how organizations and individuals can respond to the opportunities and threats which commoditization presents. In addition it includes a number of case studies which illustrate how organizations are tackling the challenges of commoditization.
- Part IV explores the future of commoditization.

When it comes to organizational design and strategy I am a great fan of contingency theory, which suggests there is no single approach that can address all situations. The classic management trap of hoping for a simple answer has long been discredited, and there are plenty of failures to support this view – downsizing is but one example. The nature of commoditization is in itself complex and is likely to change over time, so there will always be the need to revisit your response and make adjustments as the competitive landscape changes. There is no quick fix. Armed with this book you will be able to assess the impact of commoditization on your organization and career and determine the response that is most appropriate for your current business and personal circumstances. The response may appear simple, but it requires a deep understanding of the drivers of commoditization and the impacts associated with your chosen course of action. One thing is clear though, and that is: doing nothing is not an option.

References

1   Freidman, T. (2005) *The World is Flat*, London: Penguin Allen Lane, p. 344.
2   Bosshart, D. (2007) *Cheap? The Real Cost of Living in a Low Price, Low Wage World*, London: Kogan Page, p. 50.
2   Morrison R., Erickson T., and Dychtwald, K. (2006) Managing Middlescence, *Harvard Business Review*, March, pp. 1–11.
3   Bolchover, S. (2005) *The Living Dead*, Chichester: Capstone.
4   Uchitelle, L. (2006) *The Disposable American*, New York: Alfred Knopf, p. 66.
5   Handy, C. (1994) *The Empty Raincoat*, London: Hutchinson, pp. 66–79.

Foundations: The Three Waves of Commoditization

It's called commoditization, and in the wake of the triple convergence, it is happening faster and faster across a whole range of industries. As more analog processes become digital, virtual, mobile, and personal, more and more jobs and functions are being standardized, digitized, and made both easy to manipulate and available to more players.[1]

If there's one thing that microeconomics has demonstrated, it is that it's hard to keep your profit margins high if you're in the wheat-growing business. Wheat is pretty much wheat, no matter where it grows, and it's pretty easy to grow unless the Dust Bowl is raging. That means that the supply of wheat rises quickly to meet demand, which, in turn, keeps a downward pressure on prices. Wheat, in other words, is the definition of a commodity, and the market for wheat – absent government intervention – is about as close to perfect competition as you can imagine.[2]

Between 1846 and 1852, the number of telegraph miles in the United States rose more than tenfold, from 2 000 to 23 000. Excess capacity caused prices to plummet, and most telegraph companies, mainly backed by small local investors, wilted. Within a decade, most lines ended up in the hands of a single consolidator, Western Union. The country wound up with a utility that businesses of all sizes could use. And the rapid spread of cheap telegraphy set other key industrial innovations in motion: the creation of the Associated Press and a quantum leap in news gathering, national markets in stock, commodities and business information.[3]

Commoditization should be at the front of every CEO's and employee's mind. But for this to be the case they have to understand its significance and how it has affected society, industries and individuals over the past 200–300 years, and the last five or so decades in particular. As Chapter 1 alluded to, commoditization is a process that is pervasive and continuous and the wave which is currently impacting organizations and employees is merely a continuation of what has gone before.

It is possible to place the current wave, let's call it the white-collar wave, into the context of the previous two waves; let's call them the commodity and industrial waves (see Figure PI.1). There are three aspects worth drawing out from the model:

1. Each wave builds on the last as opportunities for further commoditization begin to diminish in the existing category and new targets are identified within the next. In fact many of the technological and commercial breakthroughs we have today would not have been possible without commoditization. Its ability to exert a strong downward pressure on price allows otherwise costly innovations to take hold and thrive.

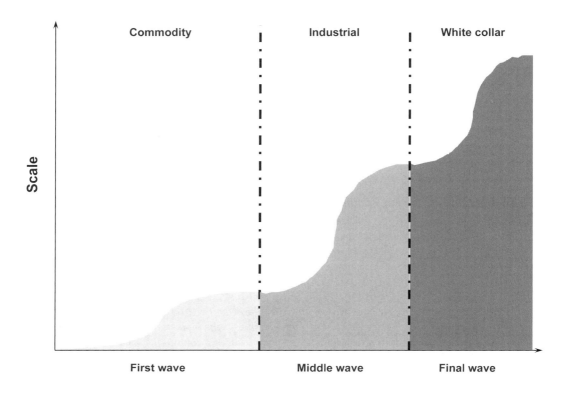

Figure PI.1 The three waves of commoditization

2. The scale and impact of commoditization increases with each wave as the previous wave sets the foundations for the next. Some of the basic commodities such as coal had to reach a level of commoditization before related industries such as rail could emerge and then, over time, become commoditized themselves. In a similar vein the latest wave of white-collar commoditization has its foundations in the industrial wave as well as the technological and economic changes that have been brought about through the Internet and globalization. This final wave of commoditization depends on the combination of stable and cheap technologies, standardized processes and the availability of a cheap and well educated labour force.
3. The speed of commoditization has increased with each successive wave.

    The purpose of Part I is to describe the three waves and through this identify the factors and underlying processes associated with commoditization.

*   Chapter 2 focuses on the commodities we are most familiar with such as cotton and coal and describes how these evolved from being obscure and limited in their application to being widespread, freely available and deeply embedded into society.
*   Chapter 3 reviews the industrial wave of commoditization and focuses on past and present commoditizations including the airline, telecommunications and information technology industries. These provide some critical insights into the importance of technology, government intervention, standards and competition in the commoditization process.

- Chapter 4 discusses how globalization and the emergence of the Internet have set the foundations for the commoditization of processes and of labour in general.
- Chapter 5 describes the process of white-collar commoditization and brings together the primary factors and market conditions that are facilitating the shift of work to the cheaper economies of the world.

Having addressed the nature of commoditization and established a common framework for its analysis, it is then possible to move on to Part II which addresses how commoditization is impacting organizations, the working environment and the nature of work itself. Armed with Part I and Part II, it is then possible to consider how best to respond to the challenges that commoditization presents. And that's what Part III is all about; the strategic response.

References

1   Friedman, T. (2005) *The World is Flat: A Brief History of the Globalized World in the 21st Century*, London: Allen Lane, p. 344.
2   Surowiecki, J. (1998) The commoditization conundrum, www.slate.com/id/2638, posted 30 January.
3   Gross, D. (2007) *Pop! Why Bubbles are Great for the Economy*, New York: HarperCollins, p. 14.

2 The First Wave: Commodities and Commoditization

Coal is a commodity utterly lacking in glamour. It is dirty, old-fashioned, domestic, and cheap…Coal does not make us think of the rich, but of the poor. It evokes bleak images of soot-covered coal miners trudging from the mines, supporting their desperately poor families in grim little company towns.[1]

The process of commoditization is something that we may not be familiar with but should be grateful for. The process through which products and services become more familiar to us and freely available has yielded significant societal benefits. If unwrapped carefully and so long as we avoid the many negative connotations which can be associated with commoditization we can see that it has contributed to the development of stable economies and the increased living standards that we have grown accustomed to. It has certainly contributed to the huge influx of cheap goods and the availability of affordable services as well as the massive rise in conspicuous consumption over the last couple of decades. Whether or not commoditization will be the undoing of our comfortable lifestyles is something I will come back to in Part IV, but for now it is important to address the nature of commoditization and how it works by focusing on a few commodities we are familiar with. How commoditization affects industries and people in particular will be addressed in Chapters 3 to 5.

Coal, coffee and cotton

As we saw in the introduction a commodity is something that we cannot easily differentiate. Take coal, for example; if I were to hold up two lumps of the stuff, one of which was bituminous and the other anthracite it is unlikely that you could identify which was which. Not only that but it is highly unlikely that you would be worried about where the coal came from because as far as you're concerned coal is coal. So whether it is from Australia, America or the United Kingdom, it really doesn't matter. You might be bothered by how much you have to pay for it and may be willing to pay a little more if it burned cleaner or provided you with more energy and heat. The key differentiator you would use when deciding on what coal you would purchase is cost and it is this which ultimately distinguishes a commodity from a non-commodity. Another aspect of the many commodities that we use every day, including sugar, salt and tea is that they are almost invisible. We pop to our local store and purchase a kilo of sugar; we ferret around in our cupboard at home and we pull out a tea bag. We don't give more than a second's thought to how or where they were produced. Why not? Quite simply because they are so much part of the fabric of our lives that they lose their significance. We assume that they will always be there, which is why there is always such a panic when there is a natural or other disaster which could affect availability. I remember bringing some sugar cane home from a trip to a Sudanese sugar plantation and showing my kids. Both were amazed as they had never fully appreciated where the sugar they put onto their cereal every morning came from or what it took to convert cane into the granulated sugar they used every day.

Most of us are familiar with commodities like copper, salt and agricultural products such as wheat and many of us would know that they are traded on the commodity exchanges around the world. However, we may be less aware that many of the products and services that we currently buy can also be considered commodities. Clearly these are not dug-up, mined, or farmed, but they are commodities all the same. Like the commodities we are familiar with they are readily available, usually produced, packaged and sold by a large number of suppliers, look much the same and are increasingly available to us at lower prices. And, as with coal, the principal basis for our decision to purchase one product or service or another is increasingly down to price. You can see this in your local computer store; customers weighing up what computer to buy even though the basic functions are pretty much the same, the components are broadly identical and the only real differentiator is price. I increasingly see this in my consulting career; if clients cannot differentiate between the services my firm provides from another's then they will make their decision as to who to employ on price. It's the nature of commoditization. But this has not always been the case. Commoditization is not an instant process; it can take years or even decades to pan out, which is why the current acceleration is worrying organizations and spurring service providers such as IBM to bring it to the attention of their customers. Even the commodities we are familiar with were not always freely available. So the process through which some of our basic commodities became just that provides us with an insight into the nature of commoditization.

COAL

When the Romans invaded Britain they came across great outcrops of coal. At first they used it as jewellery but soon discovered that it could be burnt and used as fuel. However the use of coal was not widespread and, just as before the Romans arrived, when they left in the fifth century AD, the practice of burning coal died out. It wasn't until the 12th and 13th centuries that the use of coal was more widespread, but it was the fuel crisis of the 16th century when the forests of England were being cut down to support the booming wool trade that coal came into its own. By the end of the century coal was the main source of fuel for the country. But it was not just the need for energy to feed the woollen industry that fuelled coal's growth. Other factors such as the widespread use of chimneys, once the preserve of the rich, allowed coal to extend its reach into the hearths of the lower classes. By the 18th century coal had become an essential commodity for any growing economy. Once it became something on which an industrial nation's competitiveness depended, efforts were made to make the extraction of coal a safer and more effective process. One of the most significant changes was the efficient removal of water which up until then had caused major disruptions to production and a significant number of deaths. The coal industry continued to expand throughout the 19th century; in the early part of the century production was ten times that of the 17th century and had doubled again by 1854. This expansion underpinned the transfer from water powered factories to the coal and steam powered factories that became synonymous with the industrialization of Britain. It also stimulated the mass migrations from the countryside to the towns of Northern England as well as the intensification of work. The combination of industrialization and coal spawned the shipping and railway industries, both of which relied upon the fuel to transport manufactured goods from the northern industrial cities such as Manchester to the rest of the country.

Having done its job in Britain, coal then played its part in the development and rapid industrialization of America, which by the late 19th century was well on its way to becoming the super power we now know. Coal's significance has waned considerably since its heyday, with oil and gas surpassing it as the energies of choice, but as the end of oil looms, there is talk of rekindling the depleted coal industry with its 200 plus years of reserves that still lie buried beneath the ground. Indeed, advertisements are now appearing on American television and in the press informing the general public of the merits of coal. This is a sure sign that there is still some life left in the commodity yet.

COFFEE

There is nothing like the early morning fix of a café latte to get the working day off to a productive start. Without that kick the corporate world would struggle to get going and at times it seems to be the critical fluid that runs through the veins of every organization; plots are hatched, decisions are made and deals are struck over a coffee. As a commodity, coffee is significant because it employs something in the region of 500 million people worldwide.[2] Unlike coal, coffee (as a beverage) was *discovered* much, much later. It is believed that it originated, or at least was gaining a sufficient foothold for it to be mentioned, in the Yemen around 1502 when the coffee plants of Ethiopian origin were being used to make the drink that we are now all familiar with. The drinking of coffee had a close association with Islam and, as the faith spread out along the trade routes, so did the habit of drinking coffee. The coffee house was soon to follow and it was through this that coffee became a true commodity, valued throughout the world. It wasn't long before coffee became a powerful social force as the coffee house started to replace the home as a place of entertainment and where people (mainly men at that time) of different social standings could meet and discuss the business of the day.

The coffee house encouraged the formation of numerous societies of a scientific, medical and commercial nature, but it was the centrality of coffee and the coffee house in particular to the financial and insurance markets of the 17th and 18th centuries that confirmed its importance. Lloyd's insurance started at Lloyd's coffee house, the London Stock exchange emerged from Jonathan's Coffee House in Exchange Alley and The East India Company made the Jerusalem Coffee House its unofficial headquarters.[3] The coffee house became so important that for many London merchants attendance at the coffee house became as important as attending the exchange itself.[4] It has been argued that coffee and the coffee house in particular were fundamental to the establishment of the British Empire, but this may be stretching coffee's significance a little too far, despite its role in bringing like minded people together. In modern times coffee continues to exert its power over significant portions of the global economy. At one end we have the producers, working on barely subsistence level incomes producing coffee at the lowest possible price for the markets, whilst at the other we have the well known brands such as Starbucks, Nero and Costa who charge their customers' £2–£3.50 a cup. Coffee may be a commodity, but it is deeply embedded in society and commerce. We will come back to Starbucks in Chapter 9 when we review a number of organizations who have managed to thrive in a commoditized market.

COTTON

Cotton was first domesticated some 5500 years ago in Asia, South America, India and Mexico and despite the 50 plus varieties that grew across these regions, only four were capable of producing lint that could be spun into thread which in turn could be woven into fabric. The process through which this domestication took place was very similar in each of the regions and each developed near identical tools and techniques for extracting the lint from the seeds and then spinning it into a usable form. The use of cotton as a source of fabric remained localised but as new societies came and went the process through which cotton was exploited became more sophisticated and its footprint widened. Alexander the Great clothed his army in it, the Romans considered it a luxury import and during medieval times fanciful tales were written about cotton; many in society at that time believed it had mysterious properties.

During the Inca and Aztec civilizations one variety of cotton plant came to dominate – Upland Cotton – and after Columbus discovered the New World it wasn't long before this variety accounted for the majority of cotton grown throughout the southern United States and eventually the world.[5] But once again it was the technological advances of the industrial revolution that proved to be the catalyst for significant change. Richard Arkwright's exploitation of James Hargreaves' spinning jenny revolutionized the manufacture of textiles and shifted production from a cottage and family-based industry to a cotton mill and industrialized setting that set the foundation for the booming cotton trade of 18th-century England. Further innovations followed as inventors and budding industrialists saw cotton's potential and sought to improve the efficiency and productivity of the mills. This was so successful that between 1775 and 1783 cotton production increased by 600 per cent as demand for the finished product ballooned. The United States too saw cotton's potential and in order to catch up, industrialists travelled to England to understand and then transfer the expertise of the English cotton manufacturers to their home country. But it wasn't all rosy. The use of slaves on the cotton plantations of the south became one of America's most divisive issues and precipitated the American Civil War. Once the war was over, new innovations began to transform the harvesting of cotton and the production of the cloth. The introduction of ring spinning and a perfected bobbin changer led to significant increases in productivity and more importantly reduced the requirement for expert labour. Factories could now be staffed by a low-paid inexperienced labour force and it was this that facilitated the shift in production from the north to the south of the United States. The result was catastrophic for the northern labour force which by the end of the first decade of the 20th century had contracted by 100 000 jobs.

In the same way that factory labour was gradually forced out through mechanization, the dependence on farm labourers to pick cotton by hand was gradually reduced by the introduction of the cotton-picking machine. Although invented in the 1920s and perfected during the 1930s, it was not widely used until after the First World War. But it was worth waiting for because one machine could replace 25 labourers.[6] More recent developments are equally interesting. From an economic standpoint the cotton industry is under siege from China, where near sweatshop conditions allow the production of t-shirts and other apparel to be manufactured at a fraction of the cost elsewhere. It is believed that despite the continued protectionism through the imposition of quotas by the United States government and others, the US textile industry has lost in the region of 300 000 jobs since 2000 and there are predictions of a global loss of 30 million jobs should quotas be lifted.[7] The other significant change has been the shift to genetically modified cotton. Introduced in 1996 it didn't take long for it to reach 70 per cent of United States production and it is expected to be 100 per cent by 2010.

Today 40 billion pounds of cotton are grown a year on something in the region of 70 million acres of land in over 80 countries.[8] It also finds itself in a huge number of products including gunpowder, lipstick and a wide range of foodstuffs. Cotton holds sway over the livelihoods of millions of people who attempt to compete in a crowded and commoditized market.

The process of commoditization

Tracing the history of how coal, coffee and cotton moved from scarcity to commodity is useful because we can draw out the process through which things can become commoditized. We can also start to see why commoditization is such an important process. Take coal. Without it we would not have had the industrial revolution. Without coffee we may have never had the insurance industry which emerged from the coffee houses of 17th-century London. Without cotton we may have never progressed beyond the woollen trade. All have their own paths from obscurity to commoditization and each has its own set of factors which have helped shape its own unique position in the world. Taken in the round it is possible to extract some key factors which are associated with the process of commoditization. These are:

- In order for something to become commoditized it must be plentiful. Nothing can become truly commoditized if it is in short supply. On this basis luxury goods can never become commodities because if they did, they would lose their appeal. Diamonds, which could be considered a commodity, maintain their luxury status through the control De Beers exercises over their supply. Restricting supply is one way to avoid commoditization. By the same token if the availability of a commodity begins to decline, as in the case of oil, the price may rise to a point where alternatives are sought to replace it.
- Commodities are atomic, that is, they are often the basic unit of a process, product or service and used as inputs into the completion of another task. Coal is used to create electricity in a coal-fired power station and cotton is used in the manufacture of clothes, as well as finding its way into a wide range of other products.
- Commodities become critical to other economic, social or organizational processes. Whilst the Romans may have enjoyed the intrinsic beauty of coal when they first arrived in England, it was coal's other properties that helped to avert the first energy crisis in the 16th century and embedded it into the emerging industrial processes of the 18th century.
- Once the value of a commodity is recognized new ways to exploit it are investigated and brought to market. In this way its value increases, which in turn helps to extend both its footprint and its impact, economic, social or both.
- The availability of investment capital is critical for the commodity to become widespread and useful to the broader economy. Early on this is focused on building the basic infrastructure necessary for the commodity to begin to be exploited. As the commodity's footprint enlarges capital is focused on extending its application by tying it to other economic processes and products. At the same time it is directed towards making the extraction and production processes more efficient and effective, thereby reducing the costs associated with its exploitation. And, finally, as the commodity matures, investment is focused on innovation and identifying and exploiting the remaining opportunities that the commodity can offer.
- As demand for a commodity continues to grow beyond its early exploitation it stimulates waves of innovation which are designed to increase the efficiency through which it can be brought to market or to address the threats imposed by the emergence of a cheaper alternative. Competition forces suppliers of the commodity to innovate using technology

or to seek out additional uses for it. Take coffee; if it had remained as an isolated beverage enjoyed by a few it would not have had the wide ranging social impacts it has had. The innovation around coffee was the coffee house. With respect to cotton, it was the automation of the harvesting process, the identification of additional uses for the lint and most importantly the use of trade barriers and subsidies to neutralize competition.

- Commodities can decline in their significance. Take the forerunner of cotton – wool. Wool was a staple of the English medieval economy and despite forcing commoners to wear woollen clothes in response to the introduction of cotton clothing, cotton came through mainly because it was (and still is) infinitely more comfortable. Similarly coal has been relegated by the more efficient and cleaner fuels of oil and gas and may well be further usurped by the expansion of renewable and nuclear energy sources in the future.

The route to commoditization is progressive and one that passes through five stages with the possibility of a sixth (Figure 2.1). There is of course no guarantee that the final state (i.e. commoditization) will ever be reached as there are many reasons why something which has the potential to become commoditized may never become so. Such reasons are associated with cost, availability and intrinsic value as well as deliberate strategies to avoid the commoditization trap, which includes controlling the market (as DeBeers do with diamonds – although with the sale of synthetic diamonds expected to increase tenfold over the next three years it is feasible that real diamonds will lose some of their appeal, drop in price and cost the world's mining companies in the region of $2.5 billion annually[9]), snuffing out potential competitors and regulation. Equally, once something has become fully commoditized, there is always the possibility that it could be replaced or decline in its significance if alternatives are found.

The first stage (❶) of emergence/discovery is where the potential commodity is first identified. At this stage, its usage is very limited and localized and its full potential remains undiscovered whilst those who are employing it get used to its basic facets. As we saw with

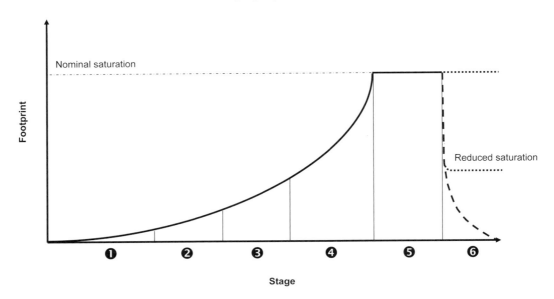

Figure 2.1 The stages of commoditization

cotton, discovery can occur simultaneously in more than one location. The important factor here is that it is localized.

The next stage (❷) is one of initial exploitation. Here the potential commodity is used in its most obvious and simplified form. With coal this was heating, with coffee it was drinking and with cotton it was spinning. Tools and techniques to facilitate this initial exploitation begin to emerge and the usage and footprint of the potential commodity expands beyond its localized origins. Expansion occurs through word of mouth but more importantly through trade. This was true of both coffee and cotton which depended on the trade routes established by the Muslims.

The third stage, extension (❸) involves a significant widening of the potential commodity as its value is recognized by a wider range of stakeholders. This is usually accompanied by further enhancements to the methods used to secure the commodity as well as advancements in the way it is exploited. With coal and cotton the extension stage was associated with improvements in mining and farming to make their extraction more efficient and mechanized. During this stage there is a greater emphasis on the commercialization of the potential commodity. Trade opens up as demand and usage increases.

The next stage (❹) is when the potential commodity is well on the way to becoming truly commoditized. It is during this stage that there is a significant shift in usage as it gains an increasingly larger foothold across society. Demand increases dramatically as the value of the potential commodity is well understood and the process through which it comes to market (sales, marketing, etc.) is capable of dealing with this increased demand. This stage is also accompanied by significant and wide ranging innovation. Typically this involves industrializing the production processes, exploiting the commodity in new ways through its integration into other processes and finding new applications for it (such as finding additional uses for cotton and integrating it into a large number of products). Competition opens up considerably as providers seek to exploit the market potential represented by the commodity. Any dominance that might have existed begins to erode. New entrants attempt to gain advantage over their rivals to increase market share, which usually involves focusing on price as the principal differentiator. Equally, the existing incumbents seek to maintain their market dominance as much as possible and as the competition hots up they may end up with little choice but to compete on price. I will discuss this in more detail in Part III, when I address elements of the strategic response.

The next stage (❺) is commoditization. This is when the commodity reaches its nominal saturation point. It is here that it has become deeply embedded within society and so readily available that it starts to lose its ability to demonstrate any value additional to that already established. The potential for innovation declines and the maximum footprint for the commodity is reached. Although additional expansion might be possible this is difficult without breaking into brand new markets such as unexploited regions of the world. The competitive environment is so intensive that rival companies fight for market share and often suffer from a death of a thousand cuts as they seek to undercut their competition. In response companies that sell the commodity seek to shift the emphasis away from the intrinsic value of the commodity to one which is based on experience or lifestyle. This is evident with coffee and the recent proliferation of cafés and coffee shops which bring together great coffee in a relaxed and convivial setting. This has been further improved by integrating cafés into bookshops which has enhanced the experience of book buying, altered the café's atmosphere by giving it a quasi intellectual feel and, of course, has created a new market for the coffee house. Once this stage has been reached, it is possible to remain in a commoditized state so long as the relationship between price and value remains at a level the market can withstand.

Where it cannot, or where alternatives emerge then it enters the last stage (❻). This is when the commodity declines and follows the conventional cycle of growth and maturity followed by commoditization and decline. Decline can be initiated by a number of different factors and can completely eliminate the commodity or reduce its footprint to a lower level where it may re-stabilize. The most obvious factor is that it becomes scarce because it has been over exploited and because of this becomes too expensive to maintain its commoditized position. When a commodity's price rises to a level where the market is unwilling to pay for it, it usually stimulates the search for alternatives, additional innovation, efforts to make better use of it or if possible find more of it. Oil is a good example. During the oil crisis in the early to mid 1970s, the automobile industry invested heavily in building more efficient engines which could provide enhanced fuel economy. The wider economy also sought out fuel efficiencies that would reduce their dependency on oil. Now we are at a similar juncture, but for different reasons. With oil now beginning to run out, the price is nearing historic highs and similar efforts are being employed to reduce the dependence on oil from the Middle East. For example, this is allowing the Canadian tar sands to become financially viable and is forcing oil majors, the automobile industry and governments to invest in renewable energy, hybrid automobiles and nuclear power. Another factor which may lead to the decline of a commodity is the introduction of an alternative. Just because a commodity is deeply embedded does not mean it cannot be dislodged. Wool had reached level five on the model during the medieval period when the European economy relied heavily upon the wool trade. At this time most people were wearing woollen clothing and wool had found its way into the homes of the vast majority of the population. The appearance of cotton as an alternative may have failed to dislodge wool to begin with, but it soon became apparent that the qualities of cotton surpassed those of wool and so wool declined. Cotton was more comfortable, it was more versatile than wool and as the tonnage under production grew it was able to complete on price. Wool of course did not disappear entirely and has instead declined to a new but reduced saturation level above which it is unlikely to increase. It is possible to view coal in the same way. It reached its zenith during the 19th and early 20th centuries and although there were still plenty of deposits capable of extraction, it was dislodged when the first oil fields were discovered in the early 20th century. Over time it became obvious that oil had many more qualities than coal and could be exploited in a lot of different ways. The use of coal declined but has yet to disappear altogether and may well find itself in greater demand in the future, especially if renewable energy sources fail to live up to the promise that they will provide an effective alternative to oil.

The wider impacts of a declining commodity are also worth noting. As the woollen and coal industries declined in their significance great tranches of employment started to disappear both in the direct and indirect sense. Those who were directly employed in the extraction or exploitation activities were the first to go. Mines were closed and woollen factories were shut and the employees thrown out onto the streets to find alternative work for which they had few skills. Those that depended on the wool and coal industries also suffered as the demand for machinery dropped, the secondary processing and exploitation of the basic commodity declined and the local economy that had relied on the income of the workers crumbled. This highlights an important aspect of commodities and commoditization. On the one hand, as a commodity becomes embedded into the wider economic and social processes the benefits of its exploitation spread far and wide, generating economic gain to a large number of people. On the other hand, as it declines in its significance either because it is exhausted or as alternatives emerge, the economic and social consequences can be devastating, especially when so many might be dependent upon it for their livelihoods.

So far we have looked at commoditization in the context of the commodities we are familiar with. In order to explore how commoditization affects us now and in particular in relation to the modern corporation and white-collar work, we first need to take a look at how the process of commoditization has played out in the industrial setting using some well known examples, including the railway, telecoms and airline industries. As with coal, cotton and coffee, each started out with a limited footprint, each has grown significantly and each has become commoditized. In assessing commoditization at industry level we can start to see that just like the basic commodities, such as coal and cotton, there are similar factors that can lead to the commoditization of entire industries. We will also see that there are some other factors to consider too.

References

1 Freese, B. (2005) *Coal: A Human History*, London: William Heinemann, p. 2.
2 Wild, A. (2004) *Coffee: A Dark History*, London: Fourth Estate, p. 1.
3 Ibid., p. 86.
4 Ellis, M. (2005) *The Coffee House: A Cultural History*, London: Phoenix, p. 171.
5 Yafa, S. (2005) *Big Cotton: How a Humble Fiber Created Fortunes, Wrecked Civilizations and Put America on the Map*, New York: Viking, pp. 15–16.
6 Rivoli, P. (2005) *The Travels of a T-Shirt in the Global Economy*, Hoboken, New Jersey: John Wiley & Sons, p. 36.
7 Ibid., p. 166.
8 Yafa, S. (2005), p. 1, see note 5 above.
9 Rossingh, D. (2007) Labs dull diamonds' lustre, *National Post*, 15 June, p. FP7.

3 The Middle Wave: The Commoditization of Industries

It is easy to forget how recently the communications revolution began. All three of today's fast-changing communications technologies have existed for more than half a century: the telephone was invented in 1876; the first television transmission was in 1926; and the electronic computer was invented in the mid-1940s. For much of that time, change has been slow, but, in each case, a revolution has taken place since the late 1980s.[1]

Travel, which was once the privilege of aristocrats and until recently a matter of prestige and pride, has now dwindled to a mere commodity.[2]

I am optimistic about technology, but not about its profits.[3]

One of the most consistent patterns in business is the failure of leading companies to stay at the top of their industries when technologies or markets change.[4]

Moving beyond the obvious commodities such as cotton and coal and analyzing how whole industries have become commoditized provides an essential perspective on how commoditization is capable of moving up the value chain and into areas that would not have been thought possible. It also begins to help to explain how and why commoditization is starting to affect a larger number of organizations and white-collar workers in particular. Clearly a basic commodity such as coal has its limitations despite its application within wider industrial processes. But what of industries; how do they fare? When we start to delve into familiar industries, both past and present, we can start to see other factors coming into play.

The rail and the telecommunications industry – past

The rail and telecommunications industries were possibly on the vanguard of the industry wave of commoditization. When comparing the two it is interesting to note how quickly both became commoditized once the basic infrastructure had been established (rails, signals and stations in the case of rail, and cables, towers and exchanges for telecommunications). The biggest difference we see today is the degree to which innovation within the rail industry has tailed off and how it has accelerated within telecommunications. Clearly this is a function of the industries themselves, but also reflects the heavy reliance on technology. There is little room for any more innovation within the rail industry and there is still some, although perhaps not that much, left in telecoms. Despite the rapidity of innovation within telecoms the advantages that come with the first mover are increasingly short-lived as no matter what suppliers do their new products and services are almost instantaneously commoditized. Unfortunately this still leaves them competing on price and desperately looking for the next big thing.

RAIL

The rail industry was born out of the Rainhill trials when George Stephenson bested all comers in demonstrating the viability of a steam driven engine. The trials took place some three years after the building of the Liverpool to Manchester Railway had started and although a lot of effort had gone into track construction, there was no means of pulling the cargo that was due to be transported along it. So in October 1829 the directors of the soon to be completed railway held a competition to find the most appropriate means of transportation. At this time there was a difference of opinion as to how. Some favoured fixed engines with ropes and pulleys, whilst others believed that a locomotive would be more effective. The competition, which was held at Rainhill, some nine miles outside of Liverpool city centre, would solve this once and for all. Of the three contestants it was Stephenson's Rocket that won and by a long chalk; his locomotive was able to haul a load 40 times over the set distance of one and three-quarter miles and did so at a top speed of 30 miles per hour. Having won the prize the engine was enhanced to suit the needs of the emerging railway industry and the Liverpool to Manchester railway was duly opened in September 1830, the first to be powered by steam locomotives. It was also the first to carry both passengers and freight.[5] It is believed that the coming of the railway increased peoples' perception of time, as the introduction of the train timetable made everyone far more conscious of their timekeeping. It has also been speculated that this was a significant factor in the adoption of the clock and pocket watch during the 19th century[6]; time had already started to become precious.

Once the basic concept of the railway had been proven, the work required to create the infrastructure to make it effective and widely available began. This focused on laying the rails that connected every major conurbation in the United Kingdom and in those countries across the world that followed the UK's lead. Enormous sums were spent on cutting up the countryside and laying thousands of kilometres of track; between 1846 and 1876 the amount of track laid globally increased from 17 424 km to 309 631 km[7] and by 1852, 6600 miles of track had been laid in Britain alone.[8] The investment frenzy that coincided with the building of the railways led to an investment boom followed rapidly by a major bust, so although by the mid-19th century most of the basic infrastructure had been established many of the speculators and banks that had funded it had failed or were in serious financial difficulty.

The first transcontinental railway was finished in 1869 in America and over the subsequent three decades the Trans-Siberian (the longest at 5338 miles[9]) and Canadian Pacific were also completed. But it took a long time for the infrastructure to become fully standardized. For example, although establishing a common gauge would have been ideal from the start, rival railway companies developed gauges that suited their own local purposes, rather than work together to create a single one. It wasn't long before two competing standards emerged. The first was Stephenson's which was based upon the width of the wagonway at Killingworth Colliery. This measured 1.44 m and was adopted by a number of railway engineers and especially those who knew or were associated with Stephenson. The second was Isambard Brunel's. He believed his much wider gauge of 2.2 m would accommodate larger trains, travel much faster and be safer at navigating bends than Stephenson's. The London to Bristol Railway (The Great Western Railway), built by Brunel, used this wider gauge. The use of alternative gauges was fine until individual lines began to connect; local lines only had to serve local populations and remained separate until the rail network began to fill out. By 1844 the Great Western railway had opened new lines from Bristol to Exeter and Bristol to Gloucester where it met Stephenson's standard gauge of the Birmingham to Gloucester line. So if you happened to be travelling from Bristol to Birmingham you had no choice but to change trains at Gloucester, which was hugely inconvenient, especially when it came to freight. The impasse between Brunel and Stephenson required government intervention to resolve. In 1845 a Royal Commission was established to review the use of different gauges and come up with a definitive standard that was to be used across the whole network. After a comprehensive consultation and analysis exercise it was decided that Stephenson's standard gauge would be adopted and The Gauge Act was passed by Parliament in 1846. Although this made the use of the standard gauge compulsory for all new railways, it took until 1892 for the Great Western Railway to adopt it. This was not the first time that governments would intervene in the industry.[10]

The turning point for the UK rail system was the First World War when the state took over the running of the entire network for the duration of the war. The principal reason for this was the need to control the transportation of munitions, troops and the other materials of war, but it demonstrated the inefficiencies that had built up in the network over the preceding 80 years. Following the war the then government decided to reduce the number of train companies to four by Act of Parliament. They felt that this would eliminate unnecessary competition and improve the efficiency and effectiveness of the whole network. As in America, it wasn't long before the British government was also regulating ticket and freight prices and forcing the rail companies to take on certain freight movements at minimal or no profit. The impact was far from positive, as both passenger and freight volume declined significantly because, thanks to this intervention, the service provided by the train companies fell below that which was generally acceptable. This was compounded by the increase in road building which allowed travelling by road to become an attractive alternative to the train.

Following the Second World War the rail network was nationalized and in response to the increasing use of the road network for passenger and freight transport was rationalized through the 'Beeching Cuts' of 1962. This reduced the number of stations by over 2300 and closed thousands of miles of track. Once the nationalized rail network had been stabilized and brought back into profit, the inevitable question of its privatization came up and as was the trend in the 1980s and 1990s, British Rail, like so many of its fellow nationalized industries (such as British Gas and British Airways) was privatized. For a short period of time the railways blossomed as passenger numbers increased in response to a series of innovations (improved rolling stock and service levels and efficiency gains from investments in processes and systems as well as changes in employment structures). However, it wasn't long before the government wanted to intervene once again and exercise some control over the fragmented rail network which the previous administration had sold off. But it was a series of fatal train accidents in the late 1990s and early 2000s that led to the demise of the operating freedom that the rail operators had become used to. In fact it was believed that the fragmented nature of the privatized industry was one of the primary causes of these accidents. Unsurprisingly, the United States railway industry has mirrored the UK's in so far as it grew rapidly and suffered from similar interventions from government. This is probably a reflection of the importance of railways to a nation's infrastructure and how vital they are to the general prosperity and smooth running of any industrialized country.

There is no doubt that the early period of the rail industry brought significant economic gains as distant parts of a country were connected together. This facilitated the rapid transportation of people and goods which in turn led to the development of new conurbations and allowed major population movements to meet the increasing needs of industrialization. The economic impact extended beyond the railways themselves as those industries that relied on them also thrived. For example, the mining, metallurgy, machine and vehicle building industries increased by nearly 40 per cent between 1841 and 1851.[11] The railways also provided the crucial platform for a whole raft of new businesses both large and small. By cutting inventory and freight costs they created the necessary foundations of the large scale retailers which started to emerge in the 1890s in towns across the world, and especially in the United States. For example, when John Wanamaker opened his first store in Philadelphia in 1876 (in a former freight building), it attracted 70 000 shoppers.[12] And it wasn't long before the retailers were reaching out to customers across the country, enabled to do so by the railway network. No longer restricted to local consumers, the mail order companies of the last quarter of the 19th century were able to display their wares through catalogues which featured thousands of items. And once ordered they could be delivered through the combination of the rail network and the postal service. This allowed companies such as Montgomery Ward to ship some 13 000 packages a day.[13]

Today the railway continues to play a vital role in transporting people and goods across a country, but it has become so much a part of the infrastructure that it no longer offers the significant economic benefits it used to. These days it is the housing market that is the primary beneficiary as stressed out executives desperate to escape claustrophobic city centres move out along the major railway routes to find villages where they can live without the problems that come with city life. With the cities acting like magnets for well paid jobs, it isn't long before house prices rise considerably along the popular routes. With faster and more frequent services, it is now possible to commute from towns and villages up to 200 miles away from the major cities. Despite this phenomenon, repeated efforts to wean people off their cars and onto the trains has failed because the majority of people would rather drive than be forced to stand or suffer the hell of other people (something I address in one of my other books – *Pains on Trains*). Rail travel may not be cheap but it is still a commodity all the same. And, with so little room for genuine innovation it is unlikely to advance much beyond its current state. This leaves little opportunity but to focus on driving out inefficiencies in much the same way airlines have done following 9/11.

The commoditization of the railway industry has in part been due to the physical constraints under which it operates. The requirement for tracks, stations, rolling stock and, of course, the land on which it sits, all serve to constrain growth. Another is the towns and cities which it serves, as once the network had filled out and connected the key towns and cities across the country there was nowhere else for it to go. Apart from these somewhat obvious physical limits, other factors such as the imposition of standards, deregulation, the opening up of competition and the alternative mode of travel represented by the car all helped to limit the growth of the railways and to ensure they became and remained commoditized.

TELECOMMUNICATIONS[14]

Man is a natural communicator. For millennia the need to communicate has driven the development of basic language, the alphabet and of course the telephone. As with so many other phenomena it started slowly and accelerated dramatically as technology caught up with the needs of those who wished to stay in contact with work, family and friends. Of all the industries that are discussed in this chapter, it is the telecommunications industry that is possibly the most commoditized and deeply embedded into today's society. Of greater significance is the rapidity with which it has penetrated society and how quickly it is converging with other forms of communication such as the television, the personal computer, the Internet and even navigation.

The origins of the modern telecommunications industry can be traced to the invention of the electric telegraph by Samuel Morse in 1838. However, it took another 12 years before the first telegraph line was opened and the first message sent. Once the technical viability of the telegraph was established, it didn't take long for it to expand, which typically occurred along existing and new railway lines. In parallel with Morse, William Fothergill Cooke and Professor Charles Wheatstone came together to create the needle telegraph, which they patented in England in 1837. Like its United States counterpart, the English Telegraph soon gained a similar foothold, especially with the railways. Two-way communication emerged in 1853 when Wilhelm Gintl was able to send signals in two directions down a single line. Further developments followed with the most significant being the laying of the first transatlantic cable in 1866.

Interest in the application of the telegraph continued, but it was the ability to transfer the human voice electronically that captured inventors' imaginations. Although a number of inventors and engineers experimented with the idea, it was Alexander Graham Bell who was able to develop it to the point where it could be patented and commercialized, which he did in 1876. Although very simple, comprising a basic microphone and speaker, it was the invention of the telephone that kick-started the telecommunications revolution – it didn't take long for other inventors to follow Bell's lead and within a few years 30 other telephone systems had been patented. However, Bell's company was by far the largest and within its first three years of operation had installed well over 50 000 telephones.

In order to complete a phone call at this time the caller had to rely on an operator who would literally build the connection between the caller and receiver. As the telephony network grew this became a major bottleneck, which wasn't resolved until 1889 when Almon Strowger invented a system that allowed the individual telephone user to make the connection himself through the use of a dialler. It was this innovation that led to the first automated telephone exchange, which no longer required operators. Mass communication had finally arrived.

The next significant innovation occurred with the introduction of wireless communication during the 1980s. The early wireless devices were poor and the technology could be classed as chunky at best. In fact the early mobile phones bore a remarkable resemblance to a brick. What they did bring however, was freedom from the fixed line, which allowed executives, salesman and other employees to maintain contact with the office whilst on the road. Within a decade of its introduction, more than one in seven of the world's telephone subscriptions were for mobile phones. With this level of demand it didn't take long for the suppliers to develop new handsets that were small enough to fit in your pocket. This, along with greater choice (with more suppliers) and increased connectivity across the world, ensured the mobile phone became one of the most ubiquitous pieces of technology on earth. More recently the convergence of the mobile phone with the Internet has allowed wireless telephony to take on an even greater significance. It is now possible to take photographs, download music, surf the net and watch movies on your mobile phone, making it more than just a communication tool.

All of these developments are clearly important to the development of the telecommunications industry, but it is cost that has been the impetus for commoditization. Without the significant reduction in the price of a basic call, it is unlikely that the phone and the mobile phone in particular would have gained the stranglehold it now has. When the first public transatlantic telephone service was established in 1927, some 50 years after the telephone was invented, it was hugely expensive; a three minute phone call cost £15, although this was reduced to £9 the following year. Over the next few decades the cost dropped to near zero as the capacity across the network expanded at breakneck speed. Cables were laid and satellites launched at such a pace that it wasn't long before capacity outstripped demand.

And as the basic call continues to lose its significance it won't be long before the call is, for all intents and purposes free. In fact with the development of VOIP (Voice Over Internet Protocol) this is already upon us. The advantage of VOIP is that you can respond to calls via the Internet using a choice of media – voice, text, or email. Without the Internet, broadband and the other technological breakthroughs associated with the Internet none of this may have been possible (more on the impact of the Internet in the next chapter).

Of course the commoditization of telecommunications is not just down to developments in technology or price, as governments have also played their part. For many years the telephone companies were in government hands and this was used to suppress competition and allowed them to control prices. However, as with other state controlled industries this did not last forever. The late 1990s saw a wave of deregulation that allowed new entrants to gain a foothold in the market. This was important because it began to break up the cosy cabal the main players (AT&T, BT and MCI) had maintained. Before then they had been able to maintain their dominance in three ways: first they never competed head-to-head, second they owned the capacity and built up enough surplus to stifle their competition by reducing prices, and finally they benefited from ongoing government protection.[15] Since deregulation was introduced, few governments have permitted an entirely free market to exist, especially given the dominance of the existing providers. Their role is now one of maintaining a level playing field and widening the competitive market by such means as reigning in BT and releasing the third generation mobile phone licences which placed the convergence of mobile phones with the Internet firmly on the agenda.

The telecommunications industry will continue to evolve and converge with other technologies and over time it is likely that the phone and its associated services will become so completely commoditized that it will be virtually free. Consumers will get more and more for less and less as suppliers compete against each other by packing ever more features onto their phones in the vain attempt to grow or at the very least retain market share.

The airline and information technology industries – present

The airline and information technology industries share some of the factors that led to the commoditization of the rail and telecoms industries; they also have some of their own. For example, both emerged after significant technological breakthroughs and as the industries' footprint expanded in response to the take-up so did the competition. This in turn increased the importance of innovation and ongoing continuous improvements. Eventually they reached the point where the focus shifted to cost and they became commodities. As we shall see, each has responded to this change in different ways, but each has found itself in a cost bind that it will never escape from.

AIRLINES

Since the Wright Brothers made their first tentative flight in December 1903 the airline industry has grown considerably. The invention of the aircraft changed the nature of travel forever and it could be argued that its effect was just as significant as that of the automobile. The commercial airline industry which emerged at the end of the Second World War literally opened up the world. Not only did it lead to the significant expansion of the travel industry and tourism in general – long the preserve of the rich – but it also facilitated the rapid growth of commerce. Even over the past 30 years this has been significant; the volume of air travel has increased 800 per cent; 1617 million passengers travel by air and nearly 30 million tonnes of freight are transported every year.[16]

The early years of the industry were dominated by government intervention. This was focused on safety, service and controlling the prices, routes and general operating conditions of the national airlines at that time. Governments also took a keen interest in developing the underlying infrastructure of the industry including engine manufacture, aircraft design and associated equipment. No wonder given that the modern airline industry was born out of its military sister.[17] Between 1930 and 1960 the aircraft graduated from the propeller driven, unpressurized, fabric covered, partially wooden construction we see in old movies to the silver metallic skinned, pressurized, streamlined aircraft we travel in today. The big technological leap that allowed this to take place occurred during the Second World War when the necessity of conflict spurred innovation after innovation. And it was this that opened up the airline industry once the war was over.

Before this leap, air travel was expensive, complicated and slow. To get to any far flung destination usually involved a series of individual legs, some of which required other modes of transport such as rail to complete. For example, to travel from London to Australia took in the region of 12 days. The introduction of the jet airliner in the 1950s and in particular the reliable Boeing 707 brought air travel into the reach of the masses. The 707 could fly at twice the height and three times the speed of its propeller-driven forebear and could transport greater numbers of passengers in a single one way flight without the need to refuel. Innovations such as fly by wire in which direct control of the aircraft by the pilot was replaced by the active control of the plane using automated systems and electronics, swept wings, inertial navigation systems, radio navigation and head-up displays followed.

As the industry matured, governments maintained their grip over nearly every aspect of the airline industry. But all this began to change in the late 1970s when the US Airline Deregulation Act came into force. This removed controls on market entry, exit and pricing policy and made it far easier for new entrants to start up new airlines. Although this led to a significant number of new carriers, few survived. There were many reasons for this, including: their relative size compared to the major carriers at the time; the shift to a hub and spoke model which served the incumbent carriers better; and innovations by the existing companies especially in terms of computerized reservation and yield management systems. As deregulation continued to play out many of the national airlines were privatized, and this had a knock-on effect within the aircraft manufacturers who experienced a wave of consolidations necessary to remain competitive in a market that could no longer rely on the orders that came from government owned airlines. The 15 or so suppliers that fed Europe consolidated into the small handful that exists today.

Towards the end of the 20th century and the beginning of the 21st the airline industry suffered a series of major setbacks which culminated in a massive downturn in air travel and a large proportion of the US airline industry going into Chapter 11 to protect themselves from their creditors and to avoid falling into bankruptcy. The industry lost something in the region of $30 billion over 2001 and 2002.[18] The events are well known and well documented: the outbreak of severe acute respiratory syndrome (SARS), the terrorist attacks on the World Trade Center in New York City, the ongoing conflict in the Middle East and the continued high price of oil. The impact of these events cannot be overstated. Apart from the significant loss, many of the major airlines were forced to economise and cut their unprofitable routes, and some of them went out of business.

Since these events there has also been significant fallout in both the number of people employed by the airline industry and, for those who have remained, significant cuts in their take home pay and benefits. Take the aircraft mechanics who worked for United Airlines. Before United went into Chapter 11 (companies in trouble and who are unable to service their debts or pay their creditors can file with a federal bankruptcy court for protection under Chapter 11 of the United States Bankruptcy Code. Chapter 11 allows the company to continue operating whilst it reorganizes itself, by protecting it from its creditors), the majority worked in state of the art facilities and were some of the highest paid in the industry. Since then the work has been outsourced and the majority of the mechanics have had to find alternative employment which paid significantly less than their previous incomes. Many left the profession altogether and had to get by on a succession of poorly paid service economy jobs.[19] The experience for many has not been a great one and the same is true across the industry; pilots, cabin crew, ground staff and others on the airlines' payrolls have all suffered – few have been spared.

The other and possibly more significant factor the major airlines had to contend with was the emergence of the cheaper alternative represented by the budget airlines. The budget airline relies on much simpler operating principles than the full service carriers. In contrast with these, the budget airlines:

- fly point to point to secondary airports
- maintain fleets which consist of one type of aircraft
- fly more hours per day
- have no frills or additional services such as airport lounges, allocated seats and so on
- make their customers pay for food and drink and increasingly luggage
- reduce staff to a minimum by using the Internet as their principal sales channel.[20]

Their success in capturing market share has been dramatic and has benefited from Internet-based booking which has highlighted the price differential between the low cost carriers and the traditional airlines. It seems that travellers are more than willing to fly for a couple of hours in relative discomfort when it costs next to nothing. When expectations are set so low it would be very difficult not to meet them, even for the most basic of services. Of course there are many who, having experienced the service first hand would never fly the budget airlines again, but there are plenty of people out there who are willing to suffer a degree of discomfort for the rock bottom price they pay. And with the recent launch of £75 flights to Hong Kong it will be interesting to see if the budget airlines can make the same headway into the long haul market as they have in the short haul.

To be successful the budget airlines have had to change and perfect the model that was used unsuccessfully in the past when the first wave of budget airlines appeared but soon failed. Concentrating on such things as simplified yield management and restricting choice were just two approaches used to great effect. When the customer compares the price of a return ticket to Milan to a full service carrier airline, such as British Airways, they see that the value proposition which comes with the higher priced ticket is at best marginal; as far as they are concerned they are dealing with a commodity and on that basis they will use price as the only differentiator. To maintain and grow market share the budget airlines are dependent on the maintenance of a low-cost base as it is this and only this that delivers the competitive advantage necessary to maintain and grow market share and most importantly keep their ticket prices low. In a commoditized world the requirement to develop low cost infrastructures is an essential strategy for those organizations which find themselves in the commoditized zone. Part III goes into this in more detail.

Of course the major airlines don't just roll over, they respond to the strategic threat as any company worth their salt would. For example British Airways have done much to close the cost advantage gap, including:[21]

- simplifying their fleet
- halving their hangar space to 26 bays
- reducing store locations from 42 to 14
- cutting headcount from 9000 to 6000
- lowering the inventory value from £630 to £340m
- eliminating process variations by adopting industry standards
- offering cheap fares for short haul flights.

When we look at the factors that have led to the commoditization of the airline industry, it is clear that not all of these were related to technological factors alone.[22] Technology was clearly important, but it was the impact of market deregulation during the 1980s and 1990s that released the industry from state control and opened up competition over routes and pricing and set the path towards privatization. But it was also the disruption caused by the events of the early 21st century that tipped the balance towards commoditization and led to the influx of the budget airlines. More recently the top-end of the airline industry, business travel, has been under attack, but not from the easyJets of this world. In this instance market share is being taken away by the specialist business travel airlines which are beginning to emerge. The focus on this group of new entrants is exclusivity; focusing on making the business traveller feel more special than they currently do with the major carriers. Using smaller jets, with fewer seats and only catering for business travellers they are able to provide an enhanced experience that is difficult to achieve with the incumbents. As a result the main airlines are being forced to continually innovate around the experience of business travel in order to maintain market share. For example, a few years ago there were no flat beds and only limited in-flight entertainment. Now both are the norm.

More recently, the European Union approved a pact with the US to start deregulating air travel across the Atlantic, known as the Open Skies agreement, which will allow greater competition, lower fares and new services. And in the longer term it could lead to cross-border airline mergers in Europe which is currently extremely difficult.[23] The principal change is that it will open up competition into the lucrative transatlantic travel that is dominated by very few players, such as British Airways and American Airlines; it is these which will face the biggest challenge.

The airline industry is bifurcating into two distinct parts, one which delivers a fully commoditized service in which the costs are low and the offering basic and the other which is experience-based, delivering a better and more exclusive service to those willing to pay. Indeed this is the primary growth engine for the full service carriers. In an increasingly commoditized industry, passengers have a simple and often stark choice; to travel in style, which comes at a price, or to travel in relative discomfort, having to pay for everything beyond the basic seat, but still a lot more cheaply than they would have had to pay in the past. But having seen the many, stressed out executives travelling on the cheap transatlantic flights out of United States hubs, I'd rather pay the premium.

INFORMATION TECHNOLOGY

There have been phenomenal changes in computer technology since its birth during the 1940s. For convenience, these changes have been labelled the first, second, third, fourth and fifth generations of computing[24] (Figure 3.1) and it is important to briefly review each of these before we discuss the recent changes in the industry, especially in relation to commoditization.

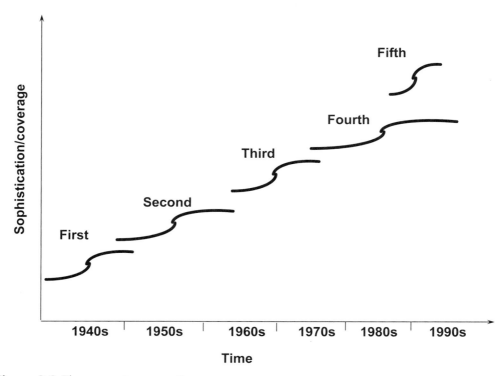

Figure 3.1 The computer generations

The first generation of computing consisted of vacuum tubes and electromagnetic relays. To ensure these large and very bulky machines operated without malfunction, special environmental conditions were needed. They also required a team with specialist knowledge and skills to maintain them. The first ever stored program computer, BABY, was completed in 1948, and ran its first program in June of that year. This machine had a limited memory of 128 bytes, weighed one ton, was over 16 feet long, and required over 3500 watts of electricity to power it.[25]

The invention of the transistor in 1948 significantly increased the speed of these early computers such as BABY. More importantly, with the transistor came reliability, smaller size and lower cost. This improvement in the price-performance ratio – more power for less money – made these devices more affordable, whilst at the same time more practical for meeting organizational needs. Critically it made it easier for organizations to consider the replacement of manual systems with computerized forms. This transistorizing of computers has been labelled the second generation of computers.

The third generation of computer technology arrived with the development of the integrated circuit board in the mid-1960s. This allowed a further improvement in the price-performance ratio and made it possible to simplify the construction of the computer and, in doing so, made it more reliable and easier to repair. The size and speed of the computer's core memory was also enhanced, making the processing of data faster. The increase in capacity and efficiency allowed the hardware developers to consider ways of making storage more accessible, resulting in the development of the magnetic disk. This combination of hardware performance improvements plus advances in storage media encouraged the development of more sophisticated operating systems which in turn led to the rapid expansion in the application of computers within organizations.

It was, however, the miniaturizing of electronics – resulting from the discovery in the 1950s, of the semi-conducting properties of silicon – that allowed computers to make their most significant impact. The mini computers of the mid-1960s to the early 1970s had all the advantages of their larger mainframe cousins, but at a fraction of the price. They were also smaller, faster, more powerful and more reliable.

The technological developments associated with the electronics industry continued well into the 1970s and 1980s with the development of the large scale integrated circuit – a small chip that contained thousands of miniature electrical components. These micro computers were lightweight, powerful, cheap, portable and widely applicable within organizations, and particularly suited to office automation. So began the fourth generation of computing. Despite the emergence of the personal computer and associated desktop applications, the 1980s also saw the continued dominance of the large centralized information systems driven by the need to process vast quantities of corporate data. This was especially the case within the financial services sector, which was at this stage, and arguably still is, the most IT dependent sector.

Towards the end of the 1980s, ever-more powerful mini, and personal computers, together with workstations, began to emerge and provide greater capability to distribute powerful computer technology throughout the organization. Continued advances in both power and miniaturization have produced yet smaller, more powerful devices including the laptop, pen-based, and notebook computers. Such devices have high speed chips, large memory capacities and are cheap, making entry level computing highly attractive to all organizations.

Then in October 1981, Japan's Ministry of International Trade and Industry (MITI) sponsored a conference to announce the Fifth Generation Project. The Japanese believed that the next generation of computer technology, the fifth, would revolutionize the computer industry and society in general. The philosophy behind the project was that a radical departure from traditional computer systems was possible. The systems which the Japanese proposed would be more like the humans that used them, in so far as they would be able to associate, make inferences and navigate through masses of information and data. The main aim of the Japanese initiative was therefore to design and develop computer hardware and software for knowledge engineering that could be used for a whole range of applications. Underlying this initiative was a belief that there was to be a shift from data processing to the intelligent processing of knowledge with artificial intelligence forming the backbone. The ultimate goal of the project was to create, by the early 1990s, a super artificial intelligence computer capable of processing up to a billion logical inferences per second, with a massive knowledge base. This failed to materialize partly because of the lack of interest in artificial intelligence at that time, but also because of over ambitious time scales, and technical problems. Despite the results of the Fifth Generation project being somewhat disappointing, the march of technology continues, and there are those who still hold onto the belief that the age of the smart machine is still possible, and that one day the technologists will be able to create artificial intelligence. Indeed, some futurologists predict by the year 2019, $1000 worth of computing power will have the computational abilities of one human brain – by 2029 this will have increased to 1000 human brains, and by 2060 to the collective brains of the entire human race. Perhaps artificial intelligence is not that far away after all.[26] And if this prediction is true, it is highly likely that work will have been automated out of existence. Of course we have seen this all before, as each successive wave of technological change and especially that associated with the computer has been accompanied by the technologists and scientists predicting the emergence of the leisure society. Despite the massive computerization of work since the 1950s, we are working more not fewer hours. All that computerization has delivered is the intensification of work (more on this in Chapter 5).

Further advances in computer technology are driven by the software companies, who in attempting to remain competitive have had to develop newer, faster and more widely applicable products, which are no longer restricted to automating existing business processes. Today such products are more integrated, globalized, easier to use and are more widely available in package form. In addition, the advent of the Internet and e-commerce in particular has had a profound effect on the way technology is applied within organizations, especially in terms of how it is developed, accessed and applied.

It is fair to assert that this technological change will continue pretty much unabated, especially if we are to believe the many books and articles on the subject of continuous technology-based change. Indeed, there are those that believe that the silicon chip is on the way out. Research being conducted by the University of California in the United States has discovered that it is possible to replicate the Silicon Chip molecularly. The scientists believe that this will allow computers to be 100 billion times more efficient than those currently available.[27] Very recently a team of engineers from the University of Wisconsin-Madison in the United States invented thin-film semiconductor techniques which promise to add sensing, computing and imaging capability to a vast array of materials.[28] Whereas the semiconductor industry has to rely upon the somewhat bulky silicon chip on which to grow and etch the thin films of material that become the electronic circuits for computers, the new thin-film techniques allow a single-crystal film of semiconductor to be removed from the substrate from which it is built. This thin layer, which has a width of only a couple of hundred nanometres, can be transferred to glass, plastic and any other flexible material and will open up a huge range of new possibilities for flexible electronics.[29] The prospect of having medicine bottles which let you know when it is time to take your next dose, or having heart and other health monitoring devices sewn into your clothes is a step closer to reality. And with Plastic Logic, a company in Cambridge, UK, announcing that it will build the first factory to manufacture plastic electronics on a commercial scale, the prospect of having thin-film technologies embedded in our day-to-day lives may be just around the corner. The facility will produce display modules for portable electronic reader devices which will enable electronic reader products to have the same utility and ease of use as a book does today.[30] Returning to BABY for one moment and comparing this machine to modern day equipment makes for an interesting comparison. The microchip, on which the modern computer depends, is 25 million times more powerful, and has 64 million times more memory than BABY. Clearly, the last 50 years have seen incredible advances in power, reliability and price, and it would be reasonable to expect the next 50 will see much the same.

The cumulative impact of the first four generations of technology has been to position IT at the heart of most business activity and set the foundations for its commoditization. The current debate within the industry is whether or not IT has become such an infrastructural technology that it no longer matters from a strategic standpoint. Nicolas Carr's book – *Does*

IT Matter?[31] in which he set out the reasons why, ruffled many feathers in the industry, but is merely reflecting how commoditized IT has become. The argument is that IT is now so deeply embedded within every business that it has become increasingly difficult to differentiate one company from another. Indeed, as IT has resolved the problems associated with reliability, connectivity and interoperability it has signed its own strategic death warrant. Carr points out that many businesses have to continue to pay for commodity resources, such as stationery and electricity as they couldn't function without them. The same is true of IT. Take it away and the majority of organizations would fail and quickly. The important point to note here is that just because IT is a commodity it does not mean that additional investments are not required to keep pace with change and to ensure the continued smooth running of the business. Organizations have invested trillions of dollars since the 1940s and although some of this has clearly been wasted (and continues to be), much of it has increased the efficiency and effectiveness of the underlying organizational processes. The price is clearly worth the pain and expense. Organizations will still need to spend significant sums on technology to maintain the digital fabric of the company, but this is no longer a strategic spend, it is infrastructural. The fundamental theme of Carr's argument is therefore around the separation of commodity from non-commodity resources. The former are incapable of providing immediate strategic advantage, whilst the latter are not. Unfortunately whilst in the past IT might have been in the latter category, today it is firmly in the former.

Carr is not alone in his views, as others point out that so much computing technology is now available and is of such a high quality that the industry is at last capable of delivering the promise of effective computing with near zero intervention to make it work properly.[32] This commoditization is reflected in the increasing pressures on the suppliers of IT and on the experts themselves. With respect to the suppliers, their number has reduced dramatically on the back of the demands for common, integrated and interoperable applications alongside the expectation of increased value for money (in other words, more power for lower cost). This has allowed the variation in platforms and operating systems, so long an issue in enterprise-wide computing, to virtually disappear, as the majority of computing needs can now be met by Intel architecture-based solutions.[33] Although there are some in the industry who still believe that IT is not quite as commoditized as commentators such as Carr like to believe, it is clear that hardware is already commoditized and software development will undoubtedly follow, especially as more Open Source software becomes available. Moreover, as computing becomes more like a utility such as gas, water or electricity, the creation of standards will ensure that the end users will be able to seek out the most cost-effective service provider thereby increasing the downward pressure on price.

IT staff are already finding it increasingly difficult to charge a premium for their services. There are at least four reasons for this. First, as discussed above, the elimination of proprietary software and operating systems means that the skills required by the market become less specialized and hence undifferentiated. Second, service providers need to keep their costs down in order to maintain their margins. Third, organizations no longer perceive IT to be adding strategic advantage and therefore are unwilling to pay such high fees or salaries for the services IT experts provide. And fourth, the huge number of Indian IT experts flooding the market is adding to the downward pressure on incomes.

These changes are already beginning to filter through to the industry itself as it begins to adjust to an era of slower and steady growth.[34] Recent earnings of the major players in the industry are reflecting this; second quarter earnings in 2006 of companies such as Dell Inc., Microsoft Corp and Hewlett Packard are all reporting lower income, earnings and profits and none predict any return soon to the double digit growth they were used to at the height of the Tech Boom. The industry, like so many others, is maturing; and despite believing that the IT industry was immune, many now recognize that the industry is as large as it is going to be. During the boom times computer companies rushed to meet the demands of its ever increasing customer bases by throwing money and resources at everything from sales through to distribution. They now find themselves saddled with fat infrastructures and too many staff at a time when they have to compete more aggressively for market share. This means keeping a much sharper eye on costs and seeking out opportunities to reduce their overall cost base through mergers and acquisitions, reorganizing and restructuring and eliminating headcount. Like its rail, airline and telecoms brethren, it too has drifted into the commoditized zone.

The process of industrial commoditization

The model of commoditization introduced in Chapter 2 is suitable to address the common commodities of coal and coffee, but it needs further enhancement if it is able to explain the process through which industries can become commoditized. Before we can rebuild the model of Figure 2.1 we need to address the impact of new and disruptive technologies and review the factors that can lead to and accelerate the commoditization process.

The impact of new technology

At the industry level any discussion about commoditization must address the role of technology and disruptive technologies in particular. Unlike basic commodities where technology is used to facilitate their extraction, processing and distribution, industries such as those discussed above are impacted by technology in different ways. As technology unfurls it has the ability to fundamentally change the nature and profitability of an entire industry. According to Cartloa Perez, technologies typically pass through two distinct periods.[35] The first, or installation period, is typified by the development of a rapid interest in the new technology, especially as a means of making a fast buck. Everyone from engineers to innovators and investors (both professional and amateur) piles in. This period involves two stages; the first, irruption, is when the technology first appears and the second is the gilded age which is where the quick bucks are made. The technology then hits the turning point which either results in it crashing and fading away or transitioning to the more stable and arguably more effective deployment period. During this period the technology once again passes through two stages. The first is the synergy or golden age when it begins to penetrate society on a much broader scale and the second is maturity when it becomes part of the fabric of an industry or, increasingly, society. Any industry which relies heavily on technology has usually passed through these two periods. It is interesting to note that, unlike the rail and airline industries, the IT and telecommunications industries have passed through this cycle on more than one occasion. For example the mad rush to come up with tin pot ideas for Dot Com companies burnt vast sums of venture capital as well as time, effort and money within many, many corporations. Some of this was clearly wasted as Philip Kaplan[36] so eloquently put in his review of Pets.com *'I'm out of dog food and my cat's box needs new litter. I know what I'll do: I'll order Dog Chow and Fresh Step online from a sock puppet and then I'll watch the dog starve and the cat shit all over the house while I wait for it to be delivered'.* Others such as Amazon.com have grown to become icons of the Dot Com age and have survived, although achieving little in the way of profits. Most of course failed, as although by March 2000, 378 Internet companies were publicly traded with a collective market capitalization of $1.5 trillion, between spring 2000 and summer 2001, 31 000 Dot Com employees were laid off, and 103 companies went bust at a cost of $1 trillion. A similar swift investment cycle has followed the release of the third generation (3G) mobile phone licenses which promised users the opportunity to use their phones for more than just voice and texting. With 3G, which is significantly faster than their 2G or digital equivalent, it is possible to surf the net and download music and videos. This was seen to provide a major revenue stream for the mobile phone suppliers who crawled over each other to get a piece of the action, only to pay way over the odds (by literally billions) and then have to write it all off later.

Another aspect of technology is its ability to disrupt incumbents. The term disruptive technology was first coined by Joseph Bower and Clayton Christensen in their seminal article in the *Harvard Business Review*.[37] Disruptive technologies are those which have the capability of meeting the demands of new, not existing customers. The argument behind this is quite simple. Successful companies tend to stay close to their customers, which mean they will carefully assess the needs of their existing customers before launching any new technology. If the new technology meets these requirements then it is launched. If it doesn't, then it remains on the cutting room floor. In fact it is very difficult for the established company to do much more than this because it is near impossible for them to gain the necessary commitment internally to do something as radical as pursuing a new and unknown customer base. This leaves the market wide open to new entrants who develop and exploit a new technology which has the capability of severely disrupting the markets of existing players. One of the many examples Bower and Christensen discuss is the emergence of desktop and Personal Computer (PC) based computing. When these low end technologies were first launched the incumbents, such as Wang, Prime and Digital Equipment were focused on mid-range technologies, which is precisely what their customers wanted. At that time there was no requirement for PCs although this changed as the power of the PC increased exponentially. Over a relatively short period, the existing players suffered as their customers switched to the increasingly powerful PC. So although the new technology, in this case the PC, had little impact to begin with and did not threaten the customers of companies such as Wang because they were sufficiently different from the existing technologies, over time the benefits provided by the PC outweighed those of the mini computer and the customers quickly switched. This raises the essential point about disruptive technologies. When they first appear they only appeal to new, not existing customers, but because of the rapid innovation that is usually associated with them, their performance trajectory soon outpaces that of the existing technologies and dislodges them as their appeal widens.

MARKET AND INTERVENTIONIST FACTORS

The factors that lead to the commoditization of an industry are best summarized as in Figure 3.2. The factors can be split into those that can be considered market related and those which are interventionist in nature. Although the factors can work in isolation they often work in concert acting as an accelerator to commoditization. For example, the freeing up of markets through government intervention, coupled with the emergence of new entrants and a desire on the customers' part to get more by way of goods and services for their money, has facilitated the commoditization of the telecommunications industry. Similarly, the combination of shock events, government intervention, new entrants and customers has allowed the airline industry to go through a period of rapid commoditization. The interventionist factors recognize that there are certain activities outside the direct control of the organization that help to drive commoditization. Although organizations may be able to exert a degree of influence on how these play out, for example if they are part of a trade body, or standards committee, the majority have to respond to them once the full extent of their impact becomes known. Market factors on the other hand are more manageable and controllable. These factors typically fall within any market-based model such as those developed by management gurus like Porter.

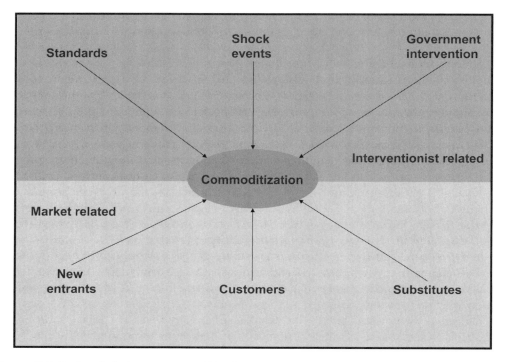

Figure 3.2 Factors in industry commoditization

Interventionist factors

There are three factors which can be considered to be interventionist in nature:

* shock events
* standards
* government intervention.

Shock events are thankfully rare, although their impact can be very significant. We are used to hearing about natural disasters, such as hurricanes, flash floods, volcanoes, earthquakes and tsunamis. Each has the capacity to cause major loss of life and disrupt normal and economic conditions. Although some communities may never fully recover, the majority gradually return to normal. Other shock events, which are not due to natural causes, are also possible and these can be equally disruptive. At its extreme the disruption caused by a shock event can be severe enough to force a company into liquidation, as we saw with the collapse of Enron which also took down Arthur Andersen. Within the context of this book, we are more interested in how shock events can lead to commoditization or at the very least increase the speed at which commoditization can occur. For example, the airline industry may eventually have become commoditized, but the combined impact of SARS, 9/11 and other factors such as the willingness of people to put up with the no frills service and the desire for second homes in other countries opened up an opportunity for the budget airlines to attack the market share of the incumbent full service carriers and accelerated the commoditization of the industry.

Standards are developed by industry bodies or collections of organizations that are keen to develop common practices for the good of an industry or the wider economy. The purpose of standards is to reduce complexity, advance understanding and generate common and consistent mechanisms for executing certain activities. Standards are also developed to enhance quality and improve safety through the adoption of common protocols and procedures. Once introduced and widely accepted and adopted they serve to normalize those activities with which they are associated. This plays an important role in helping to reduce the requirement for specialists and experts. As we saw in the introduction, the need for expert project managers has reduced over time as the mystique and complexities of the craft have been uncovered and codified. Standards and their associated codification and simplification play an important role in the commoditization process because they help to reduce complexity. As complexity is reduced and a common understanding of the standards develops, the opportunity to simplify job roles and processes is greatly enhanced. Standards in each of the industries explored above have allowed each to establish common working practices which have been adopted by individual companies and over time by the industry as a whole. This was clearly a factor when United Airlines outsourced its aircraft maintenance, and the adoption of the accepted industry standards helped British Airways respond to the threat of the budget airlines. Similarly standards have played a significant role in the rail, IT and telecoms industries. In each case they have helped to avoid the divergence that would have persisted had standards not been introduced. For example, over the 50 or so years of the IT industry, a variety of standards have been introduced to address almost every conceivable aspect of the industry including open systems, software engineering and chip manufacture. These include the Capability Maturity Model which was developed by the Software Engineering Institute at Carnegie Mellon University as well as the quality standards developed by the International Standards Organization. Standards can take years to develop and similar time spans to gain traction, but when they do, they help to reduce variation and facilitate the wider acceptance of the technology within organizations and society. Paradoxically standardization is an important and necessary factor in allowing a technology (and industry where technology is a critical component) to expand. So in the early stages of the evolution of an industry standardization provides it with the necessary fillip to allow it to expand. Then, once it is established it helps to commoditize it.

Government regulation fulfils two essential roles. The first is in supporting the build up phase of a new industry. During this time the fledgling industry is vulnerable to failure and requires significant investment or support to ensure that it survives. Although this can be provided by speculators, they are too fickle and overly concerned about securing a return on their investment to worry much about the long term fate of the industry. They want to sell at the top of the market and let the speculators who joined too late pick up the tab. As a result governments may take on this role, as they did within the early period of the airline industry. The control exerted by government allows safety and quality standards to be established and embedded within the industry and it also provides subsidies and other financial incentives to ensure the industry matures for the good of the nation. The support does not have to be purely financial, of course, as it is possible for governments to provide a brokering role as they did when addressing the question of competing rail gauges. The second role of government intervention is to stimulate or control market activity. As an industry matures, and especially one which is nationalized, the competitive environment can become stilted and end up delivering only limited value for money. In response a government may deregulate or fully privatize the industry to allow the introduction of healthy competition and through this enhance the overall value. This has been true of the airline, rail and telecoms industries. Each followed a classic government interventionist approach. Where felt necessary governments can stimulate the break up of powerful industry players, as they did with Ma Bell in the early 20th century. More recently, Microsoft has been under the spotlight. Once it had become the defacto standard for PC software in the 1990s it was clear that things would eventually come to a head and it now faces ongoing prosecution for anti-competitive behaviours. The European Union in particular believes it is engaged in illegal practices to maintain dominance of the desktop PC market. It has already paid a record fine of $613 million and is looking at another of $375 million for failing to comply with the 2004 anti-trust ruling.[38]

Market factors

There are three factors which can be considered to be related to the market:

- new entrants
- customers
- substitutes.

New entrants always pose a threat to an existing incumbent; it's the nature of competition. In order to prevent new companies entering their space, existing businesses will do everything they can to build barriers to entry. These may include the use of propriety technologies, long-term contractual arrangements, superior products, excellent service and support levels and investing in building powerful brands. All of these can certainly help, but as technology continues to make significant inroads into every industry the ability to keep the competition out becomes more difficult if not impossible. This is especially true of the high tech industries which have few barriers to entry. With sufficient capital, a good business plan and the technological know-how it is possible to take market share from even the largest corporate. The explosive growth of the Dot Com companies during the late 1990s and until the crash of 2001 is testament to how easy this can be. Thousands of companies emerged which challenged the whole concept of retail and the need to have bricks and mortar. Armed with the Internet it was and of course still is, possible to sell anything to anyone. It is here where the customer has a significant role to play in the commoditization process.

Without customers most companies would go out of business, which means every corporation has to listen to them. Increasingly they are seeking out better value for money and as with new entrants the emergence of the Internet has given them the tools with which to get the best deal. In the past, organizations could largely charge what they liked because the effort required to complete a thorough investigation of the market would be too much and would take too long. These days assessing the price of goods and services has never been so easy, which means organizations have to price more competitively than they have in the past. Apart from a few top-end brands, most businesses have to ensure they remain competitive, especially when it is so easy to shop around using the Internet. Once customers look beyond the brand and the basic features of the product or service they are seeking to buy, you know that you are in the commoditized zone. Michael Silverstein in *Treasure Hunt*[39] describes this process as the value calculus in which the consumer makes a value calculation each and every time she makes a purchase. The calculation involves weighing up a variety of factors that are financial, emotional and practical in nature. Unlike in the past when consumer decisions would match demographics and income; in other words low income families would purchase cheap goods, middle income families more expensive products and the wealthy exclusive and very expensive items, this is no longer the case. Today the consumer will compare price, technical value, functional value, the purchase excitement (how easy is it to buy), how integrated the retail experience is with support and service levels and of course the emotional impact of buying a product. The would-be consumer's socioeconomic position no longer determines what they will purchase. So a wealthy individual may well buy his next sports car from Porsche, but he will buy his stationery from Wal-Mart or Costco. This behaviour has important implications for how organizations choose to respond to the challenge that commoditization brings, as this type of consumer behaviour is increasingly reflected within corporate buying. We have to remember, however, that when every element of the value calculation is the same, the consumer and corporate buyer will fall back on price.

Substitution is not as straightforward as the previous two factors because it involves generating a new product or service that is currently unavailable. Whilst a new entrant can piggyback on existing technologies and business models, those aiming to substitute an existing product or service for a new one have a lot more work to do. As might be expected, substitution is usually simpler in the high tech industries such as IT where a new product can be taken up very quickly, or during the early stages of the evolution of an industry, when competitors fight it out in an attempt to steal as much market share as possible. Take IBM and Microsoft for example. In 1992 IBM was at a crossroads. Since its beginnings in the early 20th century, it was known for its pioneering of computer technologies, initially with punched cards and then with the mainframe computer. IBM's market share of the computing market advanced to 30 per cent. During this time, the organization's culture had evolved into a cosy world of limited competition, the result of its runaway success. IBM staffers used to be well known for their black suits and white shirts. Little variation was allowed. However, the shift to UNIX and then to personal computing managed to catch IBM unawares. In particular they failed to understand the full impact of personal computers on their customers and the wider business community, believing they would only be used by scientists and students. They also believed that personal computers would never challenge their business. As a result they allowed Microsoft to take control of the operating system and Intel to control the microprocessor. By 1993, IBM's revenues were plummeting; income from mainframes had dropped from $13 billion in 1990 to less than $7 billion. In the first four months of 1993, profit had declined by $800 million. In order to address these issues, the new CEO, Louis Gerstner, sought to reduce costs by almost $9 billion, which involved reducing headcount by 35 000. This was in addition to the 45 000 people that the previous CEO, John Akers, had dismissed. Gerstner also took action to revive the brand, which despite the problems was still strong. This involved changing the performance measurement system, shifting the company to becoming more service rather than product oriented, and expanding its offerings in its middleware portfolio (which it did by acquiring Lotus Development Corporation). All of these actions have helped to rebuild the IBM brand, which is a remarkable achievement given the sorry state it was in at the beginning of 1993.

Table 3.1 summarizes the primary, secondary and tertiary drivers of commoditization for each of the industries reviewed in this chapter. It is clear that although the path through which commoditization is achieved may be different both in terms of timing and impact; the factors are often the same. The major difference lies in the dominance of one or more of the factors that upsets the status quo within a particular industry. This is helpful to the CEO and others who are concerned about commoditization, as it begins to shed light on those factors which they need to monitor.

Industry	Primary factor	Secondary factors	Tertiary factors
Rail	Standards	Government intervention	Substitutes, customers
Telecommunications	Standards	Customers, government intervention	New entrants
Airlines	Government intervention	Shock events	New entrants, customers
Information technology	New entrants	Standards	Substitutes

Table 3.1 Drivers of industrial commoditization

A REVISED PROCESS

The stages of commoditization of Figure 2.1 are, with suitable adjustments, applicable to industries and result in an enhanced model (Figure 3.3).

Stage ❶ – the industry emerges from its roots, but its full potential is either unknown at this stage, or if recognized, is a long way off from being realized. If the industry is seen to be of national importance, governments will seek to protect it by either keeping it under national control, or establishing regulations to protect it as it grows. This is what happened with the early phases of the airline industry for example.

Stage ❷ – the industry's footprint is widened as investment funds pour in to exploit it. During this period the industry balloons as money is invested in start-up companies to take advantage of the economic potential it presents. Alternative and competing technologies and standards emerge as they did during the early period of the rail and technology industries and any differences are easily absorbed because the sophistication and footprint of the industry is still limited. Where these differences are too disruptive governments may begin to consider the need for standards as they did with railway gauges, but this is often the exception rather than the rule.

Stage ❸ – the industry passes through a period of turbulence during which many of the start-ups begin to fail. Failure results from a variety of reasons including a lack of capital, limited take-up by the market, poorly constructed or unpopular technologies and cut-throat competition. This shakeout period is also typified by the emergence of common standards which help to stabilize the industry and prevent it from fragmenting to the point where it is no longer cohesive. The stronger, more viable companies start to dominate and adopt (or drive) the standards which, over time, become accepted industry-wide. The rail industry passed through this stage quite early, whilst the IT and telecoms industries seem to repeatedly pass through this stage as new technologies and bubbles surface, such as that experienced during the Dot Com boom and bust of 2000 and 2001. For those industries that retain their government protection, this stage can be delayed until much later and may not appear until stages ❹ and

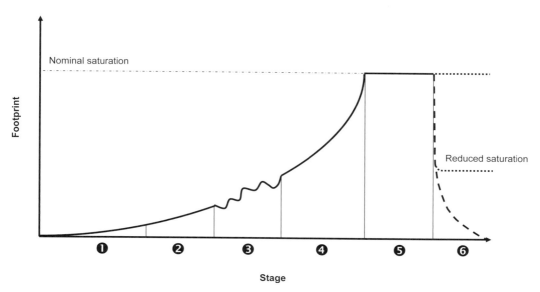

Figure 3.3 The stages of industry commoditization

❺ when governments finally choose to open up the industry to competition (more on this very shortly).

Stage ❹ – the industry, having stabilized, continues its upward path towards commoditization as the processes, technologies and infrastructure associated with it mature. In particular, the infrastructure which is vital to support its expansion is widened to provide improved interconnectivity to ensure the industry is capable of meeting the demands of a larger customer base. Such investment in infrastructure was vital in the rail, air, telecoms and IT industries to allow them the stable and connected base from which to expand their services.

Stage ❺ – the industry has now reached the point at which further growth is difficult without innovation and investment. Indeed most industries at this stage prefer to maintain a steady income stream rather than pursue new and potentially risky opportunities. As we have seen this is where disruptive technologies pose the biggest threat as new entrants introduce new products and services which can eventually undermine the incumbents. It is also the stage where the customer base has reached its natural saturation point above which it is difficult to pass unless new markets are identified and exploited. Once this saturation point has been reached industries only tend to market new products and services to existing customers rather than new ones.

Stage ❻ – as with commodities, the significance of an industry can decline over time, especially if it fails to innovate or where new competition begins to invade its market. We have seen this within the rail industry which is long past its true peak. Some industries will completely die out during this stage, especially when technology makes them redundant, whilst others will fall to a new saturation point.

In addition to the changes that reflect the specific nature of the industry wave of commoditization, the factors identified in Figure 3.2 can also change the profile of Figure 3.3. For example an industry's prospects might rise significantly following its deregulation and lead to a much higher nominal saturation than would have otherwise been reached whilst under government control (Figure 3.4). Deregulation is typically followed by a wave of new investment as companies start up with the aim of capturing the deregulated incumbent's market share. They do so through a combination of pricing strategies, innovation and enhanced service models. At the same time they also seek out new customers by bringing new products to market so that they end up playing in a much larger pool thereby making it more likely that they will succeed.

Another change in the profile might result from the introduction and adoption of standards which can result in the earlier commoditization of an industry. Because standards demystify the underlying processes and procedures associated with an industry they allow new entrants and substitutes to emerge sooner, which drives up competition and creates a downward pressure on price. This tends to shorten stage ❹ and lengthen stage ❺ (Figure 3.5). Similarly, although less often, the impact of a shock event can also result in the more rapid commoditization of an industry, as we have seen with the emergence of the discount airlines following the disruptions

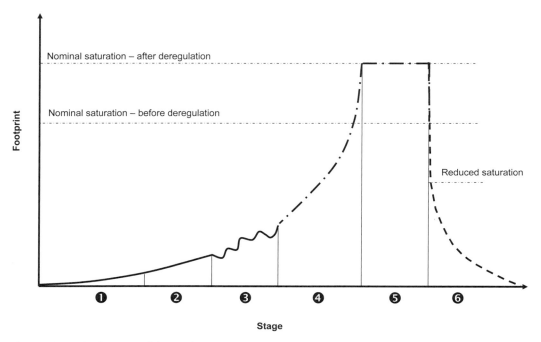

Figure 3.4 The impact of deregulation

of 9/11 and the SARS outbreak.

This chapter has discussed how entire industries can become commoditized. Most follow the same path although often at different speeds; and many can be affected by other factors that can be outside of their control, such as government intervention and shock events. What this chapter tells us is that few industries are immune from commoditization and, using history as a predictor of the future, it should be possible to spot the warning signs of impending commoditization. The next and possibly the most critical wave of commoditization, which is that of white-collar work, will be discussed once we have analyzed two of its cornerstones – globalization and the rise of the Internet.

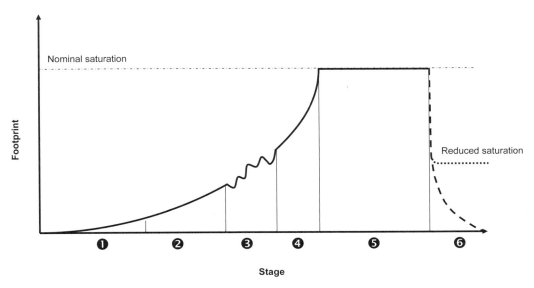

Figure 3.5 The impact of standards

References

1 Cairncross, F. (1997) *The Death of Distance*, Boston, Massachusetts: Harvard Business School Press, p. 4.
2 Bosshart, D. (2007) *Cheap? The Real Cost of Living in a Low Price, Low Wage World*, London: Kogan Page, p. 86.
3 Quoted in Standage, T. (ed.) (2005) *The Future of Technology*, London: Profile Books, p. 7.
4 Quoted in Standage, T., Bower, J. and Christensen, C. (1995) Disruptive technologies catching the wave, *Harvard Business Review*, January–February, p. 16.
5 For a more detailed description of the events surround the Rainhill Trials, see www.rainhill-civic-society. org.uk/html/rainhillHistory.html.
6 Norgate, S. (2006) *Beyond 9 to 5: Your Life in Time*, London: Weidenfeld & Nicolson, p. 13.
7 Carr, N. (2004) *Does IT Matter? Information Technology and the Corrosion of Competitive Advantage*, p. 27.
8 Murray, I. (2005) No Way to Run a Railway: Lessons from British Privatization, Adam Smith Institute, p. 5.
9 Ambrose, S. (2005) *Nothing Like it in the World: The Men Who Built the Railway that United America*, London: Pocket Books, p. 18.
10 For a detailed review of the impact of government intervention on the UK railway industry see Murray, I. (2005) *No Way to Run a Railway: Lessons from British Privatization*, Adam Smith Institute.
11 Making the Modern World – The Railways and Work, www.makingthemodernworld.org.uk.
12 Gross, D. (2007) *Pop! Why Bubbles are Great for the Economy*, New York: HarperCollins, p. 71.
13 Ibid., pp. 71–72.
14 For an excellent historical analysis of the telecommunications industry, see www.fht-esslingen.de/ telehistory.
15 Ibid., pp. 32–33.
16 PricewaterhouseCoopers (2006) *Civil aerospace in the 21st Century: Business as usual...or a fresh start?*, p. 5.
17 Hambling, D. (2005) *Weapons Grade: Revealing the Links Between Modern Warfare and Our High-tech World*, London: Constable, pp. 47–78.
18 Ibid. p. 3.
19 Uchitelle, L. (2006) *The Disposable American: Layoffs and Their Consequences*, New York: Alfred A. Knopf, pp. 49–79.
20 Alderighi, M., Cento, A., Nijkamp, P. and Rietveld, P. (2004) *The entry of low-cost airlines*, Tinbergen Institute Discussion Paper, TI 2004-074/3, p. 2.
21 BA Investor Day, 2006 – see www.ba.com.

22 Alderighi, M., Cento, A., Nijkamp, P. and Rietveld, P. (2004) *The entry of low-cost airlines*, Tinbergen Institute Discussion Paper, TI 2004-074/3, p. 2.
23 Michaels, D. (2007) 'Open skies' may spur air mergers, *The Wall Street Journal*, 23–25 March, p. 1.
24 For a fuller description of the impacts which IT has had on the organization over the last 40 years see Somogyi, E. K., and Galliers, R. D., From data processing to strategic information systems – a historical perspective, *Journal of Information Technology*, March 1987.
25 50 years of computing, *Computer Consultant*, November 1998, p. 27.
26 Kurzweil, R. (1999) *The Age of Spiritual Machines*, London: Phoenix, p. 130.
27 Saren, C., Beginning of the end for the silicon chip, *Computer Weekly*, 22 July 1999, p. 3.
28 Newswire (2006) Team invents fast, flexible computer chips on plastic, www.reliableplant.com.
29 Ibid.
30 For more information on thin-film technologies and their application see www.plasticlogic.com.
31 Carr, N. (2004) *Does IT Matter? Information Technology and the Corrosion of Competitive Advantage*, Boston, Massachusetts: Harvard Business School Press, p. 27.
32 Smoot, C-M. (2004) Computing Commoditization, www.tic.com/whitepapers.
33 Ryder, C. and King, C. (2002) Commoditization, standards and the enterprise, Segeza White Paper, March, p. 1.
34 Tam, P-W., Guth, A.,and Lawton, C. (2006) Once highflying tech industry reboots for era of slower growth, *The Wall Street Journal*, 27 July, pp. A1 & A9.
35 Standage, T. (ed.) (2005) *The Future of Technology*, London: Profile Books, p. 4.
36 Kaplan, P. (2002) *F'd Companies,* New York: Simon & Schuster, pp. 16–17.
37 Bower, J. and Christensen, C. (1995) Disruptive technologies catching the wave, *Harvard Business Review*, January–February, p. 16.
38 Acohido, B. (2006) Europe fines Microsoft $375m, *USA Today*, 13 July, Money Section B, p. 1.
39 Silverstein, M. (2006) *Treasure Hunt: Inside the Mind of the New Consumer*, New York: Portfolio, pp. 46–48.

4 *Cornerstones of the Final Wave: Globalization and the Internet*

Globalization emerged in the 1970s as if from nowhere, fully grown, enrobed in an aura of inclusivity. Advocates and believers argued with audacity that, through the prism of a particular school of economics, societies around the world would be taken in new, interwoven and positive directions.[1]

Globalization isn't just a story about a rising number of export markets for western producers. Rather, it's a story about massive waves of income redistribution, from rich labour to poor labour, from labour as a whole to capital, from workers to consumers and from energy users towards energy producers. This is a story about winners and losers, not a fable about economic growth.[2]

We hear a lot about globalization and it is one of those subjects where people take sides; there are those who believe it is an essential engine for growth, inevitable and something we should embrace, and there are those who believe it to be disruptive and damaging, allowing multinational companies to exploit the poor communities across the world and something that should be avoided and ideally rolled back. Like everything else, your viewpoint depends on where you are standing. For those who see globalization shifting their jobs overseas or feel exploited in the sweatshops of the Far East and China, it tends to be negative. For those who are running global corporations and need to develop effective business models capable of exploiting economies of scale and the numerous markets around the world, they see globalization as a positive enhancement.

Apart from providing a little bit of history about globalization, for the purposes of this book globalization is discussed in terms of how it facilitates commoditization; principally through the opening up of the global labour market. This chapter is also about the Internet and how it not only provides an essential cornerstone to commoditization but also how it is allowing it to extend and strengthen its grip. It is the combined effect of globalization and the Internet that has created an environment in which industries will continue to commoditize, and especially those that rely on a knowledgeable and connected workforce. I believe it has created the necessary foundation on which the third wave of commoditization can thrive; that of white-collar work.

Globalization

On a technology campus off the bustle of the Hosur Road in Electronics City, Bangalore, engineers are fiddling with the innards of a 65-inch television, destined for American shops in 2006. The boffins in the white lab coats work for Wipro, an Indian technology company. Wipro has a research-and-development contract with a firm called Brillian, an American company based half a world away in Tempe, Arizona. Brillian's expertise is in display technology. Wipro's job is to put together the bits that will turn Brillian's technology into a top-end TV. Wipro is sourcing the television's bits and pieces from companies in America, Japan, Taiwan and South Korea. After design and testing assembly will pass to a specialist contract manufacturer, such as Flextronics or Solectron. The buyer of the finished television might use a credit card administered from Kuala Lumpur, Malaysia. After-sales service might be provided by a polite young Indian call-centre agent, trained in stress management and taught how to aspirate her Ps the American way.[3]

We are currently in the third wave of globalization.[4] The first wave, which was long and slow, began in 1415 with the emergence of the caravel, a fast, manoeuvrable ship built by the Portuguese to explore the world, and ended with the outbreak of the First World War. It was the caravel that was used by Columbus on his many expeditions which expanded the West's knowledge of the world and extended their commercial and political reach. Over time it allowed trade to flow more freely across the globe and shifted the dominance and economic power from the countries of the Middle East to Portugal. For example, before the Portuguese arrived the Egyptians were able to control the price of pepper by restricting how much of the stuff was brought to market every year. However, once the Portuguese entered the fray pepper prices fell by 80 per cent as they wrested control away from the Egyptians and flooded the market with cheap pepper. After seeing how effective the Portuguese had been it wasn't long before the other great powers of the time, most notably the English, Dutch, Spanish and French, adopted the caravel and undertook their own expeditions to the New World, Africa and Asia. Throughout this first wave of globalization trade continued to expand and technology continued to advance, culminating in the industrial revolution. At this time the Gold Standard was conceived and adopted across the trading nations to facilitate the free flow of capital, thereby providing further fuel for the globalization of trade. This all changed with the advent of the First World War and the mincing machine that took away the lives of millions of productive workers. The Great War was followed by the Great Depression in the late 1920s and early 1930s and then the Second World War. The belief that globalization would eliminate the need for combat through the integration of the dominant nation states through trade was found to be wanting; this first wave of globalization had failed to live up to its promises.

Whereas the first wave of globalization was initiated by the Portuguese, the second, which lasted for a much shorter period (1947–2000), was championed by the Americans. The physical and economic devastation that had been wrought by the First World War required urgent attention and this was the primary focus of this wave of globalization. The secondary focus was on developing an approach to trade that was less restrictive than in the past and which was capable of providing an effective alternative to communism. Over time this also had to deal with the need to counter the emerging (real and perceived) threats that materialized with the Cold War and especially with the conflicts such as Korea and Vietnam which provided the military playground in which the two competing economic models slugged it out. During this second wave, the World Trade Organization was created with the purpose of facilitating the process through which trade barriers could be lifted and free trade allowed to emerge. At the same time, and recognizing that the United States was undamaged by the war, the dollar became the global currency with all others being tied to it at a fixed exchange rate. This was designed to stimulate trade and exports to the US, thereby helping the ruined economies of Europe and Asia to recover. In order to maintain a stable economic environment, in which extreme fluctuations in currencies were minimized, the dollar was pegged to gold.

As this second wave progressed, the American economy boomed as it became the low cost producer of its day through the supply of materials and products to the recovering nations of Western Europe and Japan. At the same time it raised the living standards of its own workforce, which allowed them to become the global consumer of choice (a position the American consumer still holds today, although with major consequences for their level of indebtedness). This created a virtuous cycle in which the United States sucked in imports from Europe and Asia which established the necessary foundations for their economic recovery. And as the global economy restabilized, the previously devastated parts of Europe boomed; it was the communist regimes that suffered, as well as those who maintained a restrictive and protectionist stance toward global trade. The period 1950 to 1973, which is often referred to as the golden age of growth, started to unravel in the early 1970s when the balance of trade between the United States and the rest of the world moved into deficit.

When the French started to exchange their excess dollars for gold, the United States government became deeply concerned and in response decided to decouple their currency from gold. The stability provided up until that point was literally lost overnight as every currency had to fix or float against the dollar and deal with the ups and downs of the dollar's value as the American economy fluctuated with the economic cycle. The beauty of the model was clear to the United States as their Treasury could print as much of its currency as it liked and the balance of trade could run at a deficit without much impact. Over time however, the trade deficit ballooned, especially with Japan, and this, coupled with a loss of manufacturing and high technology jobs to the Far East, began to raise questions about the viability of this second wave of globalization and more importantly the competitiveness of the American economy. Before this issue came to a head however, a number of events came to the rescue:

- The deal between the United States, Europe and Japan to intervene in the foreign currency markets to help the dollar fall.
- Increases in taxes which helped to offset the rise in the deficit.
- A reduction in government spending, and especially in the defence budget, which was mainly due to the fall of the Berlin Wall and the collapse of the communist economic model in the early 1990s.
- The centrality of the United States to the personal computer and micro chip industries.
- The emergence of the New Economy based upon the Internet.

However, the experiment once again failed, not on the battlefields of Belgium and France as in 1914, but with the bursting of the Dot Com bubble which precipitated a massive fall in stock markets around the world.

The final wave, which started in 2000, is where we are now. Whilst the first wave was built on exploration and second upon reconstruction, this third wave is constructed on the combination of the resurgence of the Chinese and Indian nations and the connected economy. The dominance of globalization has also shifted. While the first and second waves were driven and largely controlled by the West, today's third wave is leading to a significant transfer of power and dominance to the East. As the emerging economies become fully integrated into the global economy and exploit the new technologies developed by the West they will give the global economy its biggest boost since the Industrial Revolution. The real difference between this and the previous two waves is the sheer scale; whilst the former waves covered approximately two thirds of the world, the current one pretty much embraces the entire globe. The shift to free trade, which has resulted in a reduction in protectionist behaviour, has ensured that most nations have the opportunity to participate in the global economy, albeit in some cases the opportunity is still quite limited. This growth is reflected in the share of the world's export market held by the emerging economies which has leapt from 20 per cent in 1970 to 43 per cent currently.[5]

At the heart of the third wave is a massive influx of workers, which has in effect doubled since China, India and Russia embraced the global market, and their rapidly increasing productivity levels which are outstripping those of established economies such as America and Europe. The impact of this is being felt across the world and particularly within the industrialized economies who are facing unprecedented levels of competition and stagnating incomes. According to a number of commentators we are at the beginning of a period characterized by a significant redistribution of wealth – from West to East. As we shall see in the next chapter, the whole notion of work is changing as the newly educated masses of the emerging economies are creating significant downward pressure on incomes. This and other outcomes highlight the growing discontent with globalization identified and debated by an increasing number of authors including Robert Isaak, author of *The Globalization Gap*, who asserts that the speeding up of the economy which has accompanied globalization has increased the gap between the rich and poor principally because the rich nations are more able to respond to the demands of globalization than those which can be considered poor; and John Ralston Saul, author of *The Collapse of Globalism* who believes the globalization experiment is now well and truly dead and has over promised and under delivered. Instead of economics shaping human events, we still witness the power of politics and military force, and Joseph Stiglitz who details the failure of the International Monetary Fund and the World Trade Organization in his book *Globalization and Its Discontents*, especially in respect of their imposition of stringent economic policies on developing nations, often making them worse off. When we consider the following facts and figures associated with the impacts of globalization[6] you can begin to see why there are many out there who believe it to be a malevolent force, particularly when you view it through the lens of wealth distribution:

- The richest 50 million people in the West (primarily the United States and Europe) have the same income as 2.7 billion people in the developing and emerging economies of South America, Africa and Asia.
- The wealthiest 2 per cent of adults own more than 50 per cent of global assets, while the poorest half owns around 1 per cent.[7]
- Nearly 90 per cent of the world's wealth is held in North America, Europe, Japan and Australia.[8]
- In 1820 20 per cent of the world's people in the richest countries had three times the income of the poorest 20 per cent. In 1960 this had grown to 30 times and by 1997 to 74 times.
- A few hundred millionaires have as much wealth as the world's poorest 2.5 billion.
- The combined wealth of the world's 200 richest people reached $1 trillion in 1999, which was seven times the wealth of 582 million people living in some 43 developing countries.

Such a snapshot of the inequalities that globalization brings is possibly one reason why Warren Buffet, Bill Gates and others are turning to philanthropy in the twilight years of their commercial careers. But whatever your viewpoint, the reality is that globalization will continue to have a profound effect on countries, businesses and individuals alike. And, as we will see in the next chapter, it is already having an impact on the middle class workers of the West who are witnessing stagnating incomes and increased instability as the finite amount of capital around the world flows to the emerging economies. Working at different levels it will shift the relative importance and economic power of the nations of the world, change the internal and market dynamics of corporations and impact their very survival and alter the skills, expertise and attitudes expected of the workforce. The process of globalization is therefore leading to an increase in the levels of uncertainty for us all, as it causes corporations to reconsider their hiring policies, location and skill requirements more frequently than in the past. It is also leading to uplift in the demand for smart, versatile employees who are capable of continuous learning. This is the upside of globalization. But like everything else in life, there will be winners and losers and most of us will have to get used to continuously adjusting to the changing competitive environment in which we find ourselves. I will return to the topic of winners and losers and inequality in general in Part IV, where I take a look into the future of commoditization and its potential long-term implications and effects.

The Internet

I recently received an MP3 player for my birthday and over the course of a few weekends, I managed to load all the headache music that my friends and family detest so much (apart from my son, who seems to like even worse music than me). The ability to select only those tracks that I really liked was a godsend because it got over one of the most annoying things of owning an extensive music collection; having to purchase an album even though I only like a couple of tracks. Now, with the advent of Napster and its competitors, it is possible to download just the music you like from the Internet directly onto your MP3 player. Although I have yet to experience the joy of downloading the tracks I used to listen to in my youth, I was able to source a CD of a 12' record I currently own via Amazon's Market Place, something I could never hope to do at my local HMV store. These are just two of the many examples of how the Internet is changing the underlying economics of business and providing access to products and services which have, hitherto, been controlled by the retailer.

There is no doubt that globalization is a major force and one that will continue to exert its influence on the world economy, but its recent effects would have been far more muted had it not been for the emergence of the Internet and the communication technologies that underpin it. Whereas globalization has evened out the markets and provided everyone with a more level playing field on which to compete, the Internet has provided the access which globalization has not. If anything the Internet is proving to be an even fairer playing field than globalization has been able to achieve or perhaps ever could.

The impact of the Internet, like so many technological advances, has suffered from the over-exuberance of the technologists. Although its birth was a relatively quiet one within the academic and military communities, it was the emergence of the World Wide Web which came with Netscape that lit the touch paper of the Dot Com bubble of the late 1990s. It wasn't long before individuals and business angels, who were crazy enough to back them, were building their businesses on foundations of sand believing that their idea would change the retail world forever. Like the South Sea and Tulip Bubbles that preceded it, a significant minority made vast amounts of cash, but the majority lost their shirts. The fallout from the bursting of the bubble and the precipitous falls in the stock markets around the world that accompanied it took their toll. Some six or so years later, stock markets have finally recovered their lost ground (but let's be thankful, the UK stock market took 100 years to recover following the bursting of the South Sea Bubble). The Internet too has changed. The twenty-something MBA graduates with tin pot ideas and flaky business plans often supported by naive celebrities, have been replaced by sensible business people who recognize the significance of the Internet, but are not silly enough to believe their own press. Some of them were there at the start but have now matured and learnt from their earlier experiences. During the early days of the Internet bubble opinion was divided into two camps; those that believed that the traditional retailer was dead and those who felt that the Internet was going to be short lived. Both were wrong. What we are now seeing is a convergence of the two with traditional retailers, such as Argos offering their customers the ability to shop on line and pick-up in store and others, including Marks and Spencer, introducing kiosks within their stores so that customers can browse a wider selection of products and order them over the Internet.[9]

One of the most interesting books I have read on the impact of the Internet is Chris Anderson's *The Long Tail*.[10] What separates this from so many of the books written by consultants and academics, such as *Blur,* is that it is based upon reality rather than on prediction and ridiculous amounts of hot air and bullshit. Too much of the early material was based upon the usual hubris of gurus, consultants and commentators who predicted profound changes within short timeframes only to be proved to be very wide of the mark. In the book, Anderson discusses the impact of the Internet in terms of access and what he terms the economics of abundance. His argument is that the Internet has made it possible to sell anything, no matter what specialist niche your customer might be interested in. His long curve demonstrates that even the oddest or most bizarre niche will find customers. Although absolute sales might be very low when compared to the best selling items, when the sales of all the long tail products are combined they represent a significant market and revenue stream that can be larger than those of the best sellers combined. It is this that separates the Internet from the mainstream bricks and mortar businesses. Despite traditional retailers offering a wide range of products, they are typically only those which sell well; the rest are never stocked and hence never sold, and they remain invisible to the buying public. With the Internet, however, access to everything is possible and because the shop window is on line, retailers are able to hold items that would never be stocked in their physical stores. This long tail represents a huge opportunity to those willing to exploit it because although only a few of each product may be sold, when multiplied by the sheer number of products available it is possible to create an economically viable business. Anderson terms this the economics of abundance. What has made this possible is, according to Anderson, six themes and three forces.[11] The six themes are:

1. There are more niches than hits. In other words the number of best selling products is exceeded by that of also rans, which would have traditionally been ignored by retailers.
2. The costs of reaching the niches and those interested in them have fallen to such a low level that it is now far cheaper and hence more viable to look beyond the best sellers. The combination of increasing speed of access and more effective and targeted search capabilities is making it much easier to find even the most elusive products.
3. There need to be suitable filters and other tools in place to facilitate the ranking of products as well as the facility to share recommendations with potential buyers so that they can be guided to those products which they will find the most valuable or relevant. It is the presence of these filters that drives the demand down the curve and makes it longer.
4. As well as extending the demand curve, the presence of filters and recommendations also flattens it, allowing additional hits and niches to emerge although with a much lower demand. In other words there are multiple tails within the broad tail.

5. Taken collectively, the market for the niche products can be larger than the hits typically sold by the mainstream retailers.
6. With all this in place, demand is no longer dictated by the ability to source the product, distribution problems or a lack of information. Everything is available and all the information needed by the consumer to make an informed decision about whether to buy it or not is accessible.

The three forces which underpin the long tail are:

1. Democratizing of production which is the term Anderson uses to describe the ability for anyone to create content and product. This has been made possible through the advances in consumer electronics and especially the personal computer. This lengthens the tail by bringing to market new products and services that may have been difficult to source or service in the past through physical and analogue means.
2. Democratizing distribution which describes the role of the online retailers, such as Amazon, who bring the myriad of products together within a single location. These aggregators make it easy for their potential customers to locate what they want and, using product information plus reviews, determine if it is right for them.
3. Connecting supply and demand which is where sophisticated filters are able to take you to what you are looking for. Their job is to simply filter out everything that is irrelevant to your search so that you can focus on stuff that is. They also allow you access to those niches that would never have been visible in the past. In addition others, such as bloggers, who post reviews and recommendations about products and best sellers lists, have a significant role to play in connecting supply and demand. Mainstream stores such as Wal-Mart are beginning to recognize the value that such information can provide and are currently in the process of rolling out a system that generates television-style audience ratings for products on its shelves. This, according to one commentary, will allow them to revamp their stores to match customer preferences and buying patterns.[12]

The long tail helps to explain why smaller organizations are able to compete more effectively and service their customers in a world so often dominated by the global brands. It also begins to explain how easy it is for new competition to emerge and attack the market of established players and through this begin to erode some of the power of the brand. Over time, size and scale will become less critical than accessibility, visibility and availability. Although Anderson has focused on physical products, the principles of the long tail are just as relevant to those providing services. Therefore, in the same way you can compare the prices of new television sets, you will at some point in the future be able to compare the offerings and eventually prices of service providers (I will come back to this when I discuss the commoditization of process a bit later on in this chapter).

What has globalization and the Internet wrought?

Thomas Friedman summarizes the combined effects of globalization and the Internet incredibly well in *The World is Flat*, in which he identifies the ten events that have flattened the world.[13] For the purposes of this chapter, I have summarized them here:

1. The fall of the Berlin Wall. This was the beginning of the end for the centralized economies of the Soviet era (during the third wave of globalization), which in addition to the Soviet

Empire included India, Brazil and China, and the triumph of capitalism. Friedman also believes it allowed a wave of standardization to travel across the world based upon the sharing of best practices which was accelerated by the rise of the personal computer.

2. When Netscape went public. Netscape was the first widely available Internet browser and it was this that started the Internet revolution (the early boom and bust phase) and connected people with businesses no matter where they were in the world.

3. Workflow software. According to Friedman, connection was in itself insufficient to flatten the world; what was needed was the ability for software to talk to software and it was workflow that allowed this to happen. This took time as for workflow to be truly effective it had to wait for the IT industry to develop the necessary interoperability, common applications and network protocols, and the software developers to build the applications that would allow people to be taken out of the equation. As processes continue to be standardized, the application of workflow will undoubtedly expand.

4. Open sourcing. The emergence of open sourcing, where software developers allow their code to be used, added to and applied for free, overcame the significant barriers associated with copyrighted and proprietary software. Open Source applications such as Apache the Web server and Linux the operating system may not be able to compete directly with organizations like Microsoft (for now at least), but they are, by collaborating with corporations such as IBM, Novell and others creating an environment in which anyone can become part of the code building process and help to rapidly develop new and reliable software applications. Such collaboration is, according to Friedman, a major flattener because it makes available for free software code, development tools and applications that would otherwise have to be purchased.

5. Outsourcing Y2K. The requirement to remediate every IT application in order to hedge against the perceived risks of the millennium bug (the inability for operating systems and software to cope with the change of date from 1999 to 2000) created a huge demand for software engineers. Although many COBOL programmers came out of retirement to remediate the old green screen applications, much of the work was outsourced to the emerging Indian technology companies, who were able to follow a standard process at a very low cost. This was something the majority of Western companies were more than happy to outsource as they had plenty to do just to stay on top of managing their day-to-day businesses. After 2000 came and went without issue, the Dot Com boom and subsequent bust played right into the Indian software companies' hands. The former meant that major Western corporations found themselves shorthanded and in need of software engineers and in the latter they wanted to develop code at the lowest possible price. In both cases the Indians were willing and able to pick up the work.

6. Offshoring. Whilst India succeeded in starting the outsourcing trend, it was China that kick-started the offshoring boom. As soon as China entered the World Trade Organization in 2001 the ability to shift manufacturing under the protection of international law became possible. With their army of skilled and semi skilled labourers China has taken on the mantle of the manufacturer of the world. Factories in the West shut down as production was offshored to China where the labour was a fraction of the cost back home. The levelling effect has been to make other countries in the East, as well as manufacturers in the West, consider their own competitiveness very carefully and respond accordingly. But it is not just about offering cheap labour, as China and others are increasingly raising the bar on quality and levels of education, and moving into the service economy, which has much larger implications for the Chinese and Indian economies and especially the West.

7. Supply chaining. This is all about how horizontal collaboration between suppliers, retailers and customers can create significant value. The flattener in this case is the ability for global supply chains, such as the one developed, managed and enhanced by Wal-Mart,[14] to facilitate the creation and adoption of common standards so that global collaboration is not only possible but also highly efficient. Supply chaining involves a never ending search for more value and increased efficiency by buying directly from manufacturers, reducing costs, keeping inventories low by learning more about customers and applying new technologies such as Radio Frequency Identification (RFID). I will return to the supply chain in Part III, as in a commoditized world the supply chain is a critical component survival.

8. Insourcing. Instead of eliminating their work through outsourcing and offshoring, an increasing number of organizations are insourcing the expertise of other companies to work in the heart of their own. Friedman describes how UPS has transformed itself from being a carrier of packages to being a major player in the insourcing arena, where they work closely with their customers to run and optimize their supply chain. Such deep collaboration is not just restricted to large corporations such as Toshiba, with whom UPS works, is effective as the model for smaller organizations as well. In my mind, insourcing is a perfect example of how Handy's Doughnut Principle (see Chapter 1) works in practice and illustrates just how embedded a third party supplier can be; to the point where it is difficult to spot where the corporation ends and the supplier starts.

9. Informing. This is about how individuals are able to create their own supply chain of knowledge, contacts, collaborators and other communities via the Internet. The sophistication of search engines such as Google allows you to achieve this, but it also allows others to do the same. Some people (I met one recently) have whole sites dedicated to their achievements, not even built by them. The leveller in this case is the ability to find out about anyone and anything, which lays bare peoples' lives, their behaviours, opinions and actions; good and bad, right and wrong.

10. The Steroids. These are the technologies that help to accelerate the other nine flatteners and include such things as VOIP (Voice Over Internet Protocol), enhanced video conferencing technologies such as that being developed by HP and DreamWorks SKG, and wireless technologies. Over time, such technologies will help to transform the nature of office work, allowing the typical executive to take the office wherever he or she is. Nice idea, but as we will see in the next chapter and later on in the book, this has some very significant ramifications for both the nature of work itself and for commoditization.

Bringing Friedman's ten flatteners together and viewing them through the lens of commoditization, which we have discussed in detail in Chapters 2 and 3, allows us to draw out three themes which I believe have set the foundations for the final wave of commoditization; the commoditization of white-collar work. The three themes are:

*   connecting and conducting business anywhere and anytime
*   the 24/7 workplace
*   the commoditization of process.

CONNECTING AND CONDUCTING BUSINESS ANYWHERE AND ANYTIME

It is clear that globalization has shrunk the perception of time and distance and made it much easier to conduct business from anywhere in the world. The Internet has gone one step further and made people and businesses far more accessible because it avoids the usual constraints of face-to-face transactions and is able to transcend some of the limitations imposed by national cultures. A colleague of mine was looking to replace his old business cards and stationery. A simple task and one which it has always been possible to complete without too much effort. He followed the standard route of popping down to the high street and visiting one of the many printers that provide such a service. His quote, which included a design service, came to well over £300 and he would have to wait three weeks before he would get his new cards and letterheads. Although the price was a little high, it was the amount of time he had to wait that he baulked at. So he tried the Internet to see what was available. After a while searching, he came across one company, which was based in Mexico, that could not only design and deliver his new stationery within 48-72 hours, but also charge him less than £100. There was no contest. A straightforward example which illustrates how the Internet can connect suppliers and purchasers together no matter where they are in the world. But the Internet has of course gone much further than bringing my colleague and the Mexican printer together; it has opened up the possibility of providing previously non-tradable services such as accounting and IT from afar. As a result it has widened the pool of talent from which both the purchasers and suppliers of services can draw. For example, Accenture, the global management consultancy, operates a virtual research team that brings together 130 people across 14 countries and 27 cities. The team are able to field any question 24 hours a day, which provides a significant boost to Accenture's ability to deliver its services[15]. Other organizations, such as the Indian technology companies mentioned by Friedman are further examples of how it is possible to source professionals from anywhere around the world. As long as they have the skills and expertise, it no longer matters where they are physically located.

THE 24/7 WORKPLACE

The second theme concerns the availability and access of workers. The ability to connect and conduct business anywhere and anytime has meant that an increasing number of organizations are changing their business models to address the need to deliver their products and services across multiple time zones. As a result, a growing number of white-collar workers are working outside the traditional office hours of nine to five; about half of the 24 million American workers who work outside the hours of 7am and 7pm are in white-collar work such as technology, finance, call centres and healthcare. Many corporations are moving to three hubs – North America; Europe, Middle East and Africa; and Asia Pacific – to provide full time zone coverage and are using these to consolidate their back office activities such as finance, HR and IT as well as to provide a 24/7 service capability to their customers and clients. This growing trend is not just affecting those who are working within multinational companies, as it is also impacting those parts of the local economy that are there to support the general workforce. Many fast food restaurants and supermarkets have extended their opening hours to meet the increased demands from this segment of the workforce, as are an increasing number of call centres which can meet the consumer demands at any time of the day[16]. This ripple effect will continue to play out as more of the workforce is pulled into the global economy. Although many of us may not work in global companies we are increasingly impacted by those that do. The effect is to create a truly 24/7 workplace and workforce.

THE COMMODITIZATION OF PROCESS

But what holds everything together? It is the processes used in your organization. Processes allow you to align the way you do business. They allow you to address scalability and provide a way to incorporate knowledge of how to do things better. Processes allow you to leverage your resources and examine business trends.[17]

In a world of end-to-end, customer focused processes, what matters in the marketplace is the cost of entire processes, regardless of who owns which part of the chain.[18]

The final theme is probably the most significant because without it, the impact of the previous two would be muted. The need to deliver services at any time of the day and from anywhere in the world has necessitated the introduction of common systems and the standardization of process. Any corporation that wishes to provide a reliable service has little choice but to develop and roll out consistent processes. This of course is not easy to achieve, as processes usually develop a life of their own because the interactions of people, structure, and markets and of course politics combine to generate complexity. Despite the attempts at simplifying process, most notably during the reengineering revolution of the 1990s, organizations still find themselves tied up in knots by the inefficiency of their underlying processes. However, things are beginning to change. The shift towards standard processes is accelerating and this will allow increasing amounts of business activity to become codified, standardized and ultimately commoditized which in turn will facilitate the hollowing out of functional activity as predicted by Charles Handy in 1994 (see Chapter 1). Huge effort has already gone into developing processes that can be literally picked up and applied to any business context. For example the Supply Chain Council, which comprises some 800 members, has developed the Supply Chain Operations Reference Model (SCOR) which details the supply chain process (plan, source, make, deliver and return) to a level of detail which permits organizations to assess their own supply chain process against the model using a combination of comprehensive process descriptions and performance metrics. Those organizations that have used SCOR have seen significant changes in the performance of their supply chains.[19] Other initiatives, such as the Massachusetts Institute of Technology creation of an online process handbook containing 5,000 plus processes and activities, and the American Productivity and Quality Center's process classification framework which describes every process in a typical organization are providing the necessary tools which companies can use to both assess and reengineer their processes.[20]

Interest in creating and using process taxonomies and standards is increasing with organizations ranging from consultancies through to government institutions looking to review and enhance their process landscapes; the former because they see fee earning potential and the latter because most government organizations run outdated and inefficient process infrastructures. In general, though, organizations are recognising the impact that efficient and effective processes have on their bottom line and in fiercely competitive markets, efficient processes allow business to shave vital dollars off their operating costs. This is not the only driver that makes the commoditization of process an inevitability, as other factors such as the shift from customer as king to customer as dictator; mass production giving way to mass customization; the need for total solutions; the blurring of boundaries between industries; the locus of competition focusing on the supply and value chains and the changing nature of competition itself which is shifting from pure competition to competitive collaboration[21] are all serving to increase the interest in making processes more efficient and effective as well as standardized.

The creation of component-based architectures where processes are broken down into their basic parts and reused in a variety of other processes is also bringing a degree of standardization that has long been absent in the corporate world. For example the process of opening an account, whether it is associated with a new bank account, savings scheme or insurance policy is the same. So why should they be treated differently from a process standpoint? The impact of process standardization will be no different to how standards have impacted industries, allowing them to become first widespread and then commoditized, and has similar principles to the object orientation movement within the software industry some ten years ago.

As process standards and component-based architectures take hold they will make it much easier for organizations to pursue their outsourcing agendas on a much larger scale, allowing them to bring the full gamut of their business processes into scope. This will be possible because it will be simpler to compare the cost of executing a process in-house with that provided by a third party. Over time and as the number of process outsource suppliers increases the costs of executing business processes will drop to the point where the suppliers themselves will have become a commodity in the same way that technology outsourcers are today. When this happens, organizations will be able to compare the costs and benefits of executing their processes in-house versus outsourced and also determine which of the outsourced suppliers is best able to meet their service expectations. This of course is no different to what has occurred in the IT outsourcing arena, where the combination of competition and standardization has driven down costs to a point where the margins have been stripped away, leaving many to think carefully about how to respond in order to recover their profits. The majority are beginning to realize that their business models are unlikely to be sustainable in the medium term and they will have to fundamentally reengineer their business to survive.

The ability to conduct business anytime, anywhere and anyhow, the emergence and increasing requirement to have a 24/7 workforce and the opportunities to commoditize process are beginning to change the nature of white-collar work and are leading to its commoditization. Although globalization and the Internet can be considered to be the cornerstones of this final wave of commoditization, there are some other factors that are equally if not more important to this final wave, including shifting demographics and the availability of a cheap, well educated workforce. It seems that the economics of abundance highlighted by Anderson is increasingly relevant to white-collar work. And it is to this final wave we can now turn.

References

1 Saul, J.R., (2005) *The Collapse of Globalism*, London: Atlantic Books, p. 3.
2 HSBC research note on the global economy. Stephen King, chief economist of HSBC, and Janet Henry, the bank's global economist.
3 Standage, T., (Ed.) (2005) *The Future of Technology*, London: Profile Books, p. 112.
4 For a more a comprehensive discussion on the three waves of globalization see: Prestowitz, C., (2005), *Three Billion New Capitalists*, New York: Basic Books, pp. 9–21.
5 Woodall, S., (2006), The new titans, A survey of the world economy, *The Economist*, September 16, pp. 3–4.
6 Bonner, B., (2006) The Earth is not flat: why the rich get richer, *Money Week*, March, p. 25.
7 Giles, C., (2006) Half the world's assets held by 2% of population, *Financial Times*, December 6, p. 8.
8 Ibid.
9 Rigby, E., (2006) Stores sink or swim in the Multi-channel, *Financial Times*, July 15/July 16, p. 17.
10 Anderson, C., (2006) *The Long Tail*, New York: Hyperion.
11 Anderson, C., (2006) *The Long Tail*, New York: Hyperion, pp. 52–57.
12 Cameron, D., (2006) Shopper ratings device set to boost Wal-Mart, *Financial Times*, September 28, p. 29.

13 Friedman, T., (2005) *The World is Flat: A Brief History of the Globalized World in the 21ˢᵗ Century*, London: Allen Lane, pp. 48–172.

14 For a greater insight into Wal-Mart see Bianco, A., (2006) *The Bully of Bentonville: How the High Cost of Wal-Mart's Everyday Low Prices is Hurting America*, New York: Currency Doubleday.

15 Gascoigne, C., (2006) World domination by tiny teams that span the globe, *Sunday Times*, Consulting the next step, October 15, p. 13.

16 Rosewater, A., (2006), Around the clock, *Orlando Sentinel*, September 13, p. F1.

17 Dodson, K., et al. (2006) *Adapting CMMI for Acquisitions Organizations: A Preliminary Report*, Carnegie Mellon Software Engineering Institute, p. 4.

18 Smith, H., and Fingar, P., (2003) *Business Process Management: The Third Wave*, Florida: Meghan-Kiffer Press, p. 40.

19 Davenport, T., (2005), The coming commoditization of processes, *Harvard Business Review*, June, pp. 2–3.

20 Ibid. p. 3.

21 Smith, H., and Fingar, P., (2003) *Business Process Management: The Third Wave*, Florida: Meghan-Kiffer Press, pp. 42–46.

5 The Final Wave: Commoditization of White-Collar Work

A few years ago, the combination of technology and management know-how that makes this global network of relationships possible would have been celebrated as a wonder of the new economy. Today, the reaction is less exuberant. The forces of globalization that pushed Flextronics into China and its share price into the stratosphere in the 1990s are now blamed for the relentless export of manufacturing jobs from rich to poorer countries. Brillian's use of Indian engineers is no longer seen as a sign of the admirable flexibility of a fast growing tech firm, but as a depressing commentary on the West's declining competitiveness in engineering skills. The fibre-optic cable running between America and India that used to be hailed as futuristic transport for the digital economy is now seen as a giant pipe down which jobs are disappearing as fast as America's greedy and unpatriotic bosses can shovel them.[1]

Most of us have experienced enervating work ourselves or through family and friends. It's monotonous, homogeneous, meaningless, mindless, inconsequential, unremarkable, and underwhelming – just check your mind in at the door.[2]

The larger the available employment pool, the easier it is to control the labour force.[3]

The next wave is already upon us, although it still has a very long way to run. White-collar work is now well on the way to commoditization. The combination of an aging population, the increased codification of work through the standardization of processes, the increasing sophistication and scope and scale of IT systems and the availability of a cheap and well educated labour force from across the world means that much of the routine work that is now undertaken by well paid staffers will eventually be automated, outsourced, offshored or executed by less expensive personnel. Be warned, this is not just about the simple and routine activities undertaken by administrative personnel. As we will see later, most white-collar work is potentially up for grabs, including that of lawyers, consultants and even surgeons. In fact, any work which does not require high-touch has the potential to be commoditized.

Why now?

First, it is important to point out that the commoditization of white-collar work is part of the natural progression discussed in Chapter 2. As the successive waves have moved up the value chain, it was only a matter of time before white-collar work itself could be sufficiently codified to allow it to become commoditized. But coming back to the question, why now, white-collar work is now commoditizable for the following reasons:

- the impact of technology, especially in terms of the ability to take work out of the system;

- the development and introduction of standards, standard operating procedures and the creation of standardized and hence commoditized processes;
- the changing nature of employment and especially that which has occurred since the downsizing of corporations during the 1990s (more on this shortly);
- the changing demographic dynamics and the associated imbalances this causes within organizations (at the micro level) and nations (at the macro level).

Before moving onto the specific aspects of white-collar commoditization and the types of activity that can be considered commoditizable, as well as those which could be considered immune, it is important to explore the changing nature of work – the workplace factors, and the shifting patterns of demographic change – the population factors, in more detail.

The workplace factors

Any discussion about the commoditization of white-collar work should address the changing nature of work and of the workplace in general because both have made it easier for employers to exploit the benefits associated with labour arbitrage. The workforce factors act as a foundation on which white-collar commoditization can thrive because they set the tone, culture and precedents which permit organizations to push the boundaries and limits of the employment relationship and ultimately the flexibility of their employees. There are four factors worth discussing:

- the changing nature of work and careers;
- the end of the psychological contract and the eroding of the 1950s image of a job for life and the gold watch after 30 years of service;
- the intensification of work resulting from the increased use of mobile and connected technologies;
- the reduction in work-based benefits, which is placing greater financial risk on the employee, especially in terms of retirement (I will return to this in Chapter 7).

THE CHANGING NATURE OF WORK – THE GOLDEN AGE IS OVER

Few jobs remain static, or indeed continue forever; and many of the jobs of the past have become obsolete as technology, process and markets have shifted. For example, we see few lift attendants these days, nor do we see many petrol pump operators. Many of us may have seen them when we were growing up, but now they are a nostalgic memory or a marketing gimmick you find in upmarket department stores in New York. The same is true of the medieval period and the Agricultural and Industrial Revolutions; jobs familiar at the time are no longer present today. By the same token, as old jobs disappear, new ones emerge. For example, the invention of the computer in the mid-1940s may have started the long slow elimination of jobs, but it also created an entire industry and job families around the development and maintenance of IT applications that never existed before. So jobs come and go, but it is the nature of work itself that we are interested in here.

Organizations have always been concerned about their competitiveness. Taking this seriously has meant developing the right products and services, recruiting and retaining the best talent and keeping an eye on the future to ensure they are appropriately positioned to meet the challenges ahead. In the past this was a relatively simple exercise because the economic backdrop was one of steady growth and relative stability, especially following the Second World War; long considered to be the golden age of employment. This stability led to the creation of benevolent and paternalistic organizational cultures that looked after their staff and pretty much managed their careers for them. Employees could turn up for work in the knowledge that unless they did something seriously wrong, they would be guaranteed a job for life. They were willing to place their future careers in the hands of their employers and as long as they did a solid day's work and kept their noses clean they would gradually move up the hierarchy over the course of their career. If they were very lucky they might even reach the board of directors. Look at CEOs in the 1970s through to the late 1990s: many started out in the post room, or some very low, entry level job. Some still do, although this is becoming increasingly rare. During their careers they worked their way up through a succession of promotions to end up running the company they joined as young adults. Some took 20 years to achieve this, whilst others took 30. The very fact that such things were possible reflects the culture of the day which was concerned about the identification, retention and nurturing of talent.

It is clear that the nature of work has changed irrevocably and that the comfortable days of working with a single employer for 30 years and following a well-trodden career path are over. The business and economic environments are now more turbulent than they have ever been, with the long term cyclical patterns in the economy being replaced by uncertainty, unpredictability and short-term cycles. The current issues over energy supply, the ongoing war on terror and the US deficit are all adding to this uncertainty. This turbulence and unpredictability is increasingly reflected in our working lives. We now have to contend with information overload, heightened insecurity, reduced job tenure and the loss of the incremental steps that had previously defined our careers. In addition, the reduction in organizational hierarchies through downsizing has reduced the sources of power within the workplace, thereby making it more difficult to determine an effective and obvious path to the top.

As we have seen in the previous chapter, much of the recent change in the workplace has arisen from the combined effects of globalization and the increasingly rapid advance of technology. One could not exist without the other. With this backdrop, organizations have to consider how they can remain competitive in a commercial environment with fewer constraints and increased competition. Many have responded by merging with, or acquiring, other organizations that were better placed to deliver a truly global service. Others sought out the cheapest labour with which to manufacture their goods, leading to a massive reduction in the manufacturing sectors of the industrialized world as work was transferred to the cheaper economies of the Far East, Central Asia and, more recently, China. With further advances in technology since the 1970s, globalization is increasingly facilitating the transfer of knowledge and ensuring white-collar work follows blue-collar work around the world. And, with the emerging economies of Asia providing a ready supply of well-educated cheap labour, corporations are beginning to source their knowledge workers from overseas rather than at home, especially for those roles that do not require high levels of face-to-face contact.

THE END OF THE PSYCHOLOGICAL CONTRACT

For decades technology just affected blue-collar workers; office workers were mainly immune. They could sit in their warm offices pushing paper around their desks, attending important meetings and developing ideas and strategies for their companies in the knowledge they were far too clever or too important to suffer the same fate as their blue-collar compatriots.

The 1990s reengineering revolution put paid to that, as it stripped millions of office workers of their jobs, especially middle and senior managers. Although the impact was devastating for the many affected by the revolution unleashed by Champy and his zealots, the increase in unemployment amongst the mid-career middle managers was largely offset and hence invisible within unemployment statistics by the return to work of so many wives, many of whom were forced back into work to provide some stability to the household balance sheet. This has been highlighted by a number of observers, who claim that this shift is creating a double income trap for many married and co-habiting couples.

Whilst the Industrial Revolution only affected those whose livelihoods depended upon their physical prowess, the latter day workplace revolutions have affected those who would consider themselves middle class and who uses their brain to execute their job. With the advance of the computer, the white-collar worker, whose intellectual abilities were safe from previous disruptions, started to feel the cold wind of change. Great tranches of jobs were eradicated during the early years of computerization. As the process of automation continued, the level of uncertainty in the workplace increased. But it was the emergence of business process reengineering (BPR) during the 1990s that led to the most significant changes. BPR was designed to secure the long awaited benefits from technology and make the corporation more effective and efficient with fewer employees. Initially starting within the manufacturing sector, it soon spread into the wider economy with dramatic effects. And it wasn't long before BPR became synonymous with downsizing. As we have seen, the drivers that led to downsizing were principally associated with globalization and the impacts of technological change, but it was the fiercely competitive global economy that led many organizations – particularly in the United States and the United Kingdom – to cut costs in response to the competition coming out of the Asia-Pacific region. Given that the principal cost for any organization is its labour, it was this that bore the brunt; between 1980 and 1993 Forbes 500 companies shed eight million employees.[4] And, despite the usually positive impacts on the bottom line such headcount reductions had in the short term, many came to lament the time when they cut headcount with such gusto. For those that cut deep into their headcount, there was a realization that downsizing destroyed the psychological contract between themselves and their employees. The impact has been long lasting – organizations can no longer depend on their staff being more committed to the company than to themselves. And for many, this has resulted in poorer financial performance, plus a general lack of loyalty to the firm.

More importantly, it is also believed that downsizing destroyed much of the cultural glue that held organizations together. Downsizing has resulted in the contract between employer and employee becoming too one-sided. Instead of being balanced with the employer offering security in exchange for commitment and responsiveness, it has become one in which the employer still expects commitment and flexibility, but only offers insecurity in return.[5] Although one sided, staff are more likely to show less loyalty to their employer, as when employment markets are tight, staff are more likely to change jobs than remain where they are; something confirmed by the Society for Human Resource Management. They found that 83 per cent of employees were extremely or somewhat likely to search for a new job when the economy is high performing.[6] There is no doubt that individuals increasingly see themselves as having a series of transactions with their employers and recognize that it is they, not their employers who have to manage their own careers – however they define them. This is a real break from the past, when people were content to stay where they were and were less likely to take some risk by moving companies. What is of greater concern to employers is that employees are generally less committed and apart from those at or near the top, are no longer willing to go that extra mile, especially when they see little in the way of rewards for the extra effort. Over time this breeds mediocrity and lower performance which can have significant impacts on the bottom line because employees turn up for work, switch off and do the bare minimum to get the job done. This is not unique to Anglo Saxon countries, as similar problems are now appearing elsewhere and made the headlines with the French book, *Hello Laziness* in which the author recommended various approaches to avoiding work whilst in the office. The final problem with downsizing is that it reduces the confidence of the staff; it is well known that when staff are concerned about their job tenure they tend to be less productive and take fewer risks. This is because they believe they have lost control over their working life, have lost faith in their managers and are worried about their ability to get another job if they lose their current one. All this serves to make employees less trusting of their employer.

This loss of the strong bond between employer and employee has affected both organizations and staff alike. No longer a comfortable and cohesive place that encouraged loyalty and commitment the working environment has become one of fear and distrust with a culture of self-interest and self-preservation. Fear rules the roost for many employees; always looking over their shoulders to see if they will be the next to face the axe. Unwilling to speak out, drive forward controversial ideas or raise risks, employees are more likely to keep their mouths shut, toe the party line and keep their heads down. In a culture that supports self-interest individuals look out for number one, rather than remain loyal and true to the organization which employs them. In many organizations, points scoring and backstabbing have replaced teamwork and honesty. I will return to some of these negative effects in Part IV because one thing is sure: with the advance of commoditization, inequality will increase and many workplaces will become even more unfriendly and competitive than they are now.

There is no doubt that the end of the psychological contract has created the ideal environment in which employers can easily cut ties with their employees, and recent events at RadioShack Corporation in the US highlight just how brutal this can be. On 30 August 2006, 403 employees received an email from RadioShack's headquarters informing them they were surplus to requirements and therefore sacked.[7] Of course by the same token, such actions and attitudes have given the most talented amongst the working community the ammunition they need to cut ties without a second's thought; captured quite well in the following:

> *On these new, much vaster enterprises, workers must be specialized yet flexible; loyal to their captains yet ever ready to jump ship when new and more lucrative opportunities present themselves and always ready to man the lifeboats when a particular industry is set adrift, runs aground, or founders on high seas. Nautical courtesies of 'woman and children first' are replaced with an ethos of every man, woman and child for themselves.'[8]*

THE INTENSIFICATION OF WORK

Over the last decade or two the quality of white-collar work has gradually deteriorated. Although there have been clear and demonstrable improvements in the quality of work since the 1970s (summarized by James O'Toole and Edward Lawler in *The New American Workplace*[9]), the combined effect of technological change and globalization has resulted in the significant intensification of work which is far less positive because it serves to create new bad jobs. Intensification is evidenced by the increasing hours people are working and the degree to which work now spills over into leisure time, often referred to as job spill. Longer working hours is a common problem across Western economies and, increasingly, Eastern economies. It results from the heightened insecurity that has come with downsizing and more recently outsourcing and offshoring. Americans are working longer and harder than ever before – 25 million now work more than 49 hours a week, with a large number working a lot more besides: 11 million spend 60 hours or more at work. Women now work an average of 200 hours more each year then they did in the mid-1970s, and men work an average of 100 hours more each year.[10] The same is true for the United Kingdom which has the longest working hours in Europe; 91 per cent of British managers now work more than their contracted hours. No one is immune; in working couples nearly 46 per cent of men and 32 per cent of woman work more hours than they would like to.[11] Of course, longer working hours is not purely a Western phenomenon, as they are increasingly evident elsewhere, especially within Indian call centres, where 10 to 14-hour workdays are typical.[12] But when compared to China, all this pales into insignificance. Consider what happens at one of China's largest telecom manufacturers; every employee is issued with a mattress so that they can grab a nap beneath their desks, day or night, when they are overcome by exhaustion from their excessive working hours. This is euphemistically known as the mattress culture by the workers. Rolled up to the national level and things start to look grim as up to one million Chinese die every year from overwork. And, unlike in the West, all sectors of the economy are subject to overwork, even the cosy and rarefied world of academia, where 135 professors and other academic staff have died from overwork in the past five years.[13] According to Madeline Bunting, author of *Willing Slaves*, such overwork is having a profound effect on relationships, health and motivation. Downsizing has not helped either as the spectre of job losses, always just around the corner, fosters the long hours culture – employees believe that they have no option but to work longer and longer, because if they show any sign of slacking off, they will be the next to go.

The increasing time spent at the office is also mirrored in the amount of work that is conducted outside traditional working hours, mainly at home or on the commute to and from the office. Such job spill impacts leisure time and invades family life and makes too many workers one dimensional and boring. For example 39 per cent of Americans no longer take lunch breaks, instead favouring working through to keep up with their workload. As a commuter, I see evidence of job spill every day, with executives firing up their laptops as soon as they get on the train in order to get ahead of their busy schedule, or making incessant and often completely unnecessary calls to the office as though somehow they and the issue they are grappling with really mattered to the extent it had to be dealt with on a crowded train a mere 20 or so minutes before they physically arrived at the office. Commuting 'dead time' is thus becoming an extension of the working day, made possible by cellular phones, laptops and wireless links to the office. The same is true of evenings and weekends where workers can keep in touch with the office via cell phones, BlackBerrys and laptops. For many the office and home have merged into one. People are finding that they are being controlled by email and phones to the point of addiction; one executive could not walk past a computer without checking for messages and another had 3600 emails in the inbox. In extreme instances people send themselves emails if they feel they are not getting enough! Research by Kings College London has found that such addiction depletes cognitive abilities more rapidly than drugs – typically a 10 per cent drop in IQ, which is twice that of marijuana users.[14]

The problem is that longer working hours both inside and outside work mean that there is less time to relax. With work spilling over to weekends and evenings, white-collar workers are finding themselves squeezed with little or no time to unwind and recover from the working day. The traditional patterns of working life have changed so much, that for many it is virtually impossible to distinguish between the office and the home. Holidays too are being reduced through cost cutting initiatives by organizations as they struggle to remain competitive and by employees who believe they are too busy or too important to take them. And for many the office and their work schedule travels with them. It is not uncommon for executives to conduct teleconferences from the beach or poolside, and take their laptops on holiday so that they can deal with urgent issues and emails. I was recently with a client who told me about one of his staff who had requested a waterproof BlackBerry. Working on the assumption that this was in case the chap dropped it in the sea or swimming pool whilst on holiday, my client asked why. The response: he needed it so that he could answer his emails whilst in the shower! This clearly demonstrates just how far job spill has gone and highlights a very worrying trend about peoples' ability to switch off.

Indeed, with less time to relax workers are experiencing increasing levels of stress and there are increased health and safety concerns. Modern 24/7 workplaces put more employees at risk from health problems such as high blood pressure, cardiovascular disease and alcoholism. Research at the University of California-Irvine found that, taking into account such factors as smoking and obesity, those who said they usually worked more than 50 hours per week were significantly more likely to have been told by their doctor they had high blood pressure than those who worked fewer hours.[15] In the City of London the increasing work demands are resulting in more and more staff becoming dependent upon alcohol and drugs to relieve their emotional and psychological distress. As many as 44 per cent of men in large employers who hold senior positions regularly drink excessively.[16] Stress caused by crazy work schedules and a lack of control or no control over workload and priorities is an increasing problem for many. When this is coupled with a lack of balance and limited physical exercise it is clear that major problems are building up in the workplace and society at large. And despite all the technology which exists to make processes simpler and work easier, Americans are finding it increasingly difficult to keep up with their demanding schedules. According to the American Management Association, almost 50 per cent of Americans now feel stressed at work. Stress is a way of life for many white-collar workers irrespective of age or position within the corporate hierarchy.

WHERE HAVE THE BENEFITS GONE?

The final workplace factor to consider is the reduction in benefits from employers as they pursue shareholder value, seek ways to continue to drive up profits and reduce the long-term burden of looking after an aging workforce who may spend longer in retirement than they did in work.[17] Therefore at the same time as expecting more from their employees, employers are scaling back the rewards they provide and people are earning less not more. Middle income families in America saw their income rise by just $780 between 1988 and 1998, and although median income for US households increased by 1.1 per cent to $46 326 in 2005, earnings fell for both fulltime working men and women by 1.8 and 1.3 per cent respectively. The increase in income was masked by people juggling more than one job and the drop highlights a concern that the US economy is not generating sufficient high paying jobs.[18] Indeed, if you take into account where the bulk of the jobs are being created, you can see why; the increase in employment has not been at the top end. Far from it; most of the new jobs have been in low end service economy companies, where wages are low and opportunities limited, clearly demonstrated by the US Bureau of Labor Statistics' top ten jobs which are predicted to grow between 2004 and 2014:[19]

* waiters and waitresses
* janitors and cleaners
* food preparation

- nursing aides, orderlies and attendants
- cashiers
- customer service representatives
- retail salespersons
- registered nurses
- general and operational managers
- post secondary teachers.

Employees are therefore finding themselves trapped in what is euphemistically called the pink-collar ghetto. The societal, psychological, emotional and economic consequences of this have been well documented by a variety of observers including David Shipler (*The Working Poor*), Howard Karger (*Short Changed*), Jill Fraser (*White-Collar Sweatshop*) and Eileen Appelbaum (*Low-Wage America*).

In the United Kingdom and increasingly elsewhere, companies are cutting back on pension provision as they close down their defined benefits schemes (in which the final salary and number of years of service are used to calculate the pension that will be paid to the employee on retirement and until death) and replace these with defined contributions schemes (in which both the employer and employee contribute to a pension fund whose value at retirement depends on the level of contributions and the performance of the stock they purchase with the premiums). Every week there is another headline regarding the termination of defined benefits schemes. For example, DuPont, the chemicals giant, recently made the headlines when it stated that it would be cutting its employees' company pension benefits by two-thirds[20] and like many others it is attempting to both reduce the level of under funding that persists in its existing scheme and increase earnings per share, which will inevitably arise from reducing the funding levels. Another well known blue-chip organization, British Airways, has seen its pension deficit balloon to £2.1 billion; more than double what it was three years ago. It can no longer afford to pay its 45 000 staff the same generous pensions it gives its current pensioners and if it does then it is highly likely it will go bust. At 44 per cent of its market value, the deficit has the potential to cripple the company's ability to purchase new planes.[21] Even those companies that choose to keep their defined benefits schemes they tend to water down the benefits by using the average salary over an employees' career to calculate the pension and increasing the age at which the benefits can be taken. They also expect employees to pay more into the scheme and penalize them if they take early retirement.[22] It also appears that the trend of shutting down pension schemes is not only spreading but is also accelerating. According to a recent review of US pension provision, nearly two-thirds of employers that offer traditional pensions have closed their plans to new hires or frozen them for all employees, or plan to do so in the next two years. The latest numbers show acceleration in the decline of pensions and demonstrate that the trend is no longer confined to troubled industries such as steel, auto and airlines, but now involves healthy companies such as IBM and Verizon. Analysts have known for some time that the number of employers shutting or freezing their pension plans was on the rise. But the sharpness of the increase caught many by surprise.[23]

Unfortunately, pension deficits are significant and are impossible to tackle without this type of action. This is transferring the risks associated with funding for retirement from the employer to the employee and is creating a pensions time bomb. Fewer and fewer people will have any hope of a comfortable retirement because they cannot afford to, or perhaps are unwilling to save enough money. Plus, many of today's graduates are so burdened with student loans that most will have to delay putting money aside for their retirement, with disastrous consequences. The implications of this for the State, as well as for the individual, are enormous. The State will have to bear the burden of the increased poverty levels within the pensioner community through the provision of benefits and safety nets, whilst individuals will be faced with a stark choice of having to increase the funding for their old age, surviving on very little income for up to 30 years or working well into their 60s, 70s or even 80s in order to make ends meet. It should come as no surprise that top of American workers' worries is being able to retire comfortably; a recent survey put this at 34 per cent and a further 11 per cent were concerned about stagnant pay (thanks in part to globalization).[24] Of course there are some who have no intention of retiring because they gain most, if not all of their satisfaction from work. But they are still very much in the minority and in any case display unhealthy behaviours and typically have limited if any imagination or social connections outside work. Work for them is their home. However, they too will have to retire at some point, but theirs may be short-lived, as such people tend to die rapidly once their working life is over.

Demographic factors

Twenty years from now, what might the world's most precious, depleting, natural resource be? Oil? Steel? Lumber? How about working-age adults who are still contributing to a nation's entitlement programs rather than receiving benefits from them?[25]

Whilst the impacts of the workplace factors are significant, interest in the commoditization of white-collar work would not be as high if it were not for the more fundamental factors associated with the demographic changes playing out across the globe. The world's population is changing and fast: as the West declines into its old age, the East moves into adolescence and early maturity. The complementary spirals, one down and the other up, are acting as accelerators to commoditization. The principal factors worthy of discussion here are:

- the aging of the West
- the resurgence of the East
- economic migration.

THE AGING OF THE WEST

Europe is suffering a population collapse unseen since the Black Death of the fourteenth century[26]

The longevity of the human race has been increasing ever since we left the caves. During the Palaeolithic period life expectancy was typically 25 years and once the high death rates associated with babies and children had been stripped out this could be between 30 and 40; by 1725 this could be as high as 50 if you lived in the healthier conditions of North America, although the average was still only 32 and by 1900 Europeans could expect to live to the ripe old age of 48. This gradual increase changed during the latter half of the 20th century when, by 1950, people could expect to be still around at 68 and by 1990 77 was the average age at death.[27] The result, which had rarely been a problem in the past, is that the populations of the industrialized world are growing older at an alarming rate. The bulge of the 1960s baby boom and the secondary boom that began in the mid-1970s and peaked in 1990 is hurtling towards retirement.

This would not be such an issue if it weren't for the corresponding reduction in birth rates which are, in many Western countries, below replacement levels. One of the principal reasons behind this is that women are choosing to spend time building up a professional career prior to starting a family often to find that when they do want to have children their fertility has dropped precipitously making it near impossible to have the babies they so long for without invasive and risky infertility treatment.[28] This fall is significant if only for the simple reason that rising populations in the West have for so long equated to prosperity – the gross domestic product (GDP) of any nation is equal to the sum of its labour force times the average output per worker. When populations fall, GDP falls unless productivity increases to compensate. This is why organizations take such a keen interest in the application of technology, and governments in attracting intelligent migrants. It is clear that something has to change if the high level of prosperity that the West has enjoyed for long is to be sustained.

This double bind of aging populations and falling birth rates is causing enormous concern in Western economies. When we review the following statistics (and there are plenty more besides), we can see why:

* In the United Kingdom the number of people under 18 will fall from 7.0 to 6.6 million between now and 2011. At the same time the proportion aged 60 and over will increase from 12.1 to 14.0 million.[29]
* Unless Japanese women begin to have more children, the population is expected to shrink by 20 per cent by the middle of the century. The problem is now so critical that the Japanese have a name for it – 'shoshika' which means a society without children.[30]
* For the last ten years Germany's birth rate has been below replacement levels. This will result in the population falling from 82 million to 59 million over the next 50 years and a third of them will be over 65.[31] This is being further compounded by the departure of its qualified workers as they pursue better opportunities outside Germany.[32] It should come as no surprise that the German administration is doing everything it can to increase the birth rate, which currently stands at 1.36 children per woman. A new allowance, which became effective from 1 January 2007, pays €1,800 per month for 14 months for each child a woman has. Such economic incentives are now common across Europe and increasingly in other countries and even China.[33]
* In June 2000 the Organization for Economic Cooperation and Development (OECD) forecast that the ratio of elderly (those aged over 65) to those of working age (those between the ages of 20 and 64) would nearly double in the next 50 years.
* The European Commission projects that Europe's potential growth rate over the next 50 years will fall by 40 per cent due to the shrinking size of the workforce.[34] And within 50 years there will be 100 million fewer people living in Europe. Worse still, even if Europe can attract 600 000 new immigrants every year its population will still decline by 96 million, and if it can't, by 139 million.[35]
* The proportion of Canadians over 65 will grow from 13.3 per cent of the population to over 21 per cent, and the proportion of Canadians active in the workforce will decline from 67 per cent now to 63 per cent by 2015.[36]
* America's top 500 companies will lose half their senior managers within the next five years.[37]
* In June 2007 the OECD stated that the retirement of the baby boom generation will slow the economic growth in the United States for the next decade. They urged the US administration to pursue policies which slowed the pace of retirement and recommended that the age at which workers could receive full benefits be increased in the short term to 67 and even higher in the future.[38]

This is the current state of play, but with continued advances in medical science, especially those which are emerging since the success of the Human Genome Project, we should expect populations to continue to grow even older than they are projected to do now. Indeed there are some scientists who now believe that within a few decades we will be living well into our 100s, not as the exception as today, but as the norm.

It is clear that all industrialized countries are destined to experience similar problems as birth rates continue to fall. But it also seems that such falls in birth rate are no longer restricted to the industrialized world. Recent United Nations data suggests that the developing world is following in the West's footsteps, with families choosing to have fewer and fewer children in return for greater economic prosperity (and consumption). With birth rates across the world expected to fall below replacement levels over the next few decades, the world's population is predicted to peak at 8 billion and then start to fall in the second half of the 21st century. Some believe that the world's population will halve within 150 years. With this backdrop, companies will no longer be able to rely on a stream of fresh-faced twenty-something recruits to add to their existing pool of workers. Couple this with an aging workforce, and there are major problems on the horizon for organizations and workers alike. For example, the Federal Aviation Administration (FAA) recently announced that it intends to hire 15 000 air traffic controllers over the next ten years in response to a wave of retirements. This amount equals the current workforce because the FAA underestimated controller requirements. The National Air Traffic Controllers Association, which has been forced to accept new contracts which froze salaries for veteran controllers, believes the recruitment drive will not be able to deal with the serious crisis which is now emerging.[39] Such retirement bulges can present significant risks to organizations and even entire industries. Take the UK's power and water infrastructure. Plans to enhance and maintain this over the next 10–15 years are at risk due to the imminent retirement of many of the most experienced members of the utility sector. Although the retirement of engineers with up to 20 years of experience is bad for the industry, this is exacerbated by the limited number of engineering graduates coming through the system and the poor salaries they are paid compared to those offered within the financial services sector.[40]

This issue is particularly acute when we consider how hard it is to change an older workforce. According to the authors of *Workforce Crisis*, organizations will have to become better at managing and motivating the broad spectrum of employees they will have to employ. In their analysis, they focus on three cohorts: the baby boomers, where retirement or old age employment is a pressing concern, the generation X-ers who are mid-career, bored, stressed out, or just plain tired and the millennials who want everything their own way. Each group presents their own unique motivational concerns which have to be dealt with. As we will see shortly, employers are seeking to circumvent the problem presented by an aging workforce by filling their ranks with economic migrants and outsourcing/offshoring the problem. There are also those who believe it should be a simple matter of bringing the over 50s back into the workforce as this would not only fill the gaps in the workforce but it would also reduce the inactive and dependent population.[41] Unfortunately, with most of the developed economies hitting the same crunch, there is no easy answer or simple solution.

THE RESURGENCE OF THE EAST

China is everywhere these days[42]

Just as the West slides into old age, the East is beginning to pick up the pace and return to the position of global dominance it once held. Although some Asian nations face the same aging problems as the West, most notably Japan and increasingly China, the majority have considerably more youthful populations. It is this youth that is providing the platform for growth and the necessary energy to pick up where the US and Europe are expected to leave off. John Naisbitt, who wrote *Megatrends Asia* in 1995,[43] identified a number of trends which are now proving to be remarkably prescient. Two of these are relevant to the discussion here as they relate to the declining authority of the West and the increasing influence of the East. The first is *From Western Influence to the Asian Way*. Many Asian countries are completing the political, social and economic reforms that followed the end of the Second World War. Previously, social norms, the influence of communist regimes or similar draconian state dominance, and Western (mainly American) control prevented the Asian economies from expanding. The changes taking place are enabling the Asian economies to develop their own approaches to commerce and their own flavour of trade and ambition. Unshackled, they are booming. The second trend is *From West to East*. In the early 1960s the East Asian economies contributed around 4 per cent of the world's output. By 1997 this was 24 per cent and it is now hovering around 30 per cent. Asian countries, including China, are fast becoming the new economic leaders and as the West continues to slide into old age, the young and growing populations of the East will, as Clyde Prestowiz predicted in his book *Three Billion New Capitalists*,[44] become the consumers and leaders of the future.

It is clear that the Asian economies are no longer in awe of the industrialized nations of the West and no longer believe their own economic development has to ape the West's. They have found that following the management practices of America and other dominant nations is not as effective as developing and following their own. The reliance on export-led economies, which was long the case with China, is now shifting into consumer-led as the emergent middle classes move away from the blue-collar economy to the service and high technology industries. Like their counterparts in the West, the middle class has aspirations and a real hunger to advance and develop, which includes all the trappings and possessions one might expect middle class households to aspire to. It is China which is making the most headway. Apart from the all too familiar made in China label that accompanies most of our toys, clothes and footwear, there are other notable areas where China is advancing. As well as the aforementioned items, China is also making parts of Boeing 757s, exploring space, and making significant progress in high technology industries, including biotechnology, where it has over 300 biotech companies. Not only that, but it has somewhere between 100 and 160 cities with over one million inhabitants and by 2010 over half of its population will be living in urban areas. There is no doubt that with the country's insatiable appetite for energy, scrap metal, knowledge and development, its GDP will take it from the seventh largest economy to possibly the first in a few decades from now.[45]

The shift is not just about demographics or indeed China, but also about the rise of new corporate leaders and the long awaited benefits of globalization. The year 2005 was a milestone in global terms as it was the year when the combined outputs of the emerging economies accounted for more than half of the total world gross domestic product, which means that the developed nations are no longer dominating the global economy.[46] And although American companies initially led and dominated globalization, they are no longer the leaders they once were. The emergence of multinational companies from within China,

India, Brazil and Russia (this group of four economies has been labelled the BRICS to signify their collective importance to the balance of world trade) are changing the very nature of the global economy as they shake up entire industries. What makes many of these companies different from their earlier counterparts from Korea and Japan is that they have had to learn to survive in a highly competitive and cut throat environment, unprotected by government subsidies and protectionist policies (unlike their counterparts in the West). This has meant seeking out margins at prices that would never be sustained in the West. For example Indian drug manufacturers' charge as little as 1 per cent of what people pay in the US for their generic drugs. Others such as the Chinese Lenovo Group are big enough to buy those parts of Western companies that are no longer considered profitable, as they demonstrated when they bought IBM's PC making business in 2005 for $11 billion. Sector leaders, so long based in the US and Europe are now being superseded by companies such as Tata Consultancy Services (technology), SAB Miller (brewing), Embraer (aircraft manufacturing), América Móvil (telecoms), CNOOC (oil and gas) and Sadia (food and drink). Many of these emerging giants are using their bases in the developing world to launch inroads into the mature markets of the West and are growing at rates which can only be dreamed of by their Western counterparts.

Although their principal advantage lies in the low labour costs, there are other factors working in their favour including a larger pool of labour from which to draw their staff, a keener workforce which sees economic gain from working with prestigious multinational companies and a strong innovative streak.[47] Unsurprisingly, the Eastern economies are considering clubbing together to create their own trading bloc which will rival NAFTA (the North American Free Trade Agreement) and the EU (European Union) – see Table 5.1.

Table 5.1 Trade blocs

	Asian	**NAFTA**	**EU**
Members	Japan, China, South Korea, New Zealand, Brunei, Cambodia, Indonesia, Laos, Malaysia, Myanmar, Singapore, Thailand, The Philippines, Vietnam	Canada, United States, Mexico	Austria, Belgium, Cyprus, Czech Republic, Denmark, Estonia, Finland, France, Germany, Greece, Hungary, Ireland, Italy, Latvia, Lithuania, Luxembourg, Malta, Poland, Portugal, Slovakia, Slovenia, Spain, Sweden, The Netherlands, United Kingdom
Population	3.1 billion	430.5 million	460.1 million
Combined GDP	$10 trillion (US)	$12.9 trillion	$11.7 trillion

The free-trade idea is being spearheaded by the Japanese who are promising a ten billion Yen ($95 million) study to assess how it will work. The goal is to have the trading bloc up and running by 2015 and when fully functioning it is expected to increase the total economic output of its members by $215 billion.[48]

Russia is also on the rise and is growing rapidly off the back of its enormous energy reserves (oil, coal and natural gas). The economy has grown by 6.4 per cent every year since 1998 and has allowed them to repay the remaining $23.7 billion owed to the Club of Rome, who funded them during and after the Second World War, some nine years early.[49] Of course the economic resurgence will not help Russia with its demographic problems, which are just as bad as in the West and will limit its growth in the future; its population is expected to fall by one fifth by 2050 to less than 100 million and is currently shrinking by 700 000 per annum.[50] For the time being at least, it is able to flex its energy and economic muscles.

ECONOMIC MIGRATION

Never under any circumstances should this nation look upon any immigrant as primarily a labor unit [51]

[N]ew immigration laws should serve the economic needs of the country…[52]

These two quotes show how views on immigration have changed in a comparatively short space of time. The former was from Theodore Roosevelt and the latter George W. Bush. Both understood the importance of immigration, but Roosevelt believed that every migrant should first and foremost become an American citizen, whilst Bush clearly views each as the means of production. This reflects the inevitable consequence of the aging of the West and the youthfulness of the Asian economies with a surplus of skilled and often highly educated workers – economic migration. It also shows how workers are increasingly viewed as interchangeable commodities.

The history of the human race has been marked by major shifts in population. Whether this was the result of war, famine, persecution or just the desire to advance, migration has benefited the global economy at the micro and macro levels for millennia. According to the United Nations, the number of people living outside their country of birth has nearly doubled over the last 50 years to a record 191 million. The UN also provides an insight into the composition and destination of the migrants. Women make up almost half of the migrant population and those aged between 10 and 24 a third; one out of every four lives in the US and one in three lives in Europe. What is of greater interest is that the number of new migrants fell to 36 million between 1990 and 2005, compared to 41 million between 1975 and 1990.[53] So maybe the flow of migrants is beginning to reduce as opportunities within their home countries improve. Although it is difficult to measure the precise numbers of émigrés who move every year, estimates are helpful, as they provide us with an indication of the volume of human traffic. Approximately one million people migrate to the United States every year; Europe takes in something in the region of 2.8 million; Canada nearly a quarter of a million and Australia around 150 000.[54]

This backdrop provides some context to the position most industrialized nations now face as the level of immigration required to sustain the economies of the aging West is huge. According to the World Bank's latest *Economic Prospects* report, the pressure for migration from poor to rich countries is a permanent feature of our integrating world. The share of migrants in the populations of high-income countries has risen from 4.4 per cent in 1960 to 11.4 per cent in 2005.[55] Even Japan, which has maintained a tradition of excluding foreign nationals, has had to relax its immigration policy in light of its labour problems. Admittedly, this is still very low at 1.3 per cent of the working population and significantly below America's 15 per cent and the United Kingdom's 5 per cent, but it is a significant shift all the same.[56]

Such sustained levels of economic migration are creating significant tensions in the host nations including difficulties associated with social integration, the increasing number of illegal immigrants, and the problems the unskilled face as their jobs are taken by immigrants who are willing to work for less pay in order to gain a foothold in the economy. When you consider the significant disparities in incomes between the home and host nations, it soon becomes obvious why the immigrants want to move to the industrialized economies. Take Mexicans, who are coming to America in greater numbers than ever before. With 40 per cent of Mexico's 106 million people earning less than $2 a day, the minimum wage of $41 a day in the United States looks very attractive and presents a massive increase in income and standard of living.[57] The average immigrant ends up $20 000 a year better off and it is this disparity between the incomes of the rich and poor countries that means that graduates from poor countries are better off driving taxis in wealthy countries than following a graduate career in their own.[58] This creates issues and America, which has so long accepted economic migrants, is facing similar concerns to other parts of the world. Recent headlines highlight the increasing concern immigration presents:

- Romanians get in early for permits but say they won't flood Britain – *The Times*
- When home is not where the jobs are – *The Globe & Mail*
- Migrants job threat to British workers – *The Daily Mail*
- States try to block illegal workers – *USA Today*
- Hispanics nudge US population to 300m – *The Sunday Times*.

Much of the population growth in the West and especially the US and UK is now coming from immigrant families, both legal and illegal; in the 1960s, fewer than 10 million Americans came from other countries, today it is 36 million, nearly one eighth of the population.[59] Such changes will, over time, result in major cultural shifts with potentially significant implications for US and European societies and perhaps even their national identities, which is one of the biggest concerns reflected in many of the headlines above. But is immigration all that bad? Philippe Legrain, author of *Immigrants: Your Country Needs Them,* takes a counter view which debunks many of the concerns raised amongst the host populations. He believes that we should be welcoming immigrants, not turning them away, because they do the jobs that we don't want to, enrich society and send home billions to their loved ones literally propping up some of the poorer economies of the world. For example, Filipinos working abroad sent home a record $12.8 billion in 2006 and this is expected to increase to $14 billion in 2007. This accounts for 10 per cent of the Philippines' GDP.[60] He has a point here, as research from Duke University in the United States confirms the value which skilled immigrants in particular can bring to a nation. According to the research, skilled immigrants who lead innovation and create jobs and wealth have become a nationwide phenomenon.[61] Across the United States, immigrant founded companies produced $52 billion in sales and employed some 250 000 in 2005 and the majority of these companies were in the high technology sector, something critical to the future of the American economy.[62] And as Philippe Legrain points out, if migration were to stop, which some quarters of the indigenous populations of the West would like, the populations of Europe and Japan would fall sharply by 2050 and that of America begin to shrink.[63] This is of course an untenable situation if these economies are going to remain viable in the medium to long term. Migration is becoming one of the most significant issues within the globalization debate and it is one that will continue to run for the foreseeable future.

Economic migration has traditionally focused on the lower end of the economy. As economies grow and move away from blue-collar to white-collar work, the desire to undertake the lower forms of employment drops; people don't want to be a server in a fast food restaurant for a few bucks an hour and would rather claim unemployment benefits, where they are often better off. Migrants, however, are more than willing to do such work because it provides them with a chance to get a toehold in the economy and provide for their families back home. This highlights a major problem for many mature economies – what to do with their own unskilled, who are increasingly being alienated and pushed to the periphery of the economy.

The prevailing view is that the unskilled have a poor attitude to work, something not shared by immigrants, be they from China, Eastern Europe or India. Whilst in the past blue-collar work and the low end of the service industry were able to mop up the undereducated, this is no longer the case. In the modern economy a lack of skill is a major impediment to finding work and despite the strength of the economies in the US, UK, Germany and Canada, unemployment is rising. In part this is due to the high levels of economic migration, which includes not just the skilled migrants but also the uneducated. For example Pakistani and Bangladeshi communities in Britain suffer from high unemployment because of a combination of poor English, lack of education and low skills with little relevance for modern jobs.[64] It is also due to the shift to other forms of labour which require brains not brawn. Figures released by the US Labor Department shows that the unemployment rate for those who received education below senior high was 6.5 per cent in November 2000 but in January 2003 this had risen to 9.2 per cent.[65] It is unlikely that this trend will end any time soon. And it will continue to increase the number of working poor in the United States, which currently stands at 37 million, representing 12.7 per cent of the population, and is the highest percentage in the industrialized world.[66]

There has also been plenty of press coverage concerning the lack of workplace skills, including basic maths and English, of both school leavers and graduates. Some believe that the education system is dumbing down our future workers and because of this fewer are leaving school and university with the requisite skills to deal with increasingly global and complex working environments. Whatever the arguments for or against this perception, it is clear that organizations in countries such as Germany, the UK, America, Canada and others will continue to experience massive shortfalls in both the number and quality of employees. With insufficient home grown talent, many have little choice but to look elsewhere and many may have no choice but to consider their workers a commodity which is traded and used like any other.

Implications and changes – rise of the commoditized workforce

Dealing with the combined effects of the changing nature of work and of attitudes towards it as well as the shifts in the demographic composition of society and hence of work is not easy. But what is clear is that the economic dominance of the West over the East is shifting as downward mobility in the former is beginning to lose ground to the upward mobility of the latter (Figure 5.1).

Downward mobility, where the living standards of the workforce reduce over time, was first identified during the layoffs that came with the waves of downsizing that hit corporate America and Europe during the 1980s and 1990s. These days it is less publicized but more prevalent and no longer restricted to the working class, as middle class professionals often find themselves in this difficult position. The downwardly mobile are often themselves on reduced incomes following a forced closure, redundancy or shift to an outsourcer and this

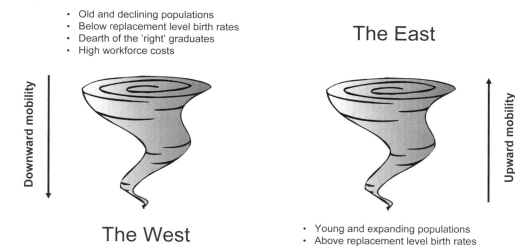

- Old and declining populations
- Below replacement level birth rates
- Dearth of the 'right' graduates
- High workforce costs

The East

Downward mobility

The West

Upward mobility

- Young and expanding populations
- Above replacement level birth rates
- Surplus of the 'right' graduates
- Low workforce costs

Figure 5.1 Changing fortunes

is often accompanied by an inability to find a new role that meets their expectations both economically and from the perspective of work content. According to one analysis wage loss due to displacement is significant and persistent.[67] Without careful management they will find themselves drifting lower in the career and work stakes whilst trying desperately to maintain the lifestyle they have been accustomed to. When coupled with high levels of debt, the situation only gets worse. Contrast this with the upward mobility of the East where incomes were and still are very low by Western standards, but for many are rising. For the workers moving into a white-collar job, even if it entails the near sweatshop conditions of a call centre, it represents a significant step up the career ladder which brings with it high rewards and benefits. For example, an Indian call centre employee may only earn $300 a month, a fraction of the $3000–$5000 earned by someone in the US, but the earnings are so good that they are considered wealthy and socially mobile.

Another factor which is also impacting the degree to which downward and upward mobility is taking hold is the supply and demand of an educated workforce, which is captured in the following quote from Robert Isaak: 'What are the symptoms of this global speed trap? Productivity growth, while promising economic growth, concentrates jobs where skills are the greatest and costs are the lowest, driving masses of people into unemployment – the unskilled, the mis-educated, and those who want to continue to be highly paid'.[68] There is no doubt that a nation's or an organization's competitiveness depends on having a constant supply of smart and committed workers. However, the prevailing view that to hold a college or university degree provided a route to well paid work and career progression is crumbling in the West and rising in the East. The mature economies of America and Europe have for a long time been pursuing a policy of sending as many as possible of their young to university where they can be suitably educated to make an effective contribution to the economy once they leave. Up until recently those with a university degree earned significantly more than those who left school without any tertiary level qualifications. In fact, by the end of the 1980s the differential was nearly 40 per cent.[69] What has changed since then is the supply of graduates, which has increased dramatically.

With the supply of graduates now outstripping demand, the bachelor degree is fast becoming the new high school diploma and, like the holders of non-tertiary qualifications, those with just a degree are no longer capable of maintaining a comfortable lifestyle. At the same time the masters degree is taking the place of the bachelors degree and it is only the super-educated (often those with PhDs) that have any chance of a full and satisfying career. This is reflected in the number of students following advanced degrees, such as MBAs, which has grown considerably, more than those taking bachelor degrees – 58 per cent compared to 25 per cent.[70] Ironically, with so many now pursuing MBAs their value is decreasing and the knowledge advantage is eroding as every MBA programme teaches exactly the same thing, which implies that the head start that knowledge once gave us is shrinking.[71] Tamara Draut in her book *Strapped* documents the impact of this rush to becoming super educated very well when she provides examples of graduates in their 20s and 30s who are struggling to get onto the career ladder whilst trying to pay off their college debts, which can take up to 20 per cent of their pay checks. Furthermore, the median annual earnings of graduates and post graduates have declined. In 1972 a male holding a graduate or post graduate qualification earned a median income of $52 087 (the female equivalent was $36 850) and in 2002 this had dropped to $48 955 ($40 021).[72] One of the reasons why incomes are dropping is the changing nature of the work available to graduates, which, as we saw earlier, is increasingly within the service sector. But there are three other reasons. The first is that economic migration and the effect of globalization in general has generated a downward pressure on the incomes of all but the most talented. A study by Harvard University confirmed this and showed that immigrant labour has reduced the wages of Americans performing low-skilled jobs by 7.4 per cent.[73] When you consider that more than one billion unskilled, low-paid workers have entered the workforce over the recent past, this shouldn't come as much of a surprise. The second, as mentioned above, is that there are just too many graduates chasing too few jobs that genuinely require graduate level skills. It is clear that the combined effects of technology, process standardization and the competition coming out of the Indian subcontinent and China are reducing the need for home-grown graduates. With Indian graduates costing approximately 12 per cent of the price of their American counterparts the economic impact is obvious. But then if you factor in the number of hours they work (2350 hours per year against 1900 for the American) you can buy almost ten Indian graduates for the price of one American.[74] The third reason is that there are not enough science and technology graduates – the right type of graduate. Although the number of graduates may be increasing, those with core science and technology subjects are decreasing and it is this that is worrying organizations and policy makers both sides of the Atlantic. The Confederation of British Industry likens this to a 'car crash in slow motion'.[75] Indeed the lack of graduates is already forcing some companies to move offshore. For example, in response to a lack of graduates in its main markets, LogicaCMG, an Anglo-Dutch computer services group, is placing greater emphasis on offshoring in order to meet client and project demands.[76]

Contrast this with what is happening in places like India and China which are churning out huge numbers of graduates, many of whom have core science and technology backgrounds. Between them, India and China produce one million engineering graduates a year compared with the 170 000 produced by the US and Europe combined, and 2.8 million Chinese students graduate every year. Chinese and Indian graduates are also more willing to relocate to anywhere around the world, which makes them the largest offshore talent pool available to any organization struggling to attract and retain the skilled personnel it needs to compete.

Companies such as GE, SAP and Google have launched Chinese and Indian research centres to tap into this highly intelligent community, but without the high costs associated with creating something similar in the US.[77]

With so many intelligent workers coming into the economy it is fast becoming a buyer's market for skill and expertise. And because of this it is unlikely that the incomes of Asian graduates will be rising anytime soon if the Chinese experience is anything to go by. Chinese graduates' incomes are dropping not increasing, and by a lot more than those of their US counterparts. On average, 2004 graduates were earning Yuan 3000–4000 ($362–483) per month which is up to 30 per cent less than those who graduated in 2003 and they too were earning up to 40 per cent less than in 2002.[78] Much of this, of course, has to do with the underlying economy which is still heavily focused on manufacturing, and hence does not require so many graduate level skills and capabilities. As workforces continue to globalize, the premium that comes with being a graduate will continue to diminish as their numbers increase. This highlights what Chris Anderson in the *Long Tail* terms plenitude in which resources can literally be wasted because they are so freely available.

This brings us to the point where the argument for commoditization becomes a very strong one. With skills and capability gaps becoming more prevalent in the West, despite the increasing number of workers with degrees, and a surfeit of skilled graduates in the East, the ability to source intelligent workers from overseas either through mechanisms such as outsourcing and offshoring or through economic migration is providing a solid platform from which white-collar work can be commoditized. As the Eastern economies mature and move into the service and knowledge industries, the requirement to pay large salaries to American, British or European staff will, at least from a purely economic standpoint, no longer be necessary. Anyone wanting to pursue a productive career must now be willing to participate in the international economy regardless of home country or employer[79]. The only fly in the ointment is the recent trend for the overseas graduates, who have been educated in the top universities of America and Europe, to return home to pursue better and more exciting opportunities. The West is fast becoming a net exporter of the intellectual capital on which the future success of its economies depends.[80] If this continues, the economic problems associated with an aging workforce will only get worse.

OFFSHORING WHITE-COLLAR WORK

They can't move snow to India.[81]

Companies offshore for a number of reasons, including:

* taking advantage of lower labour costs found elsewhere in the world;
* transferring work which their employees are unwilling to do;
* accessing other markets; taking advantage of a 24/7 working model, which uses the three main time zones of the US, Europe and Asia;
* using unique skills which cannot be sourced within the home country.

Offshoring is not necessarily new, as Henry Ford and others used it to access local markets during the 1920s and 1930s. However, back then it was rare that this displaced locally produced products or the home country's workforce. Since then outsourcing and offshoring have taken on a new and some would argue sinister role and is revealing a fundamental imbalance in the Western economies and societies. This is causing some commentators to call into question the whole ethos of outsourcing and offshoring, especially when it affects the very workers who find it difficult to find work once they have been displaced from their employment.[82] Vast tranches of the manufacturing sectors in the US and Europe have been shipped overseas where the benefits of cheap labour have allowed costs to be kept down and the companies to stay solvent as they compete in the cut throat global market.

Although once restricted to blue-collar work, outsourcing and offshoring is increasingly affecting traditional white-collar work and high-value jobs such as those associated with IT, accountancy, law, engineering design, medical diagnosis, finance and business consulting. It is predicted that up to $151 billion in wages will be shifted from the US to the lower wage countries by 2015 and 550 of the 700 service job categories in the US will be affected in one way or another[83] (I will return to this in Chapter 7). Household names like Ford, General Electric, General Motors, Accenture, American Express, AOL, Apple, Bank of America, Boeing, Cisco Systems, Coca-Cola, Goldman Sachs, Hershey, Johnson & Johnson, Kellogg, Kimberly-Clark, Office Depot and Pfizer are exploring and exploiting offshoring.[84] It is clear from this list that offshoring is affecting many organizations and it will, over time, affect many more. Pick up any newspaper and you will read about the latest trend of shipping out highly paid office work to other countries:

- To provide better value for money for its licence fee, the BBC is considering shifting support jobs – in essence, Human Resources, IT and finance – offshore to locations such as India to cut costs. At the same time it is spending more and more on its most talented employees.[85]
- Deutsche Bank will have moved almost half of its back-office jobs in its sales and trading operation to India by the end of 2007. Its plan is to triple its global market staff offshore to nearly 2000 and it is also looking to increase offshore research staff from 350 to 500. The bank is not alone in its efforts, as many others including UBS, Credit Suisse and Lehman Brothers are pursuing similar strategies. For example JPMorgan Chase is expecting to hire 4500 Indian graduates over the next two years with the aim to transfer 30 per cent of its back office staff to India.[86]
- Medical records and patient diagnoses are increasingly being sent over to India where they are transcribed and sent back as documents to be inserted into the patient's medical file by the time the doctor starts his next round.[87]
- In response to rising costs mortgage companies are starting to offshore much of the basic processing and administration to India. It is believed that between 50 and 80 per cent of mortgage related work can be offshored.[88]

US research firm Forrester Research predicts that in the region of 3.3 million US white-collar jobs in service industries will be transferred to lower-wage countries by 2018.[89] However, the ability to deliver white-collar work from anywhere in the world, the increased levels of process commoditization and the availability of a highly educated global workforce means that such predictions could be very wide of the mark. Alan Binder, an economist at Princeton University, believes that the majority of economists are underestimating the disruptive effects of offshoring and that at least two to three times as many service jobs will be at risk. This implies that perhaps up to 30 per cent of jobs could be offshored. Of greater interest, however, is that it is the middle ranking jobs and professions that are most at risk. The offshoring of this type of work has a tendency to shift relative labour demand away from the medium- and high-skill worker towards low-skill workers. So while white-collar offshoring is still small when compared to the offshoring of manufacturing, its bias against the skilled worker is a worrying trend.[90] The top end and bottom end of the jobs spectrum are largely immune from offshoring; after all you cannot offshore a cab driver. Any job which can be standardized is being squeezed the hardest by offshoring.[91]

For now at least outsourcing and offshoring is creating a clear division of labour. For those who undertake routine and repetitive tasks it is highly likely that their work will be transferred to the lower wage economies of the world. With improved technology and increasing bandwidth it is just as easy for someone in India or China to complete a routine task as an American, Briton or European. This includes routine work associated with law, engineering, IT and many other professions. It's unfortunate but anyone who works in this manner is on the path of downward mobility. For those who perform non-routine, creative or innovative tasks, such as research scientists, financiers, marketers and architects, the offshoring trend will pass them by; for now at least. However, as technology and standards continue to routinize work and the number of intelligent science and technology graduates from China and India increase, this comfortable position may well change.

COMMODITIZATION: THE BEST AND ONLY ANSWER?

The ability and the requirement to commoditize the workforce in every sense is now real. The changing demographic backdrop along with the use of the Internet is making it possible, as is economic migration, outsourcing, offshoring and the emergence of new and powerful multinational companies from China, India and South America. Articles appear almost daily which address the impacts and opportunities such commoditization presents. For example, a recent trawl produced the following:

- A journalist discussed how the Internet is leading to the dumbing down and potential elimination of his trade. The Internet, which is information rich, makes much of the traditional role of the journalist, which was geared to seeking out information from a variety of typically human sources, redundant. Many magazines, newspapers and current affairs programmes are cutting back on the number of journalists they employ (*Le Monde*, BBC's Panorama and *Time Magazine* to name a few) as the number of free newspapers increases and number of news channels expands.[92]
- McDonalds are experimenting with remote ordering where customers make their orders via a call centre, which then relays their order to the local branch via the Internet. Located in Santa Maria, California, the call centre allows the centralization and hence standardization of the order taking process, and serves local branches across the United States. The idea behind the experiment is to shave seconds off the order taking process to save millions in labour costs and to improve customer service. Like other call centres, the work is controlled by computers which prompt operatives to ask the right questions and in the correct sequence, ensure they are working off the appropriate menu (breakfast, lunch or dinner) and monitor how fast they complete the transaction, with each worker taking up to 95 orders per hour during peak times.[93]
- Building on demands from its financial customers, Thomson Financial is in the process of automating as much of its financial news as possible so that its customers can make their decision to buy or sell a particular stock within seconds of a company report being released. Very soon Thompson will be able to offer their clients a direct feed of automated reports that can be traded within a second of earnings releases.[94]
- Low-cost surgeries are beginning to emerge in India, Mexico, Taiwan, South Africa and Thailand which is leading to what is euphemistically termed medical tourism in which

those with poor medical insurance cover choose to go to have their hip replacements and heart operations overseas. With such operations costing less than a third than back home, organizations too are getting on the bandwagon in an attempt to reduce their rising health care costs. A number of Fortune 500 companies are assessing the feasibility of outsourcing non-urgent operations and health care. The cost savings can be significant and short term enough to make it worth the investment. For example, the savings on a heart bypass operation alone can be in the region of $70 000.[95]

- The College of Law of England and Wales, the largest legal training provider, is planning to eliminate lectures from its most popular courses and replace these with online tutorials which can be used by its students across the world.[96]
- Ernst & Young, the global multidisciplinary firm and the smallest of the Big Four is to move its UK tax compliance work offshore. The firm plans to recruit 200 graduates in Bangalore over the next two years to perform the largely routine work of processing company tax returns. According to Paul Davies, UK Head of Tax, the decision to offshore this work was not driven by costs, despite the fact that the hourly rate paid in India is significantly lower than in the UK. The Bangalore recruits are not accountants, but many have masters' qualifications and for the time being at least will not get involved with the higher value added tax work.[97]

Of course, not everything can be commoditized, as those roles which require significant face-to-face contact are not commoditizable. But the key point here is that a lot of work can.

Whilst it is true that commoditization in its various forms will impact the majority of organizations, it is likely that it will impact some organizations more than others and some will be more willing to pursue the commoditized route than others. James O'Toole and Edward Lawler have identified three emerging corporate models which may help to shed light onto those companies that may be affected by commoditization and hence more willing to commoditize their workforce:[98]

- **_Low cost operators_** maintain their market position by keeping their costs as low as possible and by transferring the operational savings to their customers. Because their business model is focused on continuously reducing their operational costs, staff are paid at or near minimum wage. The routine nature of the tasks also means that there is little room for advancement. And although such companies usually operate within their domestic markets, they are affected by the vagaries of the global markets because of the need to source many of their products from overseas suppliers. This is especially true of Wal-Mart.
- **_Global competitors_** are characterized by their global scope and scale and the need to compete for financial capital, technology, skills and knowledge. Typically well known corporations, they tend to be the market leaders and household names. The need to react to a constantly changing global market means that they often move their products, operations, services and people around the world and as a result increasingly hire people on a contingent basis, retaining a core of well paid employees, but outsourcing and offshoring the rest. Talent is only retained while it is of use to them, thereby creating a highly transactional relationship between employer and employee. One could argue this is high-end commoditization.
- **_High-involvement companies_** are found in most industries and are those which offer their employees challenging roles, a say in the management of the business and a commitment to low turnover and few layoffs. They value worker loyalty and attempt to build long term commitment to the organization.

Although all three corporate models could be affected by commoditization, it is likely that the first two will pursue a policy of commoditizing their workforces in order to remain competitive.

By way of a conclusion, it is useful to revisit the model we have used in Chapters 2 and 3 through the lens of employment as this will allow us to complete the discussion on the three waves of commoditization. The model of Chapter 2 still holds true at the basic level (Figure 2.1 [Figure 5.2] is repeated here for completeness).

Stage ❶ – the job emerges as one which is useful to society and or a specific industry, but at this stage the ability to perform the role is limited to a small number of individuals. The number of people either needed for or capable of fulfilling the role in the future is unknown, although projections are likely to be made. At this stage incomes are high because the specialist knowledge is limited to a small population.

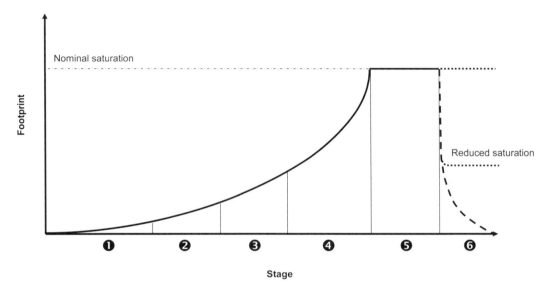

Figure 5.2 The process of commoditization

Stage ❷ – as the importance of the job increases, usually as the industry to which it relates expands, the number of people holding down the type of job also increases. At the same time the sophistication of the job may also increase in order to keep in step with the introduction of new technologies associated with the expanding industry; in other words the definition of the job still continues to develop. Incomes remain high as, although the number of people who execute the job has increased, the skills and expertise have yet to be codified or transferred to a large enough population to suppress wages.

Stage ❸ – the job has now gained sufficient importance that industry bodies, governments and others begin to recognize the need to develop standards and common activities which can help to define the job, facilitate its continued expansion through training and allow the transfer of resources and knowledge between competing companies. At this stage the job tends to stratify into two distinct parts. Those with experience are still paid well, as they retain much of the higher order understanding of the job and remain critical to its effective execution. Those with limited knowledge can be trained up as technicians who often work under the direction of the more experienced specialists. Their income is generally lower and often significantly lower than that of the expert.

Stage **❹** – the job is now sufficiently well understood and the industry to which it relates sufficiently mature that it can become fully codified. The ability to execute the activities associated with the job are so well codified that it is possible to rapidly train up a novice to be competent enough to execute the job with limited or no supervision. At the same time the numbers of people performing the job expand so that there is a large pool of resources available to execute the work. This expansion continues because there is a belief that the demand for the job will continue to grow. As expected, at this stage the incomes of the job holders stagnate and potentially drop as the competition between those with the skills to hold down the job increases.

Stage **❺** – the job has now reached its natural saturation point where it is well understood and codified. It is during this stage that it is possible to both subsume the job into suitable technologies, thereby reducing the role of the job holder, and consider outsourcing or offshoring the job. As completing the role no longer requires detailed knowledge or expertise, the need to pay those who perform the job a premium is no longer necessary.

Stage **❻** – as with all other commodities, the significance of a particular job can decline over time. This may be the result of innovation, the impact of new technology, or the loss of a particular industry, all of which can eliminate jobs. At the organizational and national level this may also be due to the transference of jobs overseas to seek out the benefits of labour arbitrage. This stage also tends to be characterized by the need to retrain and retool those sections of the workforce affected by the elimination of the job type. It is also possible that a reduced level of saturation may occur as some elements of the job may be retained which require fewer people to execute. For example, the automation of automobile factories has not completely eliminated the need for staff, although the numbers are significantly lower. Those who remain look after the machines and troubleshoot when required, and tend to get paid more than they would have in the past.

The single most important factor impacting the commoditization of work and potential elimination of jobs is technology. Technology has always had a part to play in this as the nature and type of work has changed when new technologies have been introduced. Fletchers were surplus to requirements when the musket was introduced in the 15th century and typists were no longer required when the word processor was widely taken up in the 20th century. Today,

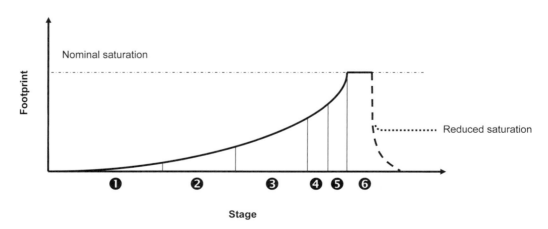

Figure 5.3 The impact of technology

however, the increasing sophistication and footprint of technology means that stages ❹, ❺ and ❻ can accelerate significantly resulting in a rapidly changing job market, which includes reducing the saturation level and possibly eliminating the job entirely (Figure 5.3). This means that skills and expertise can become outdated far more quickly than in the past.

This concludes Part I and having discussed the nature of commoditization in some detail we can now explore how it impacts organizations and their workers in general.

References

1 Standage, T. (ed.) (2005) *The Future of Technology*, London: Profile Books, p. 112.
2 Dychtwald, K. et al. (2006) *Workforce Crisis: How to Beat the Coming Shortage of Skills and Talent*, Boston, Massachusetts: Harvard Business School Press, p. 207.
3 James, O. (2007) *Affluenza*, London: Vermilion, p. 211.
4 Downs, A. (1995) *Corporate Executions*, New York: Amacom, p. 11.
5 Reilly, P. (2001) *Flexibility at Work: Balancing the Interests of Employer and Employee*, Aldershot: Gower, p. 78.
6 *The Economist* (2006) The battle for brain power: A survey of talent, 7th October, p. 4.
7 Colker, D. (2006) Read this email…then scram, *Los Angeles Times*, www.latimes.com.
8 McGee, M. (2005) *Self-Help Inc.*, Oxford: Oxford University Press, p. 30.
9 O'Toole J. and Lawler, E. (2006) *The New American Workplace*, New York: Palgrave Macmillan.
10 Frank, R. (2007) *Falling Behind: How Rising Inequality Harms the Middle Class*, Berkeley: University of California Press, p. 78.
11 Bunting, M. (2004) *Willing Slaves: How the Overwork Culture is Ruling Our Lives*, London: HarperCollins Publishers, p. 7.
12 Overell, S. (2005) Stress hits India's outsourced and overworked, *Financial Times*, 8 July, p. 12.
13 York, G. (2006) A culture of overwork exacts an extreme price, *The Globe and Mail*, 21 August, p. A2.
14 Womack, S. (2007) Recovery programme for email addicts, *The Daily Telegraph*, 21 February, p. 1.
15 Wessel, H. (2006) The cost of long work hours, Orlando Sentinel, working, 13 September, p. F1.
16 Sherwood, B. (2006) Culture of hard work and heavy drinking still drives high-flyers, *Financial Times*, 2 September/3 September, p. 4.
17 Andresky Fraser, J. (2001) *White-Collar Sweatshop: The Deterioration of Work and its Reward in Corporate America*, New York: W.W. Norton and Company, pp. 3–74.
18 Cauchon, D. (2006) Family income up, but not pay, *USA Today*, 30 August, p. 1A.
19 Dobbs, L. (2004) *Exporting America: Why Corporate Greed is Shipping American Jobs Overseas*, New York: Warner Business Books, pp. 105–106.
20 Francis, T. (2006) DuPont aims to slash pension plan, *The Wall Street Journal*, 29 August, p. A2.
21 Wilson, S. (2006) Are BA shares heading for a crash? *Money week*, 10 November, p. 18.
22 Budden, R. (2006) Employers' tweaking of final salary schemes waters down the benefits, *Financial Times*, 2 September/3 September, Money section, pp. 8–9.
23 Gosselin, P. (2007) More employers doing away with pensions, study finds, www.latimes.com, 11 July.
24 *USA Today* (2006) What Worries American Workers, 13 October, p. 1.
25 Sheppard, N. (2004) The commoditization of populations, www.intellectualconservative.com.
26 Buchanan, P. (2006) *State of Emergency*, New York: Thomas Dunne Books, p. 215.
27 Gluckman, P. and Hanson, M. (2006) *Mismatch: Why our World no Longer Fits our Bodies*, Oxford: Oxford University Press, p. 178.
28 Hewlett, S. (2002) *Baby Hunger: The New Battle for Motherhood*, London: Atlantic Books.
29 Source, The Henley Centre.
30 Sheppard, N. (2004) The commoditization of populations, www.intellectualconservative.com.
31 Buchanan, P. (2002) *The Death of the West: How Dying Populations and Immigrant Invasions Imperil our Country and Civilization*, New York: Thomas Dunne Books, St Martins Press, p. 14.
32 Benoit, B. (2006) Economy set to feel the strain as German exodus gains momentum, *Financial Times*, 2 September/3 September, p. 5.
33 Crossland, D. (2007) Happy new year for the mothers who waited for their big bonus, *The Times*, 2 January, p. 9.

34 Longman, P. (2004) *The Empty Cradle: How Falling Birthrates Threaten World Prosperity [and what to do about it]*, New York: New America Books, p. 41.
35 Sheppard, N. (2004) The commoditization of populations, www.intellectualconservative.com.
36 Scoffield, H. (2006) Amid jobs boom, hundreds of thousands left behind, *The Globe & Mail*, 21 August, p. B5.
37 *The Economist* (2006) The battle for brain power: A survey of talent, 7 October, p. 4.
38 Giles, C. (2007) Baby-boomers' farewell likely to slow growth, *Financial Times*, 30 May, p. 8.
39 Levin, A. (2007) FAA to hire 15,000 air traffic controllers, *USA Today*, 8 March, p. 3A.
40 Bolger, J. (2007) Utilities fear for future as engineers head into retirement, *The Times*, 10 April, p. 37.
41 Smallwood, C. (2006) 'Reserve army' can defuse demographic time bomb, *The Sunday Times*, 27 August, Business section, p. 4.
42 Fishman, T. (2005) *China Inc.*, New York: Scribner, p. 1.
43 Naisbitt, J. (1997) *Megatrends Asia: The Eight Asian Megatrends that are Changing the World*, London: Nicolas Brealey Publishing.
44 Prestowiz, C. (2005) *Three Billion New Capitalists*, New York: Basic Books.
45 For more on the impact of China see Fishman, T. (2005) *China Inc.*, New York: Scribner, and Hynge, J. (2006) *China Shakes the World: the Rise of a Hungry Nation*, London: Weidenfeld & Nicolson.
46 Woodall, S. (2006) The new titans, a survey of the world economy, *The Economist*, 16 September, p. 3.
47 Engardio, P. (2006) Emerging Giants, *BusinessWeek*, 31 July.
48 York, G. (2006) Asian trade bloc will rival Nafta, EU, *The Globe & Mail*, 24 August, p. B12.
49 Nicolson, A. (2006) Oil prices let Kremlin erase big debt, *The Globe & Mail*, 22 August, p. B11.
50 *The Economist* (2006) A sickness of the soul, 9 September, pp. 41–42.
51 Buchanan, P. (2006) *State of Emergency*, New York: Thomas Dunne Books, p. 72.
52 Ibid. p. 72.
53 Maddox, B. (2006) A world helped by millions on the move, *The Times*, 7 September, p. 38.
54 Legrain, P. (2006) *Immigrants: Your Country Needs Them*, London: Little, Brown, p. 9.
55 Wolf, M. (2006) Why immigration policy has to be a compromise, *Financial Times*, 22 December, p. 15.
56 Hayashi, Y. and Moffett, S. (2007) Foreign labor works for Japan, *The Wall Street Journal*, 25 May, p. 14.
57 Buchanan, P. (2006) *State of Emergency*, New York: Thomas Dunne Books, p. 121.
58 Legrain, P. (2006) *Immigrants: Your Country Needs Them*, London: Little, Brown, p. 16.
59 Baxter, S. (2006) Hispanics nudge US population to 300m, *The Sunday Times*, 9 July, p. 23.
60 Associated Press (2007) Filipinos working abroad remit record $12.8 billion, *The Wall Street Journal*, p. A8.
61 Wadhwa, V. et al. (2007) America's new immigrant entrepreneurs, Master of Engineering Program, Duke University: School of Information, UC Berkley, 4 January, p. 4.
62 Ibid.
63 Legrain, P. (2006) *Immigrants: Your Country Needs Them*, London: Little, Brown, p. 156.
64 Taylor, A. (2006) Low skills blight job prospects for some Asian communities, *Financial Times*, 5 September, p. 3.
65 Di, G. (2006) Do not blame China for job losses in US, *China Daily* 09-5, www.chinadaily.com.cn.
66 Bonner, B. (2006) The Earth is not flat: why the rich get richer, *Money Week*, March, p. 25.
67 Uchitelle, L. (2006) *The Disposable American*, New York: Alfred A. Knopf, p. 157.
68 Isaak, R. (2005) *The Globalization Gap*, Upper Saddle River, NJ: FT Prentice Hall, p. 11.
69 Uchitelle, L. (2006) *The Disposable American*, New York: Alfred A. Knopf, p. 162.
70 Draut, T. (2006) *Strapped: Why America's 20- and 30- somethings Can't Get Ahead*, New York: Doubleday, p. 54.
71 Bosshart, D. (2007) *Cheap? The Real Cost of Living in a Low Price, Low Wage World*, London: Kogan Page, p. 24.
72 Draut, T. (2006) *Strapped: Why America's 20- and 30- somethings Can't Get Ahead*, New York: Doubleday, p. 80.
73 Buchanan, P. (2006) *State of Emergency*, New York: Thomas Dunne Books, p. 33.
74 *The Economist* (2006) The battle for brain power: A survey of talent, 7 October, p. 9.
75 Eaglesham, J. (2006) CBI warns of drop in science graduates, *Financial Times*, 15 March, p. 2.
76 www.uk.biz.yahoo.com/30082006/94/logicacmg-shares-fall-line-interim-numbers.html.
77 Schrage, M. (2006) The Asian giants and the brains bazaar, *Financial Times*, 15 May, p. 17.
78 *The Epoch Times* (2004), www.english.epochtimes.com/news/4-6-29/22189.html.
79 Uchitelle, L. (2006) *The Disposable American*, New York: Alfred A. Knopf, p. 163.
80 O'Toole J. and Lawler, E. (2006) *The New American Workplace*, New York: Palgrave Macmillan, p. 197.
81 Prestowiz, C. (2005) *Three Billion New Capitalists*, New York: Basic Books, p. 4.

82 Dobbs, L. (2004) *Exporting America: Why Corporate Greed is Shipping American Jobs Overseas*, New York: Warner Business Books.

83 Ibid. p. 33.

84 Ibid. pp. 167–196.

85 Terazone, E. (2006) BBC considers shifting jobs offshore, *Financial Times*, 8/9 July 2006, p. 3

86 Wighton, D. (2006) Deutsche Bank in job exodus to India, *Financial Times*, 27 March, p. 19.

87 Dobbs, L. (2004) *Exporting America: Why Corporate Greed is Shipping American Jobs Overseas*, New York: Warner Business Books, p. 92.

88 *The Economist* (2006) Home and away, 7 October 2006, p. 82.

89 Di, G. (2006) Do not blame China for job losses in the US, *China Daily*, www.chinadaily.com.cn.

90 OECD (2007) Employment outlook, pp. 129–130.

91 Woodall, S. (2006) The new titans, A survey of the world economy, *The Economist*, 16 September, pp. 16–17.

92 Lloyd, J. (2006) The best – and worst – of times, *FT Magazine*, 1 April/2 April, p. 10.

93 Richtel, M. (2006) Drive-through takes orders from 250 miles away, *Herald-Tribune*, 11 April, p. 2A.

94 Van Duyn, A. and Gangahar, A. (2006) Finally, a reporter that always files the story on time, *Financial Times*, 19 August/20 August, p. 8.

95 Appleby, J. and Schmit, J. (2006) Sending patients packing, *USA Today*, 27 July, p. 3B.

96 Boone, J. (2006) Online tutorials to replace lectures, *Financial Times*, 10 June/11 June, p. 4.

97 Houlder, V. (2007) E&Y sends compliance work offshore, www.ft.com, 11 July.

98 O'Toole J. and Lawler, E. (2006) *The New American Workplace*, New York: Palgrave Macmillan, pp. 11–14.

PART

II *Impact*

We act as though we could wish away what is happening to new products and prices. But the fact is that the on-going commoditization of technology cannot be undone. Products will continue to get better but they will also continue to fall in price. In the face of these dynamics jobs will melt away.[1]

This is one reason why life has become so hard for established institutions and those who work for them: the ground can disappear so rapidly from beneath their feet. Competition and radical innovation can suddenly emerge to threaten the identity and purpose of established institutions. Telephone companies, which were once publicly owned, have to become fashionable Internet service providers. Public-service broadcasters have to compete in the world of digital television.[2]

Over the course of Part I we explored the nature of commoditization. We started by looking at some of the basic commodities we are familiar with such as coal and coffee and how these expanded from things with little known qualities into global industries which in many ways have shaped entire economies and societies. Tracing their development allowed us to identify the basic process through which things can become commoditized. We then moved on to industries and how these too can become commoditized. In the course of this analysis we explored the railway, telecommunications, airline and information technology industries and identified a number of factors which can influence, change and accelerate the process of commoditization, including the impact of standards, shock events and government intervention. Finally we reviewed the current wave of white-collar commoditization and highlighted how this has been heavily influenced by the emergence of the Internet, the strengthening grip of globalization and how the changing demographic patterns of the West and the East are accelerating the process through which work is being commoditized; organizations are now having to consider the commoditization of their workers out of necessity, not just because of the changing competitive environment.

Commoditization represents both a threat and an opportunity to organizations and individuals alike. Some will be immune to the direct impacts, but most will experience the indirect consequences. Before we move on to how businesses and employees can respond to the challenges of commoditization (the strategic response) it is necessary to outline how it changes the nature of the business and working environments; this is the purpose of Part II. It is intended to be relatively brief as the impacts are quite obvious. What is less obvious, because it requires some careful thought, is how to respond. Like any other strategic decision, there are pros and cons to a chosen course of action. Although avoiding commoditization may seem like a perfect strategy, this is not the only one worth pursuing, as embracing and driving commoditization, in the way that the budget airlines have done, is an effective way to address the threat. This is the focus of Part III.

Part II consists of two chapters:

- Chapter 6 focuses on the corporate environment and how commoditization affects more than just price. The chapter reviews, amongst other things, the impact on brands, how the future lies with large organizations and how businesses have to contend with not only being cheaper, but faster and better too.
- Chapter 7 looks at the specific changes that are occurring within the realms of white-collar employment including employability, skills, competencies and capabilities as well as work demands. It also looks at some additional factors such as the changing expectations of employees and how your employer may soon be a private equity house, an overseas conglomerate or no one at all.

At the end of Part II you will understand how commoditization could affect (or maybe already is affecting) your business and/or working life, and armed with this you will be better placed to consider how to respond.

References

1   Cook, G. (2003) The paradox of commoditization, www.menards.ca.
2   Leadbeater, C. (1999) *Living on Thin Air*, London: Penguin Books, p. 23.

6 *Business Impacts*

It is time to start getting used to the idea that the household names of today – whether we are speaking of IBM, Ford, and Wal-Mart in the United States; Philips, Shell and Nestle in Europe; or Panasonic, Honda and Sony in Japan – are in danger of becoming the has-beens of tomorrow.[1]

Excess, superabundance and rock-bottom prices are part of the same phenomenon. They are logical counterparts to an ascetic form of business management: be faster, better, cheaper.[2]

The power of big business over our national life has never been greater. Never have there been fewer business leaders willing to commit to the national interest over selfish interest, to the good of the country over that of the companies they lead. And the indifference of those business leaders to our long-term national welfare is nowhere more evident than in the exporting of American jobs to cheap overseas labor markets.[3]

Anyone who fails to recognize that price is a strategic instrument is probably doomed to launch continued attempts to attract more customers – and is in danger of walking into a lethal trap.[4]

In business, simply running fast is often equated with lowering prices – and then struggling to get costs under control.[5]

So far we have looked at the process through which entire industries become commoditized and at some of the factors which can speed up the process or act as the catalysts through which it can start. In addition to the general process discussed in Chapter 3, Chapter 4 outlined how the combination of globalization and the Internet have contributed to the acceleration of commoditization, especially in terms of white-collar work. Although globalization and the Internet laid the foundations for this final wave, they have also contributed significantly to how far and deep commoditization is able to penetrate organizations. The effects are wide ranging and are transforming the shape, size and focus of companies irrespective of their sector. Understanding how industries can become commoditized is important because it sets the backdrop against which the impacts on individual companies can be better assessed and it is to this which we will now turn.

The impact of commoditization on organizations can be profound and may, in extreme cases, force them out of business. However, like so many changes that affect the business world, most companies survive and find a way to respond, even if it takes a long time. For the purposes of this chapter, I will focus on what I consider to be the most significant impacts and I see these to be:

- Faster, better, cheaper. Commoditization makes products and services cheaper, but it is no longer just about price, as we also expect them to be better and faster too. This forces organizations to offer their products and services at ever cheaper prices whilst increasing their reliability, service levels (in terms of speed at least) and just about everything else. Paradoxically this fuels further commoditization.

- First margin, then brand and finally market position – the erosive power of commoditization. Although commoditization creates price pressures, it follows that it is not just price that is impacted. As commoditization takes hold it becomes harder to differentiate yourself in a crowded market and as a result your brand can become diluted. As the power of the brand reduces and the demands for lower prices increase, margins and even market position are at risk.
- Behind the steering wheel – big not small. In a commoditized world, the future belongs to those that are able to maintain their margins despite the increasing price pressures. Although small companies can fare reasonably well by carving out niches and protecting them fiercely, they often struggle against the large and lean organization that benefits from the economy of scale which comes with size.
- Mirroring Wal-Mart and passing the commoditization buck. The power of companies such as Wal-Mart is not lost on other businesses and many are mimicking their approaches to customer management, front and back office processes and general working practices. Some believe they have little or no choice but to follow suit. Of course, for those that have direct interactions with companies such as Wal-Mart, they have to mirror them if they are to survive.
- The doughnut principle and the hollowing out of organizations. As companies seek ways to maintain their competitive position they will need to focus on reducing their costs. With outsourcing and offshoring becoming easier, the opportunity to outsource and offshore non-core activity to third parties will become increasingly attractive and for some an essential part of their armoury for tackling commoditization.
- The stark choice of transform or die. The Internet, integrated supply chains and globalization all help to connect organizations together in a complex web of business activity. This creates a level of transparency which makes it difficult to justify outmoded working practices and the high costs that come with them. Increasingly the failure to transform and modernize will equate to decline, eventual takeover, or business failure.

Not just price sensitivity, but faster and better too

One of the principal impacts that organizations have to deal with when faced with commoditization is price sensitivity. As we saw throughout Part I, as the process of commoditization plays out, work becomes codified, products and services become standardized and competition increases to the point where the abundance of choice makes price the primary differentiator. It is always compelling when another supplier is willing to offer you the same service but cheaper. Why pay more if you are getting the same thing for less outlay? Of course, if the product or service is inferior, paying less can be a false economy, but with the emergence of high quality, low cost competition, especially from the BRIC economies, the argument against accepting lower prices is increasingly difficult. If organizations only had to contend with price then maybe things wouldn't be quite so bad, but there are five other facets which are critical to the low cost commodity model. And it is these that increase the overall impacts.

The first is increased efficiency and simplicity.[6] In order to survive in a commodity market, an organization, its processes and the delivery of the product or service need to be both simple and efficient. As we saw in Chapter 3, the low cost airlines could not have survived had they not simplified their operating model and the approach through which they delivered their service. Simplicity and efficiency implies complexity reduction and restricting choice, which may go against the grain for many companies, but it presents a stark necessity for organizations faced with a commodity market (I will return to the response in more detail in Chapter 8). The mantra here is less is more and to prove the point let's briefly compare Ryanair with Lufthansa. In 2003, Ryanair flew some 24 million passengers with just 2000 employees. Lufthansa flew double the number of passengers, but employed 30000 employees, fifteen times as many as Ryanair.[7] Getting the passenger-to-employee ratio as low as Ryanair necessitates an attention to detail that many organizations just don't have and without this it can be almost impossible to compete. I will return to Ryanair in Chapter 9.

The second is calculability and no frills.[8] It follows that in order to have a simplified business model anything that is not directly related to the service or product has to be eliminated, and to do this you must understand the trade-off between the cost of a process or system and its benefit. If you are to deliver a service which is low cost then you have to cut out those things which could increase its unit cost. This focus on stripping out unnecessary costs creates the basis for the current focus on no frills that is sweeping the business world. If you can persuade the consumer to accept fewer features and strip out those which add little to the overall product, then you can begin to take market share from those that offer unwanted features. We can see that this is already changing buying behaviour as the lack of interest in new options or features and the reluctance to pay for anything considered unnecessary is permeating society.

The third is predictability and no unpleasant surprises.[9] The commodity model depends heavily on the standardization of inputs. In this way it ensures there is simplicity and repeatability in the processes and systems required to generate the product or deliver the service. And with consistent, repeatable inputs we end up with consistent and repeatable outputs. When coupled with a no frills mindset it limits the variations that can lead to mismatches between expectations and outcomes. So when people travel on a low cost airline they know exactly what they are going to get and because it is a very basic service there is little or no room for disappointment. The opposite is true when you are paying for a premium service – there is plenty that can result in dissatisfaction. Keeping with the airline example, if I had paid £5000 to travel business or first class I would be on the lookout for anything that could spoil the experience, which could include check-in, my experience in the lounge, how the cabin crew treat me, the food, the seat, the in-flight entertainment and so on. When I have paid £10 I wouldn't be on the lookout for anything, because at that price I have no expectations apart from arriving on time and in one piece.

The fourth is control and repetition.[10] If you are going to provide a consistent outcome you have to eliminate all sources of error. This is where commoditization comes into its own as the ability to codify and systematize processes lies at its heart. Through this, errors can be reduced by taking work out of the system, human involvement can be minimised and everything, including customer interactions, can be made as simple and standard as possible. We see this with the scripted conversations we have with call centre staff and the almost robotic ordering processes dished out by customer service personnel.

Finally, there is overshooting. This has to do with how companies innovate faster than customers' lives change. Although peoples' lives and expectations about what they need to get done remain fairly constant over time, the same cannot be said of products, which change more frequently. As a result products become far more sophisticated than the customer requires and as each competitor seeks to out-feature and outperform its rivals this only compounds the problem. Over time there is little to differentiate one product and service from another and all products end up looking somewhat similar and therefore commoditized.[11] As products overshoot they command lower premiums for additional features – one of the most obvious indicators of commoditization introduced in Chapter 1. So as organizations continue to extend their products in an attempt to escape the trap of commoditization they are inadvertently increasing the likelihood that they will remain in the same bind. There might be a short respite during which the new product or service might enjoy being different or special, but the market quickly finds a way of making the item similar, cheaper and better.[12]

Everything about the commodity model is designed to keep the inputs and outputs as standardized and repeatable as possible. Deviations are not, and cannot be accepted, because these introduce unnecessary complexity. As these facets come together to drive down the price of goods and services, they also allow two other things to occur. The first is the ability to deliver the product or service faster and the second is to make it better. It follows that if you have taken the trouble to simplify and standardize your processes then it ought to be possible to deliver your product or service more efficiently. This is what Wal-Mart has done so that it can continue to meet its promise of everyday low prices. It also follows that if you have standardized your offering you should be able to eliminate its inherent flaws. As we saw above, one of the beauties of simplification and standardization is that errors can be eliminated more readily, thereby improving overall product and service quality.

The tensions associated with the cheaper, faster, better mentality will continue to mount as commoditization forces an increasing number of organizations to focus on more than just price. And as price competition grows, businesses will seek to outperform their rivals by adding more features, improving the quality of their products and services and delivering them more efficiently. As customers come to expect this, the bar is raised for the non-price related aspects of the product or service at the same time as the price bar is lowered. Organizations will find themselves in a bind which may be difficult to break out from.

First margin, then brand and finally market position – the erosive power of commoditization

As we can see, commoditization is not just about price. The ability of organizations to deliver low cost products and services at an acceptable or even superior level of quality means that many have to contend with the double bind of increased quality and reduced price. The immediate impact of this is the erosion of margin, as it becomes very difficult to maintain high margins when others are undercutting your prices and delivering a service that is difficult to differentiate from yours. This is further exacerbated by the unwillingness of customers to pay more than they have to or even accept additional features as a way to compensate them for higher prices. The survival of the cheapest mentality that this generates can be highly destructive and is unlikely to change for the foreseeable future. Few will be spared as the combination of globalization, the Internet and the rise of low cost competition in general will feed the ongoing erosion of margin. Even Chinese companies face the same problems. For example, Ching Hai Electronics Works Co, which produces white goods, has seen the wholesale price of its ventilators and toasters drop from seven dollars ten years ago to four dollars today.[13] Much of this fall has been down to the effect which Wal-Mart and other low cost operators have had on companies such as theirs. With their constant drive to lower their prices, Wal-Mart is able to find plenty of alternative suppliers across China who are willing to meet their stringent price expectations. For those used to charging reasonable prices for their products this means they have little choice but to reduce their prices in line with everyone else. No surprise then that average profit margin has dropped from 20 per cent to around 5 per cent over the same period.[14]

Commoditization also impacts brands. The concept of the brand emerged in the mid-1980s when the management gurus of the day suggested that successful organizations of the future would create brands, not products.[15] Since then brands have taken on significance that none would have believed possible and they are now considered to be a major source of competitive advantage. Companies take immense trouble to build and protect their brands because it allows them to differentiate themselves from their competition and provide a shortcut in buying decisions. We are all familiar with brands such as Coca-Cola, Nike, Starbucks, Ford, Toyota and many, many others and the power they have on the choices we make. Brands clearly matter and differentiation is perhaps the biggest thing that a brand can deliver as this, along with the brand proposition (position and identity) helps to create and maintain a brand that consumers can relate to. Other dimensions, including brand loyalty, awareness, associations and perceived quality are also essential foundations to building and maintaining an effective brand.

Despite the importance of a brand to an organization, commoditization is capable of reducing a brand's value in two ways, one of which is driven by the market and the other by competition. The market pressure comes from increasing choice and the reduced switching costs that come with this choice. The brands we are familiar with are being eroded by the emergence of cheap alternatives which are equally capable of delivering what the consumer wants. For example, retailers are increasingly using their own label goods to compete with well known brands. Well known products will also often be knocked-off by the competition and presented as a new and improved version of the original, and always at a lower price.[16] The same is true of proprietary and private brands; all are capable of undermining an established brand.[17] The greater the number of alternative brands, the weaker the link between an individual brand and the consumer will become. With thousands of brands appearing every year there is plenty of brand noise out there.[18] And, when there are plenty of alternatives, the costs associated with switching from one brand to another reduce considerably. Brand loyalty is therefore diminished in a commodity market.

The other way in which existing brands can be eroded has to do with their price. If you can buy branded goods at a lower price, then as the adage goes, why pay more? So if you can purchase a pair of DNKY jeans from Tesco, why would you pay more on the high street? This is exacerbated by the tendency to outsource production to far flung places like China, so whilst in the past companies would boast that their products were created locally, this is no longer the case. Smart consumers know this and they also know that similar products bearing different brand names may come from the same factory.[19] This was neatly illustrated by a colleague of mine, who was telling me of a US tool provider who was boasting about their latest machine tools, but it lost its appeal when the images sent to him had 'Made in China' emblazoned on them.

This general weakening of brands has been confirmed by Copernicus[20] who analyzed 48 categories of leading brands which ranged from hair care products through to rental cars. They found that the perception of brands was becoming more similar than different in 40 of the categories.[21] It also found that as brands become more similar, purchase decisions become weighted more heavily toward low price rather than brand.[22]

It follows that if your margins are reducing and your brand is weakening, then your market position in general is under threat. A leading position can soon turn into a lagging one, and unless you can make the necessary changes that will allow you to survive, you may end up failing or becoming an acquisition target especially for the increasingly predatory private equity firms. Commoditization has the power to change perceptions very rapidly which can make for a sudden shift in fortunes. For example car insurance has shifted quite rapidly from one which involved high street insurers providing advice to consumers, who felt they needed expert input, to one in which the majority of policies are taken out without any face-to-face interaction. The emergence of direct sales platforms, price comparison websites and a larger number of players in the insurance market, most notably the supermarkets such as Tesco, has eroded margins, made most of the brands within the sector virtually identical and reduced the market position of many insurers. With so many offering amazing deals, or offering to undercut any other insurer's quote, it's no wonder they all appear identical. The same applies to any business which can be commoditized, be it product or service oriented. Commoditization is thorough in its undermining of high prices, solid margins and strong brands.

Behind the steering wheel – big not small

The process of commoditization often starts with the emergence of low cost competition from new entrants who are willing to undercut the existing incumbents in order to grab market share. This process has been greatly enhanced by the Internet which has provided the platform from which new products and services can be launched and marketed to a much wider audience. The long tail mentioned in Chapter 4 is testament to this and highlights how it is possible to turn a profit even in the most obscure of niches. Globalization too has had its part to play through the opening up of competition by the removal of protectionist behaviours and national barriers to trade. However, although small companies can stimulate the commoditization of products and services, they often lack the resources to remain viable for the medium to long term. Many have to grow as any other organization has to if they are to continue to be successful. Amazon is a good case in point. As an Internet retailer it is one of the few businesses that managed to survive beyond the Dot Com crash of 2000–2001. It has done so by expanding its footprint and extending the range of products it sells; Amazon is no longer just about books but now includes baby ware, furniture, garden toys, office products, computers, musical instruments, groceries and many other household items. So although it could be argued that Amazon, and companies like it, stimulated the rapid commoditization of the book trade by undercutting the booksellers, its ability to survive in an increasingly cut throat market is down to its size. Having rapidly grabbed market share, it has consolidated its position through investments in technology, expansion into new product areas and by building its brand. Amazon's 2006 annual report makes for interesting reading in this respect. They recognize that their market segments are evolving rapidly and are intensely competitive. Their competition comes from many quarters including retail, e-commerce services, digital and web services. And many of their current and potential competitors have greater resources, longer histories, more customers, and greater brand recognition than they. As a result they may secure better terms from vendors, adopt more aggressive pricing strategies and devote more resources to technology, fulfilment and marketing than Amazon can. Like so many organizations today, Amazon is also expanding into China into order to capitalize on this major market. In 2004 they acquired Joyo.com, which is organized under the laws of the British Virgin Islands and operates www.joyo.com and www.joyo.com.cn in the People's Republic of China (PRC) in cooperation with a PRC subsidiary and PRC affiliates. Amazon's future may not be completely secure, but it is doing everything it can to ensure it survives in the commoditized market it helped to create. And key to this survival is its size, without which it just wouldn't have the financial muscle required to stay in business. I will return to Amazon in Chapter 9.

One of the interesting things playing out in the UK at the moment is the effect which the supermarket Tesco, Britain's largest, is having on small retailers. As it continues to expand its larger stores and its Metro stores in town and city centres in particular, many of the smaller retailers are being forced out of business. It is impossible to compete against a behemoth of a company that has immense buying power and which is able to control its suppliers and heavily influence its customers. As you'd suspect, this is creating a lot of column inches in the newspapers across the country as commentators line up to accuse Tesco of destroying the character of every high street in Britain. Of course, it is not just Tesco who are doing this, as every other big brand retailer is in on the game. Go anywhere in the UK and you could be anywhere; each town centre looks pretty much the same as any other, so if you want to go shopping these days you may as well stay at home. The same is true of Wal-Mart whose growing domination of consumers' grocery and drug spending devastates the competition. And because Wal-Mart is so vast, it's not just the smaller retailers that suffer as Wal-Mart's business model puts even the largest supermarkets at a competitive disadvantage.[23] Wal-Mart is now the Number 1 seller across a whole range of products. For example, it sells 21 per cent of the toys bought in the US, 23 per cent of the health and beauty products and 27 per cent of household goods. This stranglehold that Wal-Mart has is, according to some, suffocating market capitalism and restricting genuine choice. Moreover, Wal-Mart's suppliers cannot consider themselves to be serious players in their market segments unless they are doing business with Wal-Mart because Wal-Mart already dominates the business they are in.[24]

Looking at Amazon, Tesco and Wal-Mart it is clear that if you are a high volume producer of goods and services you may be better placed to address the challenge of commoditization, and high volume usually implies a large company. Although large organizations have their own set of issues, especially when it comes to change, they do appear to have some significant advantages in a commoditized market. The first is that they can expand into new markets more easily and take greater risks. Second, they can often cope with the financial consequences of commoditization by covering lost revenues from other parts of their business portfolio, especially if this is sufficiently diverse. Third, they can exert their purchasing power to force price reductions onto their suppliers. Fourth, as sharply reduced transportation costs and tariff barriers have taken hold, allowing all suppliers to ship their products to us more cheaply than before, the fixed costs associated with important activities such as research and development now constitute a much higher proportion of the overall product costs. This favours the larger company once again as they are able to bear the costs more readily and can benefit from their economy of scale.[25] And finally, they are able to attack the competition without completely destroying their own businesses.

General Motors provides a good example of how scale helps in a commodity market. The automobile manufacturer, which is already China's largest car maker, at 14 per cent, is hoping to push sales up to 1.3 million within the next three years.[26] This sounds like a good strategy, but there are three major hurdles that could prevent them from achieving this objective and all three are associated with the commodity market in which they exist. The first problem they have to overcome is the power of their brand; in China it is no longer capable of guaranteeing sales as it once did when they entered the market in 1997. With no fewer than 39 automotive brands vying for custom, General Motors has its work cut out as every other car manufacturer on the planet is aiming to grow their share of the Chinese market and in 2007 alone a total of 140 new vehicles were launched into an already crowded market.[27] However, it has size on its side and it benefits from the broadest range of products, which stretches from $5000 microvans through to the $95 000 Cadillacs. It also has the financial muscle to make new models and refresh old ones. The second issue they have to address is the effect that all this competition is having on their margins. As with any other commodity market, margins are being squeezed and over the past three years, the price for a new vehicle has dropped by 7 per cent per annum. To combat this, General Motors is increasing its sales volume; it is realizing savings at its assembly plants as suppliers get more competitive and reduce their prices and it is moving its facilities outside Shanghai where labour is cheaper by up to $9 an hour.[28] The final problem is unique to the Chinese market and has to do with their joint venture partner, SAIC. SAIC is the holding company which runs auto supply and commercial vehicle firms as well as partnering General Motors and Volkswagen on assembly; SAIC was China's top auto company in 2006.[29] With the Chinese government encouraging local manufacturers to start their own brands, SAIC has been making aggressive inroads in this direction and it is making solid progress; it is now spending $1.7 billion on developing its own cars. There are increasing signs that it will eventually break off from General Motors and its partners, although for the time being General Motors appears to be pretty relaxed, believing there to be plenty of room for everyone. Time will tell.

We are also seeing a general consolidation of businesses across many sectors as companies swallow each other up in order to grab market share. Such consolidation is not new, of course, but it seems to be taking on a greater significance in a commoditized world. When margins are thin, it can be a good idea to take over another company to provide additional turnover and profitability. As the new company is integrated, margin improvement may be possible as duplicate roles and positions are eliminated. It also reduces the number of competitors you have to battle with. For example, as a writer, the number of publishers I deal with has shrunk over the last few years as the large publishing houses have snapped up all the small and independent publishers. Much of this is in response to the declining trade in books and to a large extent the saturated and hence commoditized nature of the book trade stimulated to a significant extent by Amazon. One of the interesting consequences of this is that the large publishers have become more conservative and only want to sign up bestselling authors or celebrities. As a consequence, the smaller publishers end up taking fewer risks because they are gradually forced to the periphery of the book trade, as they cannot get the face-time with the booksellers who expect larger sweeteners to place new books on their shelves. Picking up small players is one thing, but we are also seeing consolidation taking place at the top end of sectors (as long as the authorities believe it is not stifling competition – something we touched on in Chapter 3). Take Mittal Steel, the Dutch listed company that is now the biggest steel company in the world. The company was built up by acquiring aging steel mills across the former Soviet Union and its satellite states, such as Poland, before negotiating the $4.5 billion buyout of International Steel Group in 2004. Then in 2006 Mittal launched a successful hostile bid for the second largest steel group, Arcelor which it purchased for $34 billion. What was significant about this deal is that it represented the consolidation between the Number 1 and Number 2 players in the market which is a break from the past when the largest companies typically acquired the smallest.[30] In another example the accounting-come-business advisory firms Grant Thornton and RSM Robson Rhodes merged in July 2007 as a means to attack the market of the established Big Four firms of PricewaterhouseCoopers (PwC), Deloitte, KPMG and Ernst & Young. It is the biggest merger since PwC was created in 1998. The combined firm will have a turnover of circa £361 million and becomes the biggest accountant outside the Big Four, albeit still a long way off in terms of its revenues, which are still one-third of Ernst & Young's, the Number 4 firm.[31] In merging, the new firm has started to open up the competition that has been ostensibly closed for a long time and through this is likely to increase the pressure on price across the industry. Subject to any competition issues, I fully expect similar consolidations to occur as a way to combat commoditization, and we shouldn't forget the impact which the private equity companies are having. I will return to this in the next chapter, as private equity businesses and mergers and acquisitions in particular have specific ramifications for the white-collar worker.

Although being large may protect you from the ravages of commoditization, it may not completely spare you, as it will not necessarily be today's large companies that will be with us 20 years from now. We are already witnessing the emergence of new multinationals from the BRIC economies (see also Chapter 5) and as these companies expand they are likely to swallow many of the big branded companies we know today and if they don't take them over, they may well take them out. One thing that is clear is that one big company will be replaced by another and it is the larger companies that could be the ultimate winners in the commoditized economy of the future.

Mirroring Wal-Mart and passing the commoditization buck

If it is to be the large organizations that will dominate the markets in a commoditized world, we should expect to see an increasing number of other organizations being pressurised into following their lead. Commoditization is clearly capable of affecting a wide range of organizations, but in today's connected economy, the effects are no longer isolated. The combination of globalization, the Internet and integrated supply chains means that if commoditization impacts one organization, it is likely to affect those that it interfaces with. The power which companies such as Wal-Mart can exert allows them to call the shots with their suppliers. Proctor and Gamble, who recently merged with Gillette, is a prime example of how even the largest suppliers have little choice but to respond to Wal-Mart's demands. With sales in excess of $68 billion per annum Proctor and Gamble is not only larger than any other consumer products company but is bigger than all but 16 public companies of any kind in the United States. And yet Wal-Mart is by a very long way Proctor and Gamble's largest customer – as big as their next nine combined.[32] With Wal-Mart being so significant, it's no wonder that Proctor and Gamble goes out of its way to keep them happy, because if they didn't the effect would be devastating. As we will see in Chapter 9, when we look at Wal-Mart's supply chain practices, suppliers, including Proctor and Gamble, have had to mirror Wal-Mart in order to meet their exacting price expectations. Companies such as Wal-Mart are at the forefront of the commoditization movement and are not only changing the way business gets done but also the way economies behave and how we perceive the world especially in relation to the products and services we buy,[33] which brings us back to the cheaper, but faster and better too discussion at the beginning of the chapter.

It is not just those who directly interface to those organizations that are driving commoditization that have to mirror them. The impact of commoditization also forces direct competitors to smarten up their act. When your primary competition operates slick back office processes or a fully integrated supply chain then you have to too, otherwise you will be carrying too much cost in the business which will prevent you from lowering price without reducing your margins. The other interesting thing about commoditization and those who are driving it is that they become the poster boys for other companies in different industries. The view here is that if Wal-Mart or Ryanair can do it in their respective industries, then we can do it in ours. Although few would want to emulate them entirely, they are happy to select those parts of the business model that are appropriate, such as the supply chain practices of Wal-Mart, or the no-frills efficiency of Ryanair. Like so many things in the business world, the opportunity to reuse other companies' practices is rarely missed. Amazon, for example, has mimicked Wal-Mart's focus on everyday low prices with its own turn on the phrase – as they stated in their 2006 annual report *we endeavour to offer our retail customers the lowest prices possible through low everyday product pricing and free shipping.*

In a recent conversation with a client of mine, it is clear that as companies mirror organizations like Wal-Mart they can become rapidly commoditized and may even become more commoditized than they realized. This particular conversation was about a major transportation and logistics company operating across North America. About 12 years ago they decided to enter the supply chain business to offset a heavy asset load (they had in the region of 180 000 depreciating assets worldwide). In one of their first service offerings, they put together a concept called dedicated contracts whereby their value proposition was to lease and maintain the truck; carry out all safety training, provide the drivers, and self insure against accidents and loss. This was designed to provide a one-stop-shop for their customers. The services were bundled together so that the customer could outsource all their transportation requirements to them. At the time, this made perfect sense, but as the business evolved, the services had to move up the value chain as competition increased and the services became more complex. Initially they were extended to include designing, scheduling and routing this was followed by cross docking services and customs and brokerage services, and eventually they extended the offering to include fourth party outsourcing, in which the transportation company acted as the lead logistics provider on major accounts. During this time, it became apparent that the value proposition had to be modified to suit different clients. For example, although a client had the transportation company as its global lead logistic provider, the company had to outsource lanes to other carriers because the full service was either not required or was too expensive to operate. The lanes for which they were responsible became commoditized to the point that contribution margins dropped to a level where lanes that were formerly held by them were no longer feasible for either them or their clients. As a result they had to unbundle their services and pass the unprofitable lanes to an alternative carrier who offered less in the way of service, but all the same bid less for the lanes. This continued commoditization forced the company into a seemingly endless round of cost reduction which has so far lasted five years. The resultant lack of spending and especially that associated with IT has caused serious issues. There is a prevailing view that in order to remain competitive with other third and fourth party providers, they should have acquired a customs brokerage firm at least five years ago. However, when brokerage firms came up for sale they were snapped up by the competition and the price of entry has now become prohibitive, which puts the company behind the major players. There has also been speculation for a number of years that they may carve out and sell the Supply Chain side of the business given the attendant issues, but this has yet to be greeted favourably by the markets especially as they would be left with only the asset-heavy side of the business which is mature, commoditizing, with eroding margins.

The doughnut principle and the hollowing out of organizations

I mentioned Charles Handy's doughnut principle in Chapter 1 because it is a helpful metaphor for the hollowing out which is occurring in many organizations. We also discussed how this is being manifested in companies in Chapter 4 when we covered amongst other things the insourcing of expertise from third party suppliers such as UPS. As commoditization continues to play out, the doughnut principle and all that it implies will take on a greater significance.

In simple terms, the doughnut principle involves identifying those activities within the business that are core and those which although important, do not add direct value to the core activities. It is these non-core activities that are the targets for outsourcing and increasingly offshoring. Although this started out focused on IT, principally as we saw in Chapter 4 because of Year 2000, it has since extended into other functional activities such as finance and HR. As more work becomes codified and its value to a company more easily assessed, it is likely that the level of outsourcing and offshoring will increase. As we saw in Chapter 4, the ability to commoditize process will greatly accelerate this trend. Indeed, there are already a significant number of jobs which have the potential to be offshored; something I will specifically address in the next chapter.

There are two very good reasons why any company should consider outsourcing.[34] The first is where a third party is able to provide the function or service more effectively for less money and the second is where the activity being outsourced is not central to the business and hence its loss is of no material consequence. There are of course other reasons why organizations pursue outsourcing and offshoring but these tend to be wrong headed – for example the me-too mentality that afflicts so many boards or the desire to get rid of a difficult or seemingly insoluble problem (which is the worst of all reasons). Outsourcing and offshoring can, of course, go horribly wrong especially if it has been poorly executed; for example, Capital One, the US credit card company, was forced to cancel a contract with Wipro Spectramind, an Indian technology company, after they discovered that the call centre staff were making unauthorized offers of credit to customers. Other similar complaints of poor service by customers have led other well known businesses, including Lehman Brothers and Dell, to bring outsourced work back inside their company in order to maintain control over quality and to avoid losing valued customers.[35] Such horror stories will not deter others from seeking the benefits that come from outsourcing and offshoring and as the markets for these services mature, the service levels will inevitably increase and problems such as those experienced above will be fewer in number. Indeed despite the known problems, the global outsourcing market continues to grow. Today it is worth something in the region of $234 billion per annum, of which 15 per cent is offshored and this is expected to grow to $310 billion in 2008, of which 20 per cent will be offshored.[36]

The nature of the focus of this outsourcing is changing as the market matures. Over time there will be fewer major IT outsourcing deals, as there will be less IT to outsource, whilst Business Process Outsourcing deals will continue to grow as back, middle and even front office processes are outsourced and offshored to reduce costs. This kind of outsourcing will continue to expand as greater tranches of business process commoditized and the work associated with is codified. For example the UK business of Prudential, the financial services group, is to outsource the back office functions related to its UK closed funds to its existing Indian operation in Mumbai. They are also considering outsourcing additional functions to Capita, the support services group. Up to 3000 jobs could be at risk.[37] When work is easily understood and hence transferable, the cheaper, faster, better mode of working facilitates further outsourcing. Cost savings can, of course, be significant and these are a major factor in deciding to outsource and offshore work. This becomes even more important when we consider just how erosive commoditization is to margins. A comparison of the costs of executing processes in the US against other countries by Accenture identified labour savings of up to 80 per cent (depending on where the process was executed) and despite the increased management overhead which can be as high as 30 per cent,[38] it is easy to see why outsourcing and offshoring in particular has gained such traction. In terms of the current destinations the lion's share goes to India at 55 per cent; the rest is divided between a variety of countries including Ireland, Russia, Mexico, China and the Philippines.[39] The locations offering Business Process Outsourcing services will continue to grow which will increase competition, help keep costs down and more importantly offer additional sites which will be more convenient to those seeking to outsource their processes.

At its extreme such hollowing out can eliminate all but the brand. For example, a small number of companies within the automotive sector have outsourced and offshored practically everything from the design to the manufacture of their vehicles leaving just the brand. Perhaps this is a bit extreme, but there is nothing to prevent other companies from doing the same. As long as the product or service is delivered according to well defined and exacting standards, the fact that all the activities, from research and design through to manufacture, are outsourced or offshored shouldn't matter. There are of course downsides to this approach as it opens you up to new competition (as we shall see when we look at the Geely Group in Chapter 9).

So we should expect more organizations to hollow out over the coming years as corporations free themselves of the unnecessary costs and overheads associated with their non-core and back and middle office activities. We will also see more third parties offering expertise in those functions and activities that companies don't want to run and are more than happy to insource if they need to.

The stark choice of modernize or die

Dramatic changes in any environment often require a dramatic response and commoditization is no exception. Organizations face major challenges when they change even at the best of times, but when it's a case of modernize or die, change takes on a whole new dimension. It might be tough to persuade people to change when times are good and business is booming, but it is much, much harder when people find themselves backed into a corner; change becomes wrenching. The problem with changing when you have to is that everyone will fight harder to hang onto what they have especially when they see that their futures are in jeopardy. Commoditization has the ability to catch you by surprise, especially if you are not paying attention to what is going on in the wider market; the sudden entry of low cost competition; the gradual erosion of margins; the loss of brand loyalty and the unattractiveness of new features, and so on. You should, of course, see it coming, but once it's caught up with you, the need to undertake wholesale change and take radical actions is not only desirable, but it becomes necessary for survival. We are seeing this with the UK's Royal Mail which is attempting to modernize in light of the increasing levels of competition following the loss of its government maintained monopoly. As low cost competition invades its markets and takes away its business, the ability to remain profitable without significant and wide-reaching changes is impossible. Unions are fighting against the need to modernize as they want to protect the 40 000 or so jobs that are at risk but each time they bring their members out on strike Royal Mail's competitors are able to secure additional business and with it market share. Royal Mail's CEO has publicly stated that they are losing revenue because the business has failed to modernize and the recent loss of an £8 million contract with Amazon is indicative of the problems they will increasingly face.[40] Ford too is still in the midst of its turnaround which will help it to navigate its way through an increasingly overcrowded and commoditized market, which is compounded by the crippling pension and health care costs it faces. The company lost $12.7 billion in 2006, equivalent to nearly $7 for every Ford share, and recently announced the sale of Volvo, the Swedish car group it bought when it was creating its Premiere Automotive Group (PAG) during the 1980s and 1990s.[41] Ford has been busy dismantling the PAG which is no longer considered core business. As well as hoping to dispose of Volvo, Ford has recently put Jaguar and Land Rover up for sale and sold Aston Martin in early 2007.[42]

Every company faced with the commoditization of its markets faces similar challenges, to be as effective as companies such as Wal-Mart, Ryanair and, increasingly the powerhouses coming from the BRIC economies, takes significant investment and time. A stark choice seems to be emerging in which organizations must change or suffer a long, or perhaps relatively short, slide into oblivion. And if you are going to change you are better off doing it in advance of commoditization, not after it has hit you. Some organizations already are. For example I have been working with one North American business which in recognition that their markets are becoming increasingly commoditized is undertaking a near $100 million transformation programme. Although they already operate very successfully in a commodity market, they see major threats from other companies outside their sector. The programme, which will take nearly two years to complete, aims to upscale the use of technology, follow a centralist path for their principal processes and to re-skill their staff so that they become more adaptive and capable of changing in the future. This is no simple undertaking, as they have to be able to protect and grow their current business at the same time. However, to a large extent they have no choice but to change because if they were to wait any longer they would have to modernize anyway. Under these circumstances the effects would be far more dramatic as it would be likely they would be changing in an environment of increased competition, falling margins and loss of brand and market share; all in all much harder to address. The upside of changing now is significant and will allow them to build a competitive advantage that will be at least two years ahead of their existing competition and more importantly will create some critical barriers to entry. Another major advantage they will have is the ability to model their margins and in doing so price their services so that that margin can be maintained or even increased in a price sensitive market. This type of response will become more common as commoditization continues to advance throughout the corporate world. I will provide some examples of what other companies are doing to combat or indeed drive commoditization in Chapter 9.

It is clear that commoditization has the power to erode some of the fundamental building blocks of any successful business, including its brand. It also seems that it will be the large organizations that stand the better chance of survival than medium to small enterprises as they have the economies of scale to cope with some of the financial implications of commoditization. That said, size is no indicator of future success, because large companies are much harder to change than small ones and as we are seeing with the Post Office and Ford, changing in response to commoditization is not simple or indeed without pain. There are, of course, choices; and understanding how to tackle the commoditization challenge is something I will be turning to in Chapters 8 and 9. However, before I can do that we need to review the impacts of commoditization on white-collar workers who, like corporations, will be feeling the cold wind of change a lot more than they have in the past.

References

1 Van Agtmael, A. (2007) *The Emerging Markets Century*, New York: Free Press, p. 14.
2 Bosshart, D. (2007) *Cheap? The Real Cost of Living in a Low Price, Low Wage World*, London: Kogan Page, p. 58.
3 Dobbs, L. (2004) *Exporting America: Why Corporate Greed is Shipping American Jobs Overseas*, New York: Warner Books, p. 1.
4 Bosshart, D. (2007) *Cheap? The Real Cost of Living in a Low Price, Low Wage World*, London: Kogan Page, p. 178.
5 Moore, J. (1996) *The Death of Competition: Leadership & Strategy in the Age of Business Ecosystems*, Chichester: John Wiley & Sons, p. 196.
6 Bosshart, D. (2007) *Cheap? The Real Cost of Living in a Low Price, Low Wage World*, London: Kogan Page, pp. 102–105.
7 Ibid., p. 104.
8 Ibid., pp. 105–106.
9 Ibid., pp. 107–108.
10 Ibid., pp. 108–109.
11 Christensen, C., Anthony, S. and Roth, E. (2004) *Seeing What's Next: Using the Theories of Innovation to Predict Industry Change*, Boston Massachusetts: Harvard Business School Press, p. 12.
12 Salzman, M. and Matathia, I. (2006) *Next Trends for the Future Now*, New York: Palgrave Macmillan, p. 146.
13 Bosshart, D. (2007) *Cheap? The Real Cost of Living in a Low Price, Low Wage World*, London: Kogan Page, p. 44.
14 Ibid.
15 Klein, N. (2001) *No Logo*, London: Flamingo, p. 3.
16 Johnston, C. Commoditization: Friend or Foe, J.C. Williams Group, p. 2 – see www.jcwg.com/downloads.
17 Bosshart, D. (2007) *Cheap? The Real Cost of Living in a Low Price, Low Wage World*, London: Kogan Page, pp. 33–34.
18 Salzman, M. and Matathia, I. (2006) *Next Trends for the Future Now*, New York: Palgrave Macmillan, p. 147.
19 Ibid.
20 Copernicus (2000) The commoditization of brands and its implications for marketers, see www.copernicusmarketing.com/about/docs/commodities.pdf.
21 Ibid., p. 4.
22 Ibid., p. 5.
23 Bianco, A. (2006) *The Bully of Bentonville: How the High Cost of Wal-Mart's Everyday Low Prices is Hurting America*, New York: Currency Doubleday, p. 200.
24 Fishman, C. (2006) *The Wal-Mart Effect*, New York: The Penguin Press, p. 234.
25 Frank, R. (2007) *Falling Behind: How Rising Inequality Harms the Middle Class*, Berkley: University of California Press, p. 96.
26 Van Praet, N. (2007) China: GM's next headache? *Financial Post Business*, July/August, p. 32.
27 Ibid., p. 34.
28 Ibid.
29 Ibid., p. 35.
30 Rushe, D. (2006) All aboard the M&A express, *The Sunday Times*, 31 December, pp. 3–5.
31 See http://ftalphaville.ft.com/blog/2007/04/30/4182/grant-thornton-and-rsm-in-merger-plan.
32 Fishman, C. (2006) *The Wal-Mart Effect*, New York: The Penguin Press, p. 234.
33 Ibid., p. 238.
34 Skapinker, M. (2004) How to control a phenomenon, *FT Management*, 1 June, p. 1.
35 Ibid., p. 2.
36 See http://itcsoftware.com/OS/globalmarket.htm.

37 Waples, J. and Ringshaw, G.,(2007) Pru revamp risks thousands of jobs, *The Sunday Times*, Business, 11 March, 9: 3–1.
38 These figures were brought to the author's attention from a lecture delivered by Dr Jeffery Sampler of Oxford University 7–9 March 2005.
39 See http://itcsoftware.com/OS/globalmarket.htm.
40 Taylor, A. (2007) Royal Mail warned users will desert it, *Financial Times*, 30 June/1 July, p. 4.
41 O'Connell, D. (2007) Ford seeks to offload Volvo in $8bn sale, *The Sunday Times*, 15 July, pp. 1–3.
42 Ibid.

7 *Individual Impacts*

Not only was the middle-class 'salariat' experiencing the full force of 'downsizing' – a well documented phenomenon – but the two pillars of the bourgeois professional's world view, career ladder and status were systematically demolished.[1]

Unlike your teacher, your boss isn't going to care much about preserving your high self-esteem. The self-esteem emphasis leaves kids ill prepared for the inevitable criticism and occasional failure that is real life...If you present a bad report at the office, your boss isn't going to say, 'Hey, I like the color paper you chose'.[2]

Therefore, the prosperity of nations, the profitability of companies and the livelihoods of individuals and their families are believed to depend on winning a competitive advantage in the knowledge-driven global economy. Britain and the US have staked their future prosperity, with all its social ramifications, on outsmarting other nations in their competition for high-skilled, high-waged employment.[3]

For many skilled and qualified workers, the fact that they have to work for Wal-Mart symbolizes their failure.[4]

It is clear from Part I and Chapter 5 in particular that the process of commoditization has now entered its most significant phase. White-collar work, long the preserve of the educated elite, is now undergoing a significant transformation as it starts to commoditize. Countries such as the United Kingdom and the United States are betting their futures on maintaining a broader, well educated workforce. But so is everyone else. The problem is that many of their competitors are likely to outsmart them with more and better educated workers who require less income to maintain a solid middle class existence. It may not happen overnight but the evidence is that it is accelerating, with major implications for today's workers and tomorrow's graduates. The collapse of communism, economic migration and the continued march of information technology have allowed China, India, Russia and many other nations to enter the global market for education, knowledge and high-end employment.[5] It is this, along with the other aspects discussed in Chapter 5 that is making the commoditization of white-collar work a reality.

Before we review these impacts in more detail it is necessary to discuss a couple of factors not addressed in Chapter 5, both of which are important backdrops because they will determine how well we are able (or not) to deal with the impacts of commoditization. The first has to do with the shift towards a culture of personal responsibility with society opting out (through legislation and other reforms) or refusing (in the case of organizations) to provide the safety net it once did for when things turn out for the worst. The second is associated with the emphasis on self-esteem which is building unrealistic expectations in the newer members of the workforce and creating a lot more narcissists who are poorly equipped to deal with the reality of being of limited importance. These two factors help to exacerbate the impacts of commoditization and make it much harder to cope with the consequences.

Personal responsibility

Many of us and particularly those of us who live in the West are taught to stand on our own two feet from a very early age. It is embedded within the Anglo Saxon culture and is something that is central to the American Dream, which encourages entrepreneurism and a winner takes all society. Cultures of course vary, as you tend to find more collective cultures across continental Europe and throughout the Asia Pacific region. Collective cultures tend to emphasise family and social connections, which is in stark contrast to those of America and the UK. National cultures aside there has been a significant trend over the recent past toward increasing our level of personal responsibility. Some of this shift has been due to the demographic changes taking place in the West, but most of it has been down to the adjustments made to the safety nets provided to the population by their governments. This is not universal, as some countries, and most notably France, still cling on to their generous social policies that are considered by many too liberal and damaging to the French economy. This may have to change over the next few years if France is to compete effectively on the global market, but only time will tell. The French economy is being dragged down by the 35-hour week, high taxation, high social costs on wages and employment and red tape, all of which is making it difficult for the French to compete. With unemployment remaining stubbornly high at 8 per cent, and youth unemployment at 22 per cent, France is facing a crisis of major proportions; and this is being compounded by the ongoing brain drain of talent that is leaving the country for London, America and Asia in order to make more money and have a better life devoid of the crushing social costs that are part of daily life in France.[6] Part of the issue facing the French is their lack of adjustment to the changing competitive dynamic which comes with commoditization and the low cost competition it brings. Whilst many other countries within the European Union, most notably the UK, have changed their employment laws and reduced their social safety nets, France has still to get to grips with the programme. Even Germany, long the bastion of a socially responsible society, is making major adjustments in order to become more market driven. Now that France has a new president, Nicolas Sarkozy, things are likely to change as he was elected on a market reform agenda, which will begin with the abolishment of the 35-hour week. So maybe France has finally got it after all, although the journey is going to be very long and no doubt rocky.

Faced with a situation of having to pay for an increasingly old population, governments have recognized that paying for pensions, medical care, education, and everything else for that matter is no longer tenable and have started to unravel many of the state sponsored safety nets that had previously protected the population against the various risks they face over the course of a lifetime. Today we are all expected to pay our way with little support; from medical insurance, to pensions, little is spared. For example as a middle aged Brit, I can look forward to having little or no state pension to keep me in my dotage and that's despite diligently paying National Insurance on my earnings which is designed to do just that. Instead I am faced with the prospect of saving a significant percentage of my income to ensure that I will be able to retire before I get too old to enjoy it. This shift towards personal responsibility has been the most marked in the US where, in the words of George W. Bush, 'America is a nation of personal responsibility where people are expected to meet their obligations'.[7] In other words, it's every man, woman and child for themselves. The underlying tenet to this change is the belief that Americans are best positioned to deal with economic risks on their own and without the benefits that government funded risk sharing had previously provided.[8] So families now have the stark choice of going without food or going without increasingly expensive medical cover. The perception that government funded safety nets made people less concerned about the risks they faced, and hence less careful in avoiding them, has been used to underwrite this argument. In other words, if you make it too easy for people by protecting them through state protection against loss, they will only pull back in terms of their effort, and are more likely to buck the system and act fraudulently.[9] It follows therefore that if people self-insure against the hazards they face, they will be more diligent in avoiding them.[10] Well this is the theory, but the reality is that this shift is making the life of the average person far riskier than ever before and, as we saw in Chapter 5, the majority of employees are now not only having to make ends meet, they are also having to save more in order to survive into old age and insure against a range of eventualities such as the loss of a job or serious illness. And when Warren Buffett believes the whole thing is a red herring then there must be something wrong.[11]

When combined with the increasing turbulence within the job markets (see a bit later on in this chapter) you can begin to understand why the levels of insecurity within the working population are going up, not down. Being responsible for every eventuality places a large burden on the average family, as there is no longer the cushion that would have protected them in the past. Economic security is the cornerstone of economic opportunity and people only invest in their future when they have protection against their greatest downside risks. So the more insecure workers feel, the less productive they will be in the long run and the less they will invest in specialized training and commitment to their employer. Play this out into the family setting and we can see that the more insecure the family is the less likely they will be able, or willing to invest in their future, which includes education.[12] In the end the emphasis on personal responsibility is creating high levels of insecurity within the workplace, which is probably going to increase as the momentum of commoditization continues to build. Faced with a declining tax take (from the suppressed income of the middle classes) and an aging population, governments will be seeking to push more risk onto the shoulders of the workforce rather than providing them with the state funded safety nets that they could really do with.

The self-esteem movement and the rise of narcissistic behaviour

There has been another major shift over the last decade or so but this time towards a greater emphasis on maintaining high self-esteem. The term wasn't used much until the 1960s when the Boomer generation started to push the boundaries of behaviour. Self-esteem as a deeply embedded concept did not take hold until the 1990s. By the middle of the 1990s most adolescents took it for granted that everyone knew what self-esteem was and how to assess their own levels of self-esteem. Since then it has become big business for the self-help movement who make millions peddling their sickly blend of you can be anything you want, so long as you believe you can.[13] Of course having a degree of self-esteem or self-respect is important, as we all need to be comfortable with ourselves if we are to succeed both in the workplace and in our lives in general. However, there is a point where self-esteem can be too high, especially when it leads to extreme behaviours such as narcissism. We are beginning to see both the effects of the self-esteem movement and a rise of narcissistic behaviours within the newest working generation – Generation Y – according to one study seven times more prevalent than they were in the 1950s.[14] This cohort has been brought up to believe they are mini deities who can do whatever they want. The future is their oyster and they believe everyone else – parents, teachers and employers – is there to massage their ego and support their aspirations. They pass through life with the firm belief that they are important and that they will get everything they want.[15] This self-absorption is helping to replace the belief that hard work leads to success with the Californian self-help approach that chooses self-gratification and instant results over effort and self-sacrifice. Although much of the blame can be placed at the door of the modern day parents who exhibit appalling parenting skills, the problems run much deeper than this as they extend into the education system with its grade inflation; the lack of competition (and the distinction between winners and losers – when no one is allowed to lose at school anymore); the self-help movement which gives the false impression that everyone is capable of becoming the next president of the United Nations; and the fact that everyone is meant to be special, gifted and talented. This is patently not the case, as you only need to look around you to work that one out. The other problem this seems to be creating is a disconnection between high self-esteem and performance and an increased tendency to cheat in order to ensure people get what they want.[16] This does not bode well for a future workplace where softer skills such as teamwork will have a much greater significance than they do now (see Chapter 9 and the Semco case study for an example).

The fundamental problem with the self-esteem movement is that the emphasis on self-importance sets unrealistic expectations. These are going to be impossible to meet in a world where workers are going to be treated as commodities and will have few opportunities for progressing to the heady heights of president of the United Nations. For example, when a bunch of teenagers were asked in 1999 how much they expected to be earning by the time they were 30, the average income cited was $75 000. The actual income for 30-year-olds at this time was $27 000.[17] In another example, a new employee, who when asked what his career expectations were, told his boss that he expected to be a Vice President in two years. When he was reminded that most of the Vice Presidents in the organization were in their 60s and had grey hair, the new intern was most upset and told his boss that he should be helping him to achieve his objectives, not pouring cold water over them. The poor kid really had no idea that working life was going to be quite a bit different from the cosseted world of the family home and school, where no matter how bad he was, he was always led to believe he was the cream of the crop. It is clear that the emphasis on self-esteem does nothing to serve the children and young adults in the long run and in fact there is an increasing number of academics and social scientists who believe that children should spend more time focusing on developing real skills and using these to accomplish something more tangible than feeding and inflating their egos. In the long run self-discipline and self-control are the true predicators of success.[18] One has to ask just how successful the next generation of workers is going to be. With many of the typical professions of the middle classes, such as accountancy, being eroded by commoditization, there won't be much in the way of opportunities.

We are already witnessing some of the problems that the self-absorbed Generation Y are presenting to their employers. Take the United Kingdom which churns out over 250 000 graduates a year. With graduate-entry level posts standing at 20 000 you would have thought the employers would find it relatively simple to fill their vacancies. However, this is not the case because it seems that many of candidates have a so-what attitude and believe that potential employers need to sell themselves to them, not the other way around.[19] One could argue this attitude could be marginally justified when there is a scarcity of graduates, but this is no longer the case. And with a surfeit of smart, highly motivated and willing graduates within the global employment market, such an attitude is completely unjustified. It should come as no surprise therefore that this cohort is the most depressed, suicidal and lost we have ever seen. They have been sold a future that just doesn't exist and have not been furnished with the skills or capabilities to deal with the inevitable disappointment and sense of under-achievement that comes with unfulfilled dreams.[20] No wonder then that the self-help movement continues to thrive.

The impacts of the continued commoditization of white-collar work on the very foundation of a solid middle class existence are wide ranging, and the effects of the rise in personal responsibility and the self-esteem movement will exacerbate them. The principal impacts on the white-collar employee include:

*   One company but many owners as the impacts of foreign ownership, buy-outs by private equity and takeovers by rivals continue to change the patterns of company ownership and employment. Few of us can expect to remain within a single company that retains its ownership for a lengthy period of time and with this comes additional uncertainty and insecurity.
*   The potential for most if not all white-collar jobs being at risk from commoditization; perhaps not now, but certainly in the future. Remember, any job that can be codified is potentially at risk.
*   An increase in low level, routine work at the expense of the intrinsically interesting work most white-collar workers have come to expect. This does not necessarily mean that work will be any less pressured. Evidence is pointing to the intensification of routine white-collar work which is becoming more demanding not less, something we touched on in Chapter 5 and something I will return to in Chapter 11.
*   The loss of an obvious career path making it much harder to navigate through your working life. This is further compounded by the weakening of the relationship between education and employability which has until very recently been central to a successful career.
*   Economic instability and income stagnation as the China Price moves to the white-collar labour market.

One company but many owners

The past few years have witnessed a massive increase in the levels of takeovers and acquisitions. The number of mergers and acquisitions in 2006 exceeded the highest annual figure on record, which was at the height of the Dot Com mania in 2000. Back then the deals totalled $3332 billion[21] and by the end of 2006 this figure had reached a record $3760.[22] Not only are the number of deals greater now, but their size is also increasing with a larger number over $10 billion and the average deal coming in at around $200 million. Most sectors are targeted and indeed most companies these days seem to present viable opportunities for takeover. Deals are also increasingly driven by the Private Equity houses such as Texas Pacific Group and Kohlberg Kravis Roberts who are becoming increasingly bold in their targets.

Making small companies private and improving them is generally thought to be a good thing because it shakes up the often complacent management team. However, many are now chasing the largest companies in the attempt to gain significant returns. Companies such as Alliance Boots the global wholesale/retail drug supplier (which has now been sold to Kohlberg Kravis Roberts and Co. for $29.4 billion[23]), Sainsburys, one of the UK's largest supermarkets, EMI the record company, Qantas the Australian airline and the London Stock Exchange have all been targets. Another interesting trend is the increasing number of hostile bids which is making life difficult for the target companies and forcing them to take very costly actions to defend themselves.

Unions are becoming increasingly unsettled at the scale of private equity operations, especially in terms of their impact on the livelihoods of their members and intend to publish their own data, which will contest those of the private equity houses, who claim to create, not destroy jobs. Typical of the complaints made by the unions are those associated with the Automobile Association (AA) in the UK. Staff and unions have expressed concerns that core services are being cut in order to maximize the profits of Permira and CVC the private equity owners. Once a mutual owned by its members, the AA was bought in 1999 by the multinational Centrica, before being sold to Permira and CVC, in 2004. If the company is sold in 2008 it may net the equity partners £1.75 billion in profits. To achieve this, the AA's 10 000 workforce has been cut by a third, which includes some 600 patrolmen.[24] No wonder then that many amongst union ranks believe private equity to be a cancer that must be stopped. In more recent moves the big Service Employees International Union has started researching and blogging about corporate buyout deals[25] and in March 2007 union officials from 15 nations called on industrialized countries to impose greater regulation, and are lobbying the Organization for Economic Cooperation (OECD) and other bodies such as the International Monetary Fund.[26]

Of course private equity has a role to play and if companies were well run in the first place, they would never be targets. It should be remembered that private equity companies will only take on a new acquisition if they can see value from the deal. And such value comes from four sources: earnings growth (which is revenue and/or margin driven); multiple expansion (of earnings multiples and hence valuation); hidden value (such as forgotten divisions or restructuring), and financial leverage.[27]

In parallel with this is the rise of the new conglomerates of the world that are equally hungry for a piece of the action. As we saw in Chapter 5, many of the global powerhouses now hail from the emerging economies of the Far East, South America and Africa. Few commentators on free trade would have predicted that such a rise would ever occur and now companies such as Hyundai and Cemex are becoming the next global employers who are replacing the household names most of us have grown up with. Today, there are at least 25 world-class multinationals that originate from emerging economies and this is expected to increase to over 100 within the next ten years.[28] Like all other multinationals these emerging leaders are keen to expand into new markets, take over Western businesses and build their brands into something that is as recognizable as Coke and General Motors. They are making steady progress. For example French electronics giant Thomson was purchased by Chinese consumer electronics company TCL, Siemens Mobile was acquired by Taiwan's BenQ and Germany's Grundig was acquired by the Turkish company Beko. In 2005 these emerging multinationals spent $42 billion on takeover deals in Europe alone.[29] It shouldn't come as a surprise that foreign ownership of UK firms has risen from 30 to 50 per cent over the past decade and there are no signs of this trend slowing down.[30]

So what does this mean for the average worker? First it generates a lot more uncertainty within the workforce because all mergers and acquisitions expect to produce significant savings from the synergies created by the joining together of two companies. Such savings are primarily associated with a reduction in the number of employees, which can be in the tens of thousands. For example the takeover of ABN Amro, the Dutch bank, by Barclays, one of its UK rivals, will result in a reduction of 12 800 jobs and the offshoring of a further 10 800 to low cost countries such as India.[31] Although Barclays pulled out, it is still a useful example. As more companies consolidate there will be a continued downward pressure on headcount and increased levels of uncertainty. Second, staff will have to get used to regular changes of ownership. On face value this shouldn't create too much of a problem, as once the headcount reductions that typically follow any acquisition have ended it will be back to business as usual. Indeed many acquired companies are left alone to just deliver the numbers. However, any shift in ownership creates turbulence, be it in changes in leadership and the various layers of management across the organization, in process, location and systems and even culture. Newly merged companies tend to battle it out between the legacy businesses and the culture clash that results often lasts a considerable amount of time, and much longer than most companies believe it should. So although there may be some short-term uncertainty about the immediate loss of a job, the uncertainty does not end there, as staff will feel uneasy about their medium and long-term futures. With new management also come new options to be explored, such as outsourcing and offshoring. Private equity ownership also creates medium term uncertainty because few if any will hold on to their acquisition for long. Apart from a very few exceptions, a private equity house will have its exit strategy defined at the time of purchase, so don't expect there to be certainty once the acquisition is completed.

All white-collar jobs at risk

Ever since downsizing hit the corporate world in the1990s we have been told that we should not expect to have a job for life. And although it has taken a long time to adjust to the changes which downsizing heralded, many of today's workforces have finally come to accept that mantra. It is certainly true that few of us can really expect to have a job for life in the same way the Boomer Generation had and many of us change our careers a number of times over the course of a 30–40 year working life. So what's new and why is this something we need to worry about? First, job churn is increasing at a much higher rate than in the past. Despite the massive layoffs that came with the downsizing projects it wasn't long before many corporations re-stabilized and continued much as before – just a bit leaner and meaner and with a generally much less committed workforce. When it comes to job churn, we usually assume that it is the West that is losing their jobs at the fastest rate as they move to the cheaper economies of the East. However this is not the case. When the global job market is taken into account and particularly its growth, we find that although the global economy continues to expand there is little or no growth in actual employment. Jobs are being lost everywhere, even in China. For example, the Chinese manufacturing sector is losing jobs at a faster rate than anywhere else in the world. This comes as a surprise to many I am sure. At the same time global unemployment is rising, especially amongst the younger workers. Job churn is also affected by the ownership changes discussed above. As the revolving door of ownership continues to turn, and the new owners seek efficiencies and the subsequent reductions in headcount which follow the level of job churn and job losses will continue to mount. Second, as the combined impacts of an increasingly educated global workforce and advancements in technology play out, more of what we class as solid white-collar work will come under the scrutiny of commoditization.

I have personally witnessed how the impacts of commoditization have affected the project management profession, which has gone from being something quite important to just another middle or back office job. The same is true of IT. As profits come under pressure from increased competition and as organizations seek to simplify and standardize their activities we will see the numbers of traditional white-collar jobs shrink. It's unavoidable. And if we are to believe some of the latest research into the offshoring of white-collar work, those of us who hold down respectable middle class jobs should be very concerned indeed.

Alan Blinder of Princeton University has attempted to place a figure on the number of American jobs that could potentially be offshored, and in doing so has highlighted a whole raft of jobs that already are or could become commoditized. His main argument is that it is the occupation, not the industry, that can be offshored and that those jobs which require no physical contact are most at risk.[32] Blinder breaks the total United States jobs market into four categories:[33]

*   Category I – Highly offshorable. These are the jobs that do not require the worker to be physically close to a specific work location or in the United States. They encompass 59 occupations and some 8.2 million workers.[34] Typical occupations include computer programmers, actuaries, statisticians, technical writers, insurance claims processing clerks and economists.[35]
*   Category II – Offshorable. These are the jobs that need to be physically close to the work unit but do not have to be located in the United States and in this case include 151 occupations and 20.7 million workers.[36] Typical occupations in this category include tax preparers, electrical engineers, chemists, procurement clerks and medical scientists.[37]
*   Category III – Non-offshorable. These are the jobs which have to be physically close to the work unit and must also be carried out somewhere within the United States; a total of 74 occupations and 8.8 million workers.[38] Typical occupations which fall into this category include broadcast news analysts, producers and directors, aerospace engineers, purchasing managers and training and development managers.[39]
*   Category IV – Highly non-offshorable. These are the jobs where the person needs to be close to a specific work location in the United States and encompasses 533 occupations and 92.6 million workers.[40] Typical occupations which fall under this category include health and safety engineers, advertising sales agents, business operations specialists and nurses.[41]

His analysis suggests that between 22 and 29 per cent of all United States jobs could be offshored and the same is probably true of many of the industrialized nations of the West. So, just because the work is well paid today there is no guarantee that it will continue to be well paid in the future.

Fewer interesting jobs, but demanding all the same

Following on from the above, it is clear that the commoditization of white-collar work will mean that there will be fewer opportunities for employees to genuinely exercise their intellect within the average workplace. Indeed, whilst we are being led to believe (mainly by our governments, it has to be said, and perhaps the HR departments of many corporations) that the demand for knowledge work will increase dramatically; it appears that there is little evidence to support this assertion. As we saw in Chapter 5, the largest growth in jobs is at the lower end of the service economy and most people will continue to work in occupations that require low levels of education and training; some 70 per cent of the workforce in fact.[42] Indeed, it appears that the proportion of workers who hold qualifications above those required for the jobs they do is growing, not shrinking. This has increased from around 30 per cent in 1986 to nearly 40 per cent in 2002[43] and will undoubtedly go much higher as the effects of commoditization play out and an increasing number of highly qualified workers flood the job market. Such a mismatch impacts the quality of the working experience for the well educated and ultimately suppresses income.[44] It also forces more and more of the less qualified to the periphery of the economy with all the issues and problems this brings. Some of this peripheral work will entail serving the richer cohorts of society and this is already happening with the return to the servant class who clean floors, pack bags and cook our meals.[45] As the cash rich but time poor executives find it increasingly difficult to cope with the domestic side of their lives, they are turning in greater numbers to the time rich and cash poor to carry out these basic activities. All this and the other evidence suggests that the knowledge economy has failed to deliver on its promises because most jobs are de-skilled as managers exercise tighter controls over the labour processes.[46]

Some of the reasons for this have been discussed in Part II, with technology playing a significant role in dampening down the demand for knowledge work. With computer applications becoming ever more sophisticated the need for clever people reduces. Technology is fantastic at eliminating the need to think and equally good at forcing us to follow a set of computer driven processes (no matter how bad they might be and no matter how much they tie an organization up in knots). We have already mentioned the problem of the living dead – people turning up for work that is mind numbing, pointless and dull; but there is another problem for white-collar workers: whilst job quality may well reduce over time, the demands placed upon them seem to be increasing. People are working more intensely than ever before and experiencing greater mental strain and higher levels of exhaustion (see Chapter 5).[47] The reasons for the increasing demands placed upon white-collar workers are varied and are not purely related to the introduction of new technology, although this does have a major part to play as we saw in Chapter 5 when we highlighted the phenomenon of job spill. A secondary factor associated with technology, which also impacts the level of demand placed upon employees, is the impact of workflow. For those people who work within a call centre this will be more than familiar to them. The call routing technology used within call centres acts as a modern day production line in which different types of calls are routed to the operatives one after another, so that as one call is finished the next one starts.[48] This creates significant demands on the employee and it is well known that Indian call centre operatives suffer from stress and burnout because of the demanding nature of their work, even though they follow predefined scripts and procedures when dealing with the calls. As technology becomes more sophisticated and as work becomes more codified and commoditized it doesn't stretch the imagination too far to see how the same increase in demand can be placed on other white-collar workers.

Another factor which has increased the demands of work has been the rapid shift to the service economy which has entailed a greater number of white-collar workers' work being dictated by the customer.[49] Workers need to respond to customer needs as they arise and to cater for that demand employers will roster their staff accordingly so that there is little downtime. They will also increase the demands on their staff through multi-skilling so that when demand is lower in one area, they can be used to meet the demands in another. Nurses in the UK have seen this first hand with the widening of their role to encapsulate supervisory, management and even minor surgical activities in addition to their basic nursing tasks.[50]

Employers also have another trick up their sleeves which can result in greater demands being placed upon their workers and that is the ability to monitor the work as it is executed. One of the most significant benefits which commoditization brings to the employer is transparency of work-based activity. Commoditization is capable of making previously invisible work visible and through this facilitates its monitoring by management, who are able to assess an individual's effort and contribution more precisely. And finally as employers gain the upper hand in the ongoing struggle between themselves and their workers, it is likely that the checks and balances provided by organized labour will diminish. When faced with the stark choice between keeping jobs which are more demanding and which may pay less or seeing them pass over to cheaper labour elsewhere, many unions find they have little choice but to accept the harsh realities of the changing world of work. In the UK for example, the proportion of unionized workers fell by 0.6 per cent in 2006 to 28.4 per cent, its biggest drop for eight years.[51] This is of course even worse for the white-collar worker, who very often is without the support of a union – only 16.6 per cent of private sector workers in the UK are unionized.[52] The ability to dictate terms to employees is one reason why Wal-Mart would rather close its stores and give up business than cede control to the unions. For example in August 2004, a union was given authority to negotiate on behalf of the 190 staff at a store in Quebec, Canada. Ten months later the 130,000 square foot store was closed down and everyone lost their jobs.[53] Workers are increasingly finding that unions have little weight when addressing the impacts of globalization and commoditization.

Recent surveys support the combined effects of all of the above and suggest that employees are working harder, faster and with increasing levels of tension than ever before and this is something that is increasingly reflected in most economies.[54] There is nothing to suggest that this will change over the foreseeable future, as the effects of technology, a surplus of intelligent employees and the need to compete against low cost competitors will continue to play out. And with these will come more demands on the average worker who, in order to remain economically viable over the course of their working life will have little choice but to pick up the pace.

The loss of the traditional career path

When I started work some 20 years ago as a fresh faced graduate, I was full of expectation and had pretty much mapped out my career ahead of me. Like most careers, things never turn out quite how you expect them to, as I have not continued along a single career path and probably never will. As my career developed I moved from surveying and mapping (something I had decided to do at 16 and studied in my first degree), into software development (something I drifted into and continued to advance through my Masters degree), then project and programme management (because I got a bit bored with building and maintaining IT systems and was failing to use the skills and knowledge I had acquired in my second degree) and finally into management consultancy. I also recognized the value of continuous learning, which is why I picked up a Masters Degree, and have continued to feed my brain ever since. Despite the many changes and companies I have worked for, the one thing I was pretty certain of was that I would have a career and this would involve opportunities for developing new skills and capabilities and involve promotions and advancement (which it did). I also believed it would remain on an upward course for the majority of my working life. Much of this confidence was based upon the stability of my employers and the belief that the skills and capabilities I brought with me would always (with some adjustments) be in demand.

Things are undoubtedly changing in that traditional career paths are gradually disappearing. The obvious and previously strong link between education and long-term employability and career advancement, is as we saw in Chapter 5, becoming much weaker. The significant investment in time, money and energy no longer has its obvious payback. Although education still remains a principal plank in the ability to compete and outsmart others who work within the knowledge economy, the sheer number of graduates available in the market makes this much harder and there are fewer guarantees of success. With 90 per cent of the world's scientists expected to be living in Asia by 2010[55] even those who believe that following a career path in science or indeed engineering is a cast iron way of protecting themselves may be mistaken. The expectation that many of the emerging nations would take a long time to build the infrastructure necessary to generate a high-skilled workforce has proved to be wide of the mark. For example, although Singapore initially pursued a low-skilled strategy to economic advancement, it has since moved to a high-skilled agenda and within a comparatively short space of time has become the world's second most competitive nation.[56] This is not to say education is unnecessary, but longevity in one's career is no longer firmly linked to it.[57] Instead, education will become a defensive mechanism which will be used to gain a seat at the employment table.[58] It may not, of course, keep you there without a focus on continuous learning and what I call cycles of experience (more on this in Chapter 10). To some extent we are already seeing some of this defensive stance with the increasing numbers of post graduate qualifications. As we saw in Chapter 5, more and more of the workforce is gaining additional qualifications beyond the level which would have been perfectly adequate in the past. Without them it is unlikely that they will be able to secure the better jobs.

Just as the direct correlation between education and employability is weakening the traditional career on which it was predicated is also disappearing. Apart from the small number of people who appear to be blessed by their organizations, career progression for the majority of workers is slowing. The global oversupply of labour which is increasingly educated creates the backdrop for white-collar commoditization and the threat to the traditional career path most of us had expected to pursue. This exacerbates the self-esteem issue discussed at the beginning of the chapter, as it creates a massive disconnect between the expectations of the younger workforce and what turns out to be reality. Fewer can expect the glittering career promised them when they were young. Most will end up in mediocre jobs with few real prospects for advancement. But there is more to this issue than meets the eye as there are some other factors which are affecting the traditional concept of a career path. First, the flattening of organizational hierarchies which followed the downsizing of corporations has meant that there are fewer layers to pass through to get to the top. That's fine if there are plenty of opportunities at the top of the organization, but that is rarely the case. Without the perceived progression that comes with deep corporate structures staff will be left at the same position for long periods of time which may not be good for them or the business without some creativity on the company's part to keep them engaged (more on this in Chapters 8 and 9). Second, technology as we saw above allows the flow of work to be more effectively controlled and as it continues to become more sophisticated and capable of subsuming business processes it is likely that there will be less need for supervisors. Third, as the impacts of market consolidation through mergers and acquisitions continue to play out, there will be fewer positions to fill. When two similar companies come together there is no need for two CEOs, two marketing departments and so on, so duplicate positions and functions disappear along with the opportunities for career progression. Fourth, the hollowing out of the corporation, as discussed in the previous chapter, is also reducing the career path for many workers. Eliminating the bulk of your finance, IT, HR, legal and any other function for that matter, means once again that there are fewer opportunities for advancement. With a single outsource organization running the finance or HR activities for many other companies, those finance and HR professionals who would have previously worked in-house, no longer have a job. And finally, the impact of commoditization on job classes will itself also limit the opportunities for a typical career as work goes overseas and as technology and general changes in the nature of work remove the need for certain jobs. In summary then, the notion of a mapped out career path continues to be replaced with a random walk with advancement no longer predicated on character and conduct.[59]

Economic instability and income stagnation – the China price moves to white-collar labour

One of the central drivers of commoditization is price competition. As we saw in Chapter 1, and throughout Part I, as soon as price becomes the primary factor for negotiation then you have been commoditized. The ability to differentiate yourself from the millions of other graduates and white-collar workers is hard and when we consider that the billion plus populations of India and China are beginning to compete for the high-skilled work that has been the preserve of America and Europe, it is easy to see how white-collar and skilled work will be subject to long-term price competition. According to some commentators this is leading us towards a high-skill, low-wage economy.[60] Others believe that the doubling of the global labour pool from 1.46 billion to 2.93 billion when China, the ex-Soviet countries and India are included will create the biggest challenge since the Depression of the 1930s.[61] The economic impacts of commoditization on the middle classes are already showing up in the stagnation of incomes (something I touched on in Chapter 5 and will return to in Chapter 11) and the increasing fragility of household balance sheets. Even when we strip out peoples' desire to live beyond their means and to emulate their favourite celebrities, the number of bankruptcies is increasing dramatically as workers find themselves on a path of downward mobility and struggle to make ends meet on a lower income. Although economies continue to grow and create jobs, many of these as we have seen do not require highly skilled individuals to execute them. There is also no evidence to support the assertion that a low inflation environment leads to jobs and income growth, in fact the opposite appears to be true.[62] Add to this an increase in the share of workers who find themselves without work, which has increased to levels not seen since the recession of the early 1980s and you can see that there are problems ahead as the unemployed increase the downward pressure on incomes.[63]

Another important aspect of earnings is that incomes now rise and fall more sharply than ever before and such volatility is more of an issue than income inequality.[64] Evidence for this comes from the Panel Study of Income Dynamics (PSID) which is an American survey that has been tracking thousands of families each year from the late 1960s.[65] What this survey shows is by how much a family's income can rise and fall and how the range between the lowest and highest has risen over the recent past. For example, the difference between the highest and lowest in the 1970s was 43 per cent (in other words the lowest income for a given year was 43 per cent of the highest) whilst in the period 1993–2003 this had dropped to 25 per cent, itself a significant reduction from the near 36 per cent difference that was typical of the previous decade. The trend is clearly downwards. The fact that people are doing well one year and badly the next is missed in the annual snapshots of income and therefore hides the true levels of volatility that exist in many households.[66] This instability in income is at an all time high and is now five times greater than it was in the 1970s. Like every other trend associated with commoditization, it is not only the blue-collar workers who are having to cope with the issue, as many white-collar workers are now facing the rollercoaster ride of income volatility from which they thought themselves immune,[67] and which they believed they had been protected against by a solid education. Some of the increased volatility and its associated insecurity will undoubtedly come from the changes in ownership which not only result in a loss of income through redundancy, but also a reduction in upward mobility. Other sources will include outsourcing and offshoring which always result in a lowering of income (after all that's what they are really about aren't they?).

The China Price which is so expertly used by Wal-Mart to suppress wages and ensure their suppliers can match their price expectations exerts a powerful downward pressure on incomes. In the recent past this has been restricted to the manufacturing sector, but as the full force of the global workforce is felt, the China Price will start to invade the world of the middle class white-collar worker. As a result real income volatility may increase and real income growth may become a thing of the past for many. When there is someone out there who is both willing and able to do your job, but for a fraction of the price, what do you do? You do what Wal-Mart's suppliers do, you conform and accept a lower income or you fold and take your chances elsewhere. It's often that binary. The problem is of course that we would all rather have a stable income than no income at all and the unfortunate thing with commoditization is that it makes everything far more unstable for us all. This is of course extreme but the oversupply of graduates means that, as we saw above, all white-collar jobs are potentially at risk from commoditization and the longer-term impacts of this may be significant, as we will see in Chapter 11.

When I sit down with my son Tom and quiz him on what he wants to do when he is grown up he often says he would like to become a biochemical engineer. Sometimes he is less sure, but that should be expected of someone who has yet to reach the point at which the decision has to be made. He may be uncertain, which is expected, but I am increasingly unclear of what his or his sister's future holds both in terms of career and economic stability. The future is increasingly cloudy and holding down a job gets much harder as time goes by. It's hard enough right now, but what will working life be like in 15 years time? This is a very difficult question to answer and will depend upon a range of factors we have introduced and discussed in this book and how individual economies and organizations respond. As we saw in the previous chapter, commoditization creates instability in the system and just as companies need to respond, so do individuals. Of course, there are still many opportunities for those with the right skills, capabilities, expertise and experience to progress and follow a successful and varied career. For example, those who are in the middle of their careers may well find themselves partially insulated from the worst effects of commoditization by the immediate skill shortages that will result from the demographic changes we are beginning to experience and as the global economy rebalances to one which is less dependent upon America and the West in general. However, it is getting harder and will continue to do so over the next decade as many of the issues I raised in Chapter 5 begin to bite.

Although all of this may feel a bit depressing, it is becoming the reality to which we must all face up. But that's enough on the impacts. It is now important to turn to Part III where we explore what organizations can do to respond to the challenge of commoditization and what you can do as an individual to protect yourself from the impacts of the commoditization of white-collar work. The former will require a range of responses, some of which will be more focused on staff than costs, and the latter will require a greater emphasis and commitment on your part to build a portfolio of transferable and saleable skills. What we will find in Part III is that there are still plenty of opportunities to remain profitable and grow a business and that for many workers there are lots of opportunities to have a fulfilling working life – it just means that it has to be more actively managed.

References

1 Elliot, L. and Atkinson, D. (1998) *The Age of Insecurity*, London: Verso, p. 128.
2 Twenge, J. (2006) *Generation Me*, New York: Free Press, p. 68.
3 Brown, P., et al. (2006) Towards a high-skilled, low-waged economy? A review of global trends in education, employment and the labour market, in Porter, S. and Campbell, M. (eds.) *Skills and Economic Performance*, London: Caspian Publishing, p. 55.
4 Bosshart, D. (2007) *Cheap? The Real Cost of Living in a Low Price, Low Wage World*, p. 69.
5 Ibid., p. 59.
6 *The Business* (2007) The best France can hope for is the ambiguous Mr Sarkozy, pp. 8–9.
7 Hacker, J. (2006) *The Great Risk Shift*, Oxford: Oxford University Press, p. 37.
8 Ibid., p. 39.
9 Ibid., pp. 52–53.
10 Ibid., p. 47.
11 Ibid., p. 195.
12 Ibid., p. 178.
13 Twenge, J. (2006) *Generation Me*, New York: Free Press, pp. 44–45.
14 Ibid., p. 69.
15 Ibid., p. 49.
16 Ibid., p. 66.
17 Ibid., p. 79.
18 Ibid., p. 66.
19 Braid, M. (2007) Why today's graduates don't make the grade, *The Sunday Times*, Appointments, 25 February, pp. 4–15.
20 Twenge, J. (2006) *Generation Me*, New York: Free Press, pp. 104–136.
21 Armistead, L. and Rushe, D. (2006) Boom time as M&A deals reach an all-time record, *The Sunday Times*, Business, 19 November, p. 3–1.
22 Rushe, D. (2006) All aboard the M&A express, *The Sunday Times*, 31 December, pp. 3–5.
23 Craven, N. (2007) KKR, Pessina win Boots chain with £11.1 B bid, *National Post*, 25 April, p. FP16.
24 Calvert, J. and Ungoed-Thomas, J. (2007) AA 'cutting services' to boost profits, *The Sunday Times*, 24 June, pp. 1–10.
25 Sender, H. and Lueck, S. (2007) Tax plan adds to the pressure on buyout firms, *The Wall Street Journal*, 16–17 June, p. A1.
26 Arnold, M. (2007) Unions vow to fight the 'cancer' of hedge funds, *Financial Times*, 17–18 March, p. 6.
27 Sanderse, M. (2007) Private Equity and Transport: Alchemist or turbo charged investors, *Morgan Stanley*, p. 13.
28 Agtmael, A. (2007) *The emerging markets century*, New York: Free Press, p. 15.
29 Ibid., p. 25.
30 West, K. (2007) The 'winner takes all society', *Daily Mail*, 11 July, p. 5.
31 Thal, P., et al. (2007) Scepticism greets Barclay's figures, *Financial Times*, 24 April, p. 22.
32 Blinder, Al. (2007) How many jobs might be offshorable? Princeton University, CEPS Working Paper No. 142, March 2007, p. 5.
33 Ibid., p. 18.
34 Ibid., p. 19.
35 Ibid., pp. 38–39.
36 Ibid., p. 19.
37 Ibid., pp. 39–42.

38 Ibid., p. 19.
39 Ibid., pp. 41–43.
40 Ibid., p. 19.
41 Ibid., p. 43.
42 Agtmael, A. (2007) *The Emerging Markets Century*, New York: Free Press, p. 65.
43 Green, F. (2006) *Demanding Work: The Paradox of Job Quality in the Affluent Economy*, New Jersey: Princeton University Press, pp. 40–41.
44 Ibid., p. 41.
45 Ibid., p. 6.
46 Ibid., p. 35.
47 Ibid., p. 1
48 Ibid, p. 70
49 Ibid., p. 6.
50 Ibid., p. 72.
51 Smith, D. (2007) Workers count cost of a global labour flood, *The Sunday Times*, 29 April, p. 3–4.
52 Ibid.
53 Fishman, C. (2006) *The Wal-Mart Effect*, New York: The Penguin Press, p. 8.
54 Green, F. (2006) *Demanding Work: The Paradox of Job Quality in the Affluent Economy*, New Jersey: Princeton University Press, pp. 44–65.
55 Brown, P., et al. (2006) Towards a high-skilled, low-waged economy? A review of global trends in education, employment and the labour market, in Porter, S. and Campbell, M. (eds.) *Skills and Economic Performance*, London: Caspian Publishing, p. 62.
56 Ibid.
57 Ibid., p. 63.
58 Ibid., p. 84.
59 Elliot, L. and Atkinson, D. (1998) *The age of insecurity*, London: Verso, p. 131.
60 Brown, P., et al. (2006) Towards a high-skilled, low-waged economy? A review of global trends in education, employment and the labour market, in Porter, S. and Campbell, M. (eds.) *Skills and Economic Performance*, London: Caspian Publishing, p. 73.
61 Freeman, R. (2007) The great doubling: The challenge of the new global labour market, in Edwards, J., et al., (2007) [eds.], *Ending Poverty in America*, New York: The New Press, p. 55.
62 Elliot, L. and Atkinson, D. (1998) *The Age of Insecurity*, London: Verso, pp. 238–239.
63 Hacker, J. (2007) The risky outlook for middle-class America, in Edwards, J., et al., (2007) [eds.], *Ending Poverty in America*, New York: The New Press, p. 67.
64 Hacker, J. (2006) *The Great Risk Shift*, Oxford: Oxford University Press, p. 2.
65 Hacker, J. (2007) The risky outlook for middle-class America, in Edwards, J., et al., (2007) [eds.], *Ending Poverty in America*, New York: The New Press, p. 69.
66 Ibid.
67 Ibid., p. 71.

PART III *Response*

> *However, this is a basic fact of life in all industries: left to the competitive strains of a free market, all products will be reduced to being a commodity over time.*[1]

> *We will fight our battles not on the low road to commoditization, but on the high road of innovation.*[2]

The impacts of commoditization are far reaching and are exposing the inefficient underbelly of organizations as they grapple with the need to remain competitive in a world of increasing and highly efficient competition. At the same time the power of commoditization is shifting the nature and composition of the employment market, propelling those with the adaptability of skills and capabilities to the top of the food chain whilst pushing everyone else further down the income scale, making downward mobility a reality for millions of middle class, white-collar workers.

Responding to the challenge of commoditization depends on where you stand and what your perspective is. It is unlikely that the low cost airlines would complain about the commoditization of the airline industry and it would be doubtful that the emerging Indian, African and Chinese multinationals would claim the competitive landscape is unfair given they have managed to not only survive but also to thrive in a very uneven global market often heavily weighted against them. However, for those industries and workers who are feeling the impacts of commoditization the need to adapt is vital. Although it would be very easy to suggest that everything will become commoditized and that the only way to address the challenges it presents is to pursue a commoditized path, this would be too simplistic a response. A better way is to view commoditization as a continuum (see Figure PIII.1) along which you operate and which ranges from near zero commoditization at one end to fully commoditized at the other. Where you are along the continuum defines the operating environment in which you compete (at the commercial level if you are viewing this from an organizational perspective and at the individual level if you are considering this from an employability and career standpoint). Understanding where you lie along this continuum allows you to develop a response that best suits your current context and which will help you understand where you might want to be or what threats might be on the horizon which you need to address.

| Full commoditization | Partial commoditization | Limited or no commoditization |

Figure PIII.1 The commoditization continuum

Like so many things within organizational and working life you may find not extremes but a mix; some parts of the business may be more commoditized than others and some of your skills may be more repeatable or transferable than others. Of course you may find that your entire business lies at one of the two extremes of the continuum and the same might apply to your skill set. Although understanding where you are along the continuum is important, as is recognizing where you sit in relation to the process of commoditization discussed in Part I, it is the response that really matters. It is this that defines whether you will be choosing to invest in new products and services or perhaps divesting parts of your business. And it is this that will determine which skills you will be choosing to grow and which you may decide to drop. The strategic response to commoditization is as much about now as it is about the future. The now should focus on the immediate nature of your response, whilst the future should consider in what markets you want to compete and how. As I mentioned in the introduction, when it comes to commoditization taking no action is not going to be an effective response.

Part III consists of three chapters:

- Chapter 8 focuses on the corporate setting and describes the range of responses that can be chosen. It identifies the questions the CEO and the board must consider in order to remain competitive, irrespective of whether or not they believe they are operating within a commoditized market, and outlines the areas where they will need to focus their response to address the challenges which commoditization presents.
- Chapter 9 uses a series of short case studies to illustrate how organizations are responding. These case studies are designed to highlight what companies focus on and whether they decide to attack or avoid commoditization.
- Chapter 10 reviews the options open to the individual. In this instance it will address some of the actions open to those who find their skills have become or are becoming commoditized, and will discuss how to avoid the trap of becoming part of a commoditized workforce (if they want to of course, as some will be happy to be treated as a commodity).

At the end of Part III you will have an understanding of what strategic choices can be adopted to address the impacts of an increasingly commoditized corporate and working environment. Armed with this you can decide how to respond; to fight it and work with commoditization, or to flee it and pursue a path predicated on innovation.

References

1 Smith, G. (2004) Winning at the commodity game, www.marketingprofs.com/4/smith10.asp.
2 Stringer, H. (2006) quote in Expanding the innovation horizon, The global CEO survey 2006, IBM, p. 10.

8 *Business Responses*

An increasing number of commodity businesses – blood collection products, replacement motors, and steel strapping, among others – are becoming consistently profitable by knowing how and when to differentiate their products through innovation, service, and customer partnerships; and how and when to offer a 'no-frills' product and seek cost leadership.[1]

Commoditization will not displace that portion of your business that requires substantial judgment, the exercise of discretion and the skill to differentiate your enterprise from your competitors.[2]

We are witnessing an era for business around the world in which engaging employees makes the difference between success and failure.[3]

Human capital will go where it is wanted, and it will stay where it is well treated. It cannot be driven; it can only be attracted.[4]

Innovation is like a virus and we are expert at stamping it out.[5]

The enemy? *Commoditization*

The victim? *Every company who fails to lead in innovation*

The penalty? *First growth. Then profitability. Ultimately the right to exist.*[6]

Mr. Needham of ATTIK says 'It's a 24/7 headache' to constantly come up with the new thing that most people haven't heard about yet. 'Today it's cool, but tomorrow it's not,' he says.' So we have to move that quickly to retain credibility. As soon as I start hearing about something too much, I'm over it.[7]

The pressure of commoditization will continue to exert itself on organizations everywhere: the increasing impact of demographic change; the requirement to maintain a keen eye on costs in order to compete effectively within the global market; the continued advance of technology; the ability to standardize processes and eliminate major inefficiencies; the pressure to outsource and offshore business activities in order to exploit the cost advantages of cheaper labour, and the opportunity for your competition to attack your markets and replicate your products and services more freely. Responding to the pressures will depend on many things, not least where you sit in relation to the commoditization continuum introduced at the start of this part of the book.

Critical conversations

Getting to a position where you can respond to the threats and opportunities that commoditization presents requires what I term critical conversations. They are critical because they require a hard look at the strategic, competitive and operational contexts of the business and will undoubtedly necessitate difficult decisions. These are important discussions which cannot be deferred because the pressures of commoditization will continue to mount and the longer it takes to respond the greater and perhaps more radical and wide reaching the response will have to be.

The starting point for any board level discussion has to be an understanding of the current state as well as the future direction of the organization. Given the nature of commoditization, this has to encompass every part of the business, from the front office functions such as sales and marketing through to the supporting activities such as order processing and HR. A broad assessment is important here because of the potential for commoditization to creep up on you, but perhaps more critically because it forces you to take the long view, in the same way that Shell did with its much heralded scenario planning technique which they first applied in the 1970s.

One of the issues with those organizations that may be particularly at risk from commoditization is that they fail to take the long view. Unfortunately more and more organizations are falling into the short-termist trap as the market economy, stock markets, shareholders and competition compel boards of directors to focus on the next quarter to the detriment of the long term. This is often due to a variety of factors including a singular focus on the bottom line (especially the case within the Private Equity industry), a commanding position in the industry or sector which leads to arrogance and short-sighted behaviours, or just a lack of forward thinking executives in senior positions. Having spent the majority of their careers focused on the short-term goals of their bosses and the markets, many just don't know how to operate any other way.

Tackling commoditization in a fragmented or short-termist way will not allow you to understand its effects and neither will it provide the solid platform required to build an effective response. So when it comes to considering the potential impacts of commoditization you need to ask yourself the following two questions:

1. Can all or part of our business become commoditized? It is easy to believe that you are immune to the effects of commoditization and that you don't need to respond to something that may not even be on your horizon. But there are some useful lessons we can take away from Shell's experience with scenario planning, especially in the way it allowed them to prepare the business for a number of alternative futures. When responding to this question the best approach is to start from the position that everything you do is capable of becoming commoditized if not now, then certainly at some point in the future. Of course you may find that not everything can be commoditized, but it is far better to come to this conclusion after completing a thorough analysis of your business than to make assumptions based upon a limited perspective or worse still, gut feel.

2. How should we respond to the threat of commoditization? In particular should we embrace it or avoid it? This is a crucial question to answer once you have understood the threats and opportunities commoditization poses to the organization. As with any strategic decision it is likely to have significant operational implications. In some cases you may find that you have little alternative but to become more commoditized yourself,

whilst in others you may be able to adopt a more flexible approach. When considering the response, you will need to think about such things as:

- How can we insulate ourselves from the threat of commoditization?
- Given the choice what parts of our business should we allow to become commoditized?
- Where and in which markets should we innovate as a way of avoiding the commoditization trap?
- Where should we target our investments – with our customers, on our back office processes, in research and development, on acquisitions or all of the above?

In order to answer these with a sufficiently open mind you need to do two things. The first is to accept that commoditization is a genuine threat as well as a potential opportunity and the second is to be vigilant because commoditization is not a static threat, but one which will evolve and become more significant over time. Armed with this information you can then consider how best to respond. Generating a suitable response requires a broad and connected strategy which will require the input from a broad range of stakeholders, including HR, Research and Development, Sales, Marketing and operational heads.

What to do when faced with low cost competition

Before we look at the types of actions companies can take to address the challenges of commoditization in some detail, it is useful to review the broad strategies organizations can follow when faced by a low cost competitor. The emergence of low cost competition is one of the most obvious signs that a business and the products and services it sells are capable of becoming, or indeed already are, commoditized. The argument I would make here is that it is far better to be in a position to predict the emergence of such competition ahead of time rather than to have to react to it. Reacting leaves little room for error and can lead to major problems if the response is flawed or ill judged.

Taking a deliberate strategy of competing on cost is always simpler when starting a new business or moving into a known commoditized market, but what options should be considered in those organizations that are facing the prospect of competing with low cost rivals? One thing is clear and that is that ignoring them is a recipe for disaster as it usually forces the incumbent to vacate entire market segments principally because the low cost rival is able to completely change consumer behaviour.[8] There are three options open to organizations when faced with price cutting competitors. First, they can differentiate their products so that consumers are willing to pay a premium over and above those offered by their cost focused rivals. This can be achieved through a number of ways including continuous innovation such as Gillette do with their shaving products or designing cool products and offerings as Apple continue to do with their IMac and IPod product ranges.[9] Second, they can set up a low cost subsidiary to compete head-to-head with their low cost competition. In this instance it is essential to use the same tricks used by the low cost rival, focus on making money, avoid attacking the principal business' markets and achieve synergies between the mainstream business and the low cost subsidiary. British Airways failed to leverage its low cost airline Go because it kept it separate and lost the natural synergies that would have resulted had it been more integrated with its parent; it was eventually sold to easyJet. When Dow Corning created Xiameter it decided on fully integrating this into its core business so that it could, for example, use idle production time to manufacture their products; and it restricted the product range to the 350 which faced the most intensity from Dow's competitors. In this way it was able to protect the margins of its principal business. This strategy has allowed the parent company to turn a $28 million loss in 2001 to a $500 million profit in 2005.[10] The third option involves changing the business model to address the threat. There are two choices here. The first is to switch from products to solutions and this is what many corporations decide to do when faced with the threat of low cost competition. The problem with this is that the switch from a product to a service focused business is not that simple and in fact can be highly damaging as Xerox found when it attempted to promote itself as a document solutions business. And for those organizations which have managed to transform, the process has been difficult as we saw when IBM had to restructure and reengineer its business in response to the rise of Microsoft and the shift away from mainframe computers.[11] Dell is finding that it too is having to respond to a change in market sentiment as consumers shift to using laptops and retail prices for technology products continue to slump. With Michael Dell back at the helm after ousting chief executive Kevin Rawlins, shareholders hope that he will return the company to its glory days.[12] Successful transformation necessitates a near 180 degree change in direction, and recognition that the approach to building and selling solutions is very different to building and selling products. Most critically, it is essential to understand the fundamental difference between product and service focused businesses. A product focused business tends to start with the products and then seeks ways to match these to customers' needs and when customers want something new an additional feature is added to the product to satisfy that need. The reverse is true of a solutions based approach which begins with the desired outcome before developing the solution to meet that need. Being successful at selling solutions also requires greater integration and transparency with others in the supply chain, and changing the customer base, which often means dropping existing customers and seeking out new ones, perhaps outside the traditional market.[13] Key to success is the near complete transformation of the business from the front office through to the back, which has to encompass the skills and capabilities of the workforce as well as the many other strands of the organization such as channel strategies, suppliers and management behaviour, all of which can be incredibly uncomfortable. The second approach to changing the business model is to beat the low cost competitors at their own game by becoming one yourself, but this is even more difficult to achieve than moving to a solutions or pure services based organization and few companies have been successful. Whatever strategy is adopted, when faced with competition from a low cost rival it is essential to consider many of the factors discussed in this chapter, and especially those associated with the cost base and the elimination of unnecessary and overly complex processes.

Exploring the elements of the strategic response is where we will now turn. To achieve this, the remainder of this chapter outlines the areas which organizations will typically need to focus on and integrate into their response. Chapter 9 highlights a range of companies that are already working at each of the three key points along the continuum, namely:

- Those companies which operate within a near or completely commoditized environment – inside the commoditized zone.
- Those who operate within an environment which has little or no commoditization – outside the commoditized zone.
- Those who find themselves with a more complex setting in which part of the business falls within the commoditized zone and part outside.

At this stage it is helpful to refer back to the commoditization model introduced in Part I and the three emerging types of business briefly mentioned in Chapter 5. The former is helpful because it can be used to position your products and services along the model and will allow you to determine both how far down the commoditized path you might already be and what your options could be when it comes to addressing the opportunities and threats associated with commoditization. The latter helps to position you within one of the three broad categories of organization mentioned above and is useful because it identifies some of the attributes of those organizations that are already successfully addressing the challenges that commoditization brings. This gives you a sense of the art of the possible. If we recall, the emerging business types were:

- Low-cost operators. These organizations are the closest to the fully commoditized end of the spectrum introduced at the beginning of Part III. They are used to working within a cost focused environment and have become expert at squeezing out efficiencies and containing their costs throughout their supply chain and back office functions.
- Global competitor corporations. These companies work across the full spectrum of the continuum and are arguably the closest to the mixed operating environment midway across it. The global footprint of such organizations usually means that they will need to compete on costs in some parts of their business whilst in others they may retain a degree of freedom from the tyranny of commoditization. Working in a part commoditized, part non-commoditized business requires a complex approach because unlike those within a fully commoditized business, cost containment is not the only driver; innovation takes on a more significant role.
- High-involvement companies. These organizations place a greater significance on their people and take their contribution and engagement very seriously. Although such businesses can operate across the full commoditization continuum, we can argue that their singular focus on their human capital allows them to concentrate more effectively on areas which may be difficult to commoditize. We will see just how important this is a bit later, because if you want to survive outside of the commoditized zone you cannot afford to treat your staff like a commodity.

Areas to consider when developing your response

With the impacts of commoditization being so wide ranging, organizations have a variety of means through which they can respond, including:

- process simplification and optimization
- cost containment and management
- outsourcing and offshoring
- supply chain management
- talent management and labour management
- innovation
- branding.

When looking down this list it becomes clear that there are two broad thrusts to the response. The first is to have a cost and efficiency focus and the second is to have a value creation focus. The two should go hand in hand as concentrating purely on cost and efficiency can lead to problems downstream, as we saw with the business process reengineering movement of the 1990s. Although many of the areas listed above are potentially relevant to every organization, it is their relative importance that is pertinent here, as some will be more essential and indeed more relevant than others. It is also necessary to recognize that the specific response may also vary according to where the organization sits along the continuum. So although there may be a need to focus on innovation the nature of this will vary depending on whether the business is operating in a fully commoditized environment or exists at the other end of the spectrum where little of the business is currently commoditized. In addition there are some strategic choices which have to be made in order to prioritize the usually limited capital available for projects and programmes. Ideally each of the areas identified above needs to be fully considered and integrated into any change that is to take place, but organizational reality normally means some degree of compromise is necessary and indeed essential. As we will see in the next chapter when we review some of the organizations that are operating within each of the three positions along the continuum, few have addressed each and every one of the areas about to be discussed. It is also important to recognize that building an effective response will require connectivity between many of the areas above. For example, pursuing process simplification is fine of itself, but it is best achieved under a wider cost containment and outsourcing strategy. Finally and for the purposes of clarity, at the end of the discussion for each area I will indicate the importance and focus of each for the three key points along the continuum (inside the commoditized zone, outside the commoditized zone and those who work with a mix of both). The importance will be rated as being:

- critical
- advisable
- optional.

PROCESS SIMPLIFICATION AND OPTIMIZATION

Business process reengineering may have led to mass layoffs after it was hijacked by overzealous consultants and business leaders, but it has left us with some powerful tools and techniques with which to analyze and improve process. Apart from the obvious failings of the business process reengineering movement, another was the desire to follow the big bang approach to implementation. Attempting to literally obliterate the business model and redesign everything simultaneously resulted in just as many failures as we see in major IT programmes. So although a focus on process is a critical element to surviving in a commoditized market, you are far better taking a series of steps to get there. Naturally if you have suddenly found yourself confronted by low cost competitors you may not have the luxury of time, but for the majority it is better to take a little longer and get it right than go to guns too early and end up in a worse position

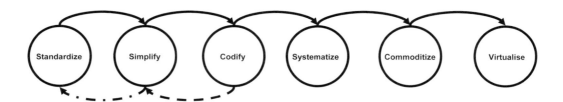

Figure 8.1 Achieving process commoditization

than before. How far along the process simplification and commoditization route you choose to go will reflect your strategic positioning in relation to commoditization.

There are six steps towards total process commoditization (Figure 8.1) and each brings greater benefits because the more a process is standardized and commoditized the greater the savings in time and headcount will be. The process through which this is achieved is not completely linear, as there are opportunities to revisit the earlier steps as clarity around the process increases.

1. Standardize – the majority of businesses still operate non-standardized processes despite there being plenty of opportunity to leverage the work done by others, such as MIT and SCOR (see Chapter 4). In a commoditized business the need for standardized processes is particularly important because significant savings can be made through the removal of redundant steps associated with localized processes and unnecessary human intervention. Such tardiness, which generates unnecessary complexity and with it costs, is something a commoditized business cannot afford to have. Standard business processes also allow the free movement of staff and prevent them from becoming locked into processes which only they can perform. They also, of course, facilitate commoditization.

2. Simplify. Once you have a standardized set of processes you should be aiming to simplify them as much as possible. Although many companies attempt to standardize and simplify simultaneously, it is better to standardize first because it is generally easier to simplify a standard process than a collection of non-standard processes. The simplification approach typically involves getting into the detail of the processes and the business activities which they support. Processes are often complex because of the way the underlying business model operates, so it might be necessary to tweak the business model in order to deliver the required simplification targets. The objective of the simplification exercise is to make the processes run more efficiently and to engineer work out of the system; essential if you want to be in a better position to combat the impacts and risks associated with commoditization. Once you have simplified your processes some additional benefits can be gained from a further round of standardization by rolling out the newly simplified processes.

3. Codify. As we have seen throughout Part I, the ability to codify and make visible the intricacies of industrial and human processes is key to allowing them to become fully commoditized. Making processes transparent and easily understood by everyone allows you to both reduce the reliance on the experts who may have been involved with the execution of the process in the past and also to widen the pool of resources who can execute the work going forward. As the process of codification plays out, the opportunities to reduce the costs associated with its execution increases, so there is a significant prize to be had here. The other important aspect of codification is that it then allows further simplification because more about the process is known and the more that is known, the easier it is to simplify.

4. Systematize. As this step suggests, to achieve further process efficiencies it is necessary to use technology. Technology has been eliminating manual processes ever since it took hold during the Industrial Revolution and will continue to remove human contact from work processes as these become more simplified and codified. Once a process is sufficiently transparent and standardized the opportunity to then automate it increases significantly. So in the same way that most of the project management processes that used to be executed by expert project managers have been subsumed into professional services automation software the same

is true of other processes which rely on experts such as accountancy and law. One of the problems with many IT projects is that they attempt to implement existing processes, which makes the task almost impossible. Far better to get the processes to a level of simplification and standardization so that standard, off the shelf software can be used. This was after all, the principle behind the business process reengineering movement before it was hijacked.

5. Commoditize. Once you have systematized your processes you are then in a position to commoditize them. As we saw in Chapter 4, treating your processes as a commodity provides you with more choices and flexibility over who should manage and execute them and allows you to compare the costs of their execution more readily. In other words it allows the process to become independent of its execution. This gets over one of the biggest hurdles within organizations; believing that processes are unique to the company rather than common to everyone. This has more to do with emotional commitment than with the process itself, but once you overcome this hurdle you can then take the decision to move the bulk of your processes into a shared services environment, as an increasing number of corporations are doing with their finance, IT and Human Resources activities.

6. Virtualize. This should be the ultimate aim of any focus on process and where the greatest benefits lie. At this level you should have the confidence that no matter who executes the process or where it is executed, it will produce consistently reliable results. This opens up the opportunity to fully outsource the execution of the processes either to a local supplier (nearshore) or (offshore) to another country, such as India. This allows you to fully exploit the benefits of labour arbitrage, and in the same way that Wal-Mart continues to shift its production deeper and deeper into China in order to squeeze additional savings from its supply chain, you can shift the execution of the process to a location with a cheaper labour force. Also, when costs rise, as they invariably do, you can always shift the management of processes to where the costs are lowest. Once a process is a commodity, this is a comparatively simple exercise.

Table 8.1 Process focus across the continuum

Full commoditization	Partial commoditization	Limited or no commoditization
Critical All back office processes should be simplified, standardized and eventually virtualised to keep costs to a minimum. Front office processes should be simplified as much as possible so that any inefficiency is eliminated. Being critical to the business these processes should be maintained in house, or insourced so that control is maintained locally.	**Advisable** As some parts of the business will be more commoditized than others it is likely that process simplification and standardization will be necessary to remain competitive. Although less critical to the less commoditized parts of the business, the opportunity to leverage the simplified and standardized processes across back office activity, for example, should be exploited.	**Optional** Although process simplification is not a big issue for such organizations some processes on which the business survives, such as innovation, should be simplified and standardized to ensure these critical activities can proceed as rapidly and efficiently as possible. The same applies to the customer management processes.

COST CONTAINMENT AND COST MANAGEMENT

The management of costs is an issue for every organization. Whether a global major or a small localized manufacturer, every business has to worry about the costs it incurs to deliver its products and services into its chosen markets. Despite this common need to control costs, organizations struggle to establish a permanent cost management ethos amongst their workforce. We only need to witness the periodic cost cutting that takes place to understand that few are really expert at maintaining an effective balance between cost control and the more laissez faire attitude to cost management. Although some of this may be due to sudden changes in fortune or the impacts of a changing economic cycle, most of it is down to a difficulty companies face in trying to keep a lid on costs, especially those associated with labour.

This attitude was reflected in a global survey on cost management I was involved with.[14] What was clear from this survey was that few businesses were equipped to truly control costs; they would reduce them only to find them creeping back again once the economic cycle picked up. Few it seemed were willing to address the cost challenge strategically, instead preferring to adopt a knee-jerk approach to their cost base. That was then and this is now, and I am sure there are still plenty of corporations who still follow the slash and burn approach to managing their costs, but with the continued advance of commoditization many are finally realizing the importance of addressing their cost base strategically in the same way that Wal-Mart and the low cost airlines have done. For example, Pfizer recently announced that it would cut 10 000 jobs and close at least five of its facilities in order to reduce its annual costs by $2 billion. This latest round comes on top of a previous announcement that indicated the company would cut $4 billion in costs by 2008, so that's $6 billion in total. So why the huge cuts? Pfizer is suffering from three major issues. The first is that many of the patents for its blockbuster drugs are coming to an end which typically means that revenues fall off a cliff as patent protection disappears and the generic drug providers enter the market. For example when their antidepressant Zoloft lost patent protection in 2006 its sales sank by 79 per cent. One of the biggest advantages the generic drug providers have over companies such as Pfizer is the emphasis they have on efficient manufacturing.[15] The second is the generic drug makers themselves, whose competition is fierce and cost focused; they are more than happy to work under such conditions because they always have. And finally, the insurers and the large purchasers of medicines are no longer willing to pay such high prices and are demanding significant reductions. In the absence of new drugs coming through the research and development process, the effects have been devastating, leading to deep cuts across the business.[16]

Although all organizations across the commoditization spectrum have to be competent at managing their costs, it is those within the commoditized zone that have to place a much greater significance on cost management because failure to address the underlying cost base can mean the difference between a market leading position and operating within the knife-edge conditions of near bankruptcy. Indeed this is beginning to be the case within the IT outsource service providers who are increasingly having to address the risks associated with razor thin margins. Those that are able to address their internal costs will out-perform those that can't, as the one thing you come to realize is that there is always someone else out there who is willing to compete on price. However, as we saw earlier, responding to the challenge of low cost competition can be both difficult and very painful. The effective management of the cost base is therefore one way in which the organization can control its competitive position and this is becoming more critical as more companies enter the same markets, price and quality competition increases, product lifecycles become shorter and mass customization necessitates a more tailored approach to customer needs.[17] Although it is seductive to cut back office costs across the board, some recent research suggests that it might be better to reconfigure them instead. The research reviewed a number of companies across a range of industries that typically followed one of three strategies: to reduce costs, to redesign processes or to fundamentally restructure. Reducing costs is usually straightforward and usually yields plenty of quick-win savings. Redesigning processes, as we saw earlier, may take longer, but can result in higher savings. But it is restructuring that presents the biggest opportunities for cost savings, albeit harder to achieve, especially as it may involve outsourcing (see later section). Taken as a range, reduction leads to 25 per cent of the total that could be saved, redesigning yields up to an additional 35 per cent and restructuring brings in another 40 per cent.[18]

Addressing the cost issue has to start with an understanding of the types of costs which the business is incurring, be they production, trading or operating costs; direct or indirect; capital; employee, and so on. It is also essential to get a clear picture of costs by each functional area so that it is possible to model how the costs of the function translate into outcomes and ultimately the bottom line. The use of benchmarking and activity based costing can be very helpful in this respect. Benchmarking provides you with the necessary yardstick against which your costs can be compared with other companies and helps to identify areas for cost reduction. Benchmarking should always be used with a degree of care, however, as it is easy to think that your costs have to match those who are considered best in class. Without an understanding of the context of these other companies, benchmarking can only give you a sense of where you lie on a comparative basis. But used with care benchmarked costs can be a good way to target where you should be. Activity based costing allows you to focus on the costs associated with individual activities and how these activities are used to deliver the products and services (that is, outputs) of the organization. This is an essential feed into building an effective response to commoditization and helps you to identify where you might need to reduce costs on a more targeted basis rather than attempting to cut costs universally. When it comes to cutting costs there are up to 20 areas to look for cost savings including: renegotiating contracts, strategic sourcing, outsourcing (as discussed shortly), controlling the payroll (a euphemism for headcount reductions), leasing instead of buying and managing your inventory more efficiently.[19]

Companies which operate within the commoditized zone have a ruthless focus on cost so that any cost is directed to adding value to the delivery of the products or services they provide to their customers. Take the low cost airlines as one example. As we saw in Chapter 3 in order for easyJet and Ryanair to compete against the major carriers they had to redefine the nature of air travel so that their customers were willing to accept fewer frills and add-ons in return for very cheap fares. EasyJet was one of the first airlines to go completely ticketless and Ryanair has recently reduced the baggage allowance for their customers and will be charging them for items which fall outside the allowance. All of this is designed to reduce costs so that they can maintain some of the lowest fares in the industry. It should come as no surprise that every nickel and dime saved helps to maintain a profitable business and what is fascinating about the low cost airline model is that customers are willing to put up with the reduced comfort and service levels. Take food and drink, which was once a standard offering in all airlines. Such perks are becoming a rarity for travellers; what started in the US is now gaining a firmer footing across Europe. This is because some of the financial concerns that bedevilled the US carriers a number of years ago are now affecting their European counterparts, are forcing a greater number to reduce the perks of air travel (free newspapers, hot towels, drinks, food, and so on). Scandinavian Airlines System (SAS) limit their economy travellers to just one alcoholic beverage, rescinding their previous policy of allowing customers to drink as many as they wanted to, and they have now started to charge for food and drink on their intra-European flights; Iberia has taken free meals out of its economy cabin on all of its short- and medium-haul services and Aer Lingus charges for food on all of its European flights.[20] Air travel has become mass market and commoditized and in this environment cost management is king. The customers may not always like it, but the profits of easyJet and Ryanair continue to please the investor community, which suggests they are getting something right.

Wal-Mart also shows us how a ruthless focus on costs is imperative when working within the commoditized zone. Wal-Mart was one of the first companies to exploit the benefits of offshoring and has been in the vanguard ever since. The company is continually looking to gain additional savings within its supply chain and manufacturing processes so that it is able to maintain its cost advantage and ensure its customers are able to continue to buy their products for next to nothing. Although critics of Wal-Mart like to refer to such ruthless behaviour as the China Price, it makes sense to Wal-Mart and their customers (I will return to both Wal-Mart and Ryanair in the next chapter to highlight some of the specific actions they have taken to succeed within commoditized markets).

Table 8.2 Cost containment focus across the continuum

Full commoditization	Partial commoditization	Limited or no commoditization
Critical Without the ruthless focus on costs it is unlikely that businesses operating at this end of the continuum would survive. Every aspect of cost has to be analyzed and where it adds no value, eliminated. Cost management has to be part of the culture so that it is everyone's responsibility.	**Critical/ advisable** Depending on the mix of the commoditized and non-commoditized aspects of the business, the need to focus on cost management will vary. However it is a good idea that the cost discipline established within the more commoditized parts of the business are adopted elsewhere to ensure the company is capable of tackling (or even driving) low cost competition.	**Advisable** No matter how untouched by commoditization, it is increasingly important to focus on managing costs. It is too easy for costs to creep into a business that depends on innovation and high end service provision and if there is a need for a sharp reduction in costs, this can be very damaging and very difficult to achieve without affecting the frontline services and the innovative qualities on which the business depends.

OUTSOURCING AND OFFSHORING

The decision to outsource and offshore work is something that should not be taken lightly, as the impacts can be highly damaging if the execution is poor. If we are in any doubt about this we only need to witness some of the current backlash against the offshoring of American jobs to understand just how emotive this can be – something discussed in Chapter 6. Despite such backlash, one of the benefits of commoditization comes from the ability to reduce costs through outsourcing and offshoring work, even though corporations and political commentators refuse to admit that this is often the primary reason why they are considering outsourcing and offshoring in the first place. Both are now significant factors in any organization's arsenal of addressing the persistent issues associated with the costs of their human capital. In many respects the desire to outsource reflects the inevitable rise of Business Process Outsourcing (BPO) which is driving the specialized economy and is causing many CEOs to fundamentally rethink the boundaries of the firm. BPO naturally follows the optimization of process and the transparency that comes with the development and promulgation of standards, whilst its success depends on the dual impacts of globalization and the rise of the internet discussed in Chapter 4.

When thinking about the opportunities which outsourcing and offshoring present it is important to consider how far you want to go. Whilst in the past much of the outsourcing and offshoring was aimed at the lower order activities, such as call centres, today there is a lot more on offer and the option to outsource high end activities is now available. The best way to view this is as a range from low to high value activities as below:[21]

- low value – call centres and basic order processing;
- medium value – accounting, interpretation of X-rays, graphics;
- medium to high value – engineering, insurance claims;
- high value – underwriting, equity research, market research.

This shift reflects the general changes in how outsourcing is now perceived. Although in the past it was considered a tactical move to tackle costs or a difficult organizational function, principally IT, it is now considered to be part of the strategic armoury which organizations can use to address their market position. And as we saw in Chapter 4, some companies are insourcing their supplier's expertise. The shift also highlights the degree to which customers are becoming more comfortable with the remote delivery of services.[22]

As there are plenty of advisors, books and seminars available to those who wish to investigate and pursue the outsourcing agenda I will not go into immense detail on how to approach it. However, for the purposes of this book I will highlight a few factors that should be addressed when considering your response in the light of commoditization. First, it is vital to understand why you are pursuing the outsource and offshore route in the first place and to ensure the necessary debates have been had with the principal stakeholders and decision makers. Second, it is necessary to determine how far up the process value chain you wish to proceed and this depends on how the board perceives the threats and opportunities associated with commoditization and how it defines its response. Third, nearshoring opportunities should be considered when seeking an offshored solution. Nearshoring offers some advantages over the fully offshored model including: cultural affinity; better language skills; a reduction in trade associated costs (by remaining within a single trading bloc, such as NAFTA for example); security and legal protection; improved control and ease of intervention should issues arise and reduced impacts of time zone differences.[23] Fourth, if considering going completely offshore it is important to take your time to select the right country to offshore to, as mistakes can be very costly. Such things as supply of the right labour, prevailing salaries, cultural variations and differences, the level of geopolitical risk, the level of sophistication of the services offered within the country and their experience and expertise in managing offshored business processes all need to be considered before arriving at the decision.[24] And, finally, make sure you follow a tried and tested process, supported by experts in the area of contract negotiation and service management and who have had prior experience of helping organizations outsource their processes.

Table 8.3 Outsourcing focus across the continuum

Full commoditization	Partial commoditization	Limited or no commoditization
Critical/advisable Likely to use outsourcing and offshoring as a strategic tool to ensure costs are kept to an acceptable level. Most, if not all, back office functions should be outsourced and any non-critical business processes can be outsourced to ensure costs are focused on those aspects of the business that drive performance and customer experience.	**Advisable/ optional** Requires careful exploration to understand how best to address outsourcing and offshoring. Likely to outsource principal back office functions such as IT and finance and potentially HR. Other mid-office activities may be worth outsourcing to provide a strategic cost advantage over rivals, but care needs to be exercised to ensure activities core to the business are retained in house.	**Optional** Although not essential, some back office functions could be outsourced or offshored. Can exist largely untouched by outsourcing – high margins/ profitability make the requirement to outsource because of cost pressures less likely. May pursue offshoring for efficiency reasons.

SUPPLY CHAIN MANAGEMENT

Supply chain management is a concept that came into vogue around 20 years ago to crystallize the idea of managing an organization in terms of the resources, activities and strategies of those companies on which it depends.[25] Viewed in simple terms the supply chain links the organization and its processes to its suppliers at one end of the chain (who provide raw materials, semi-finished products and so on) and the customer at the other. This belies the underlying complexity of many supply chains which can be difficult to unravel and are rarely linear. However, as a concept it is increasingly important as it is often viewed as a strategic process within organizations and especially those which have a global footprint. Building a strong supply chain is considered to be an essential component of business success[26] and as organizations grapple with low cost competition and a commoditized market, the requirement to make the supply chain work as smoothly as possible is a very real one. This is not a simple task as it requires the suppliers to be intimately involved with any changes because without mutual benefits it is unlikely they would want to play ball. Wal-Mart has been very successful in this respect, and not just because of their immense buying power. We will look at Wal-Mart and its supply chain management practices in the next chapter.

When it comes to addressing the supply chain it is recommended that you follow a three step process.[27] Step one involves understanding the supply chain itself, its internal dynamics, characteristics and relationships. There are some 15 dimensions along which the supply chain can be defined and understood, including the product life cycle, the number of channels and the material flow, the volume per order/product and the mix of products in terms of movement, costs and inventories.[28] Having mapped, modelled and understood the supply chain the next thing to do is to build in the operational and management practices so that it is efficient and effective. Such operational and management practices include data integrity, enterprise-wide demand and supply management and building lean processes. Once this step is completed and the supply chain is stable you can then begin to innovate around it by exploring other means of enhancing it and making it even more effective. The purpose behind all this is have a supply chain that is agile (capable of responding to abrupt changes in market conditions), adaptable (collecting and tracking key data that identify trends and patterns which may require a response) and aligned (the interests of the organization and its suppliers are fully aligned).[29] When in place the triple A (agile, adaptable and aligned) supply chain can provide a strategic advantage over rivals in so far as it is easier to:

- respond to new demands and get new products to market;
- adapt to crises and interruptions due to war and natural disasters and recover much faster;
- adjust to structural changes in the supply networks which arise from political, economic, demographic and social change;
- run multiple supply chains to meet the needs of particular market segments.

With the emergence of radio frequency identification (RFID) there will be even greater opportunities for building efficient, effective and triple A supply chains. RFID allows organizations and their suppliers to identify and track any physical object within their supply chain and, more importantly, track it right through to the end consumer. Although this is creating issues for those concerned about privacy,[30] for those organizations willing to invest, RFID will prove a boon as it will yield near real time information on where components and finished products are across the entire supply chain. Technologically based innovation around the supply chain is likely to continue as organizations recognize the importance of managing it as efficiently as possible.

Table 8.4 Supply chain management focus across the continuum

Full commoditization	Partial commoditization	Limited or no commoditization
Critical For those organizations which are product focused or which have an integrated product/ service mix, an effective supply chain is critical to maintaining a lean and efficient cost base. This is especially important for those businesses which have to source their components and products from overseas or from a wide range of suppliers.	**Critical/ advisable** Operating in the partially commoditized space will require an efficient and effective supply chain because of the need to adapt to changing market conditions, either through the threat of low cost producers or shifts in market sentiment.	**Advisable** Even for those organizations which operate outside the commoditized zone, there are significant advantages to be had from running an effective supply chain, not least the ability to pick up new trends and respond to them rapidly.

TALENT AND LABOUR MANAGEMENT

As we saw in Chapter 5, the world of work continues to evolve as the combination of technology, demographic change, changes in the economic balance and globalization impact the nature, quality and composition of employment. As work increasingly becomes a commodity, either through the changes which are already taking hold, or through deliberate employer strategies, the need to revisit the relationship between the worker and the organization will increase. As the difference between those at the top of the talent pool and those in the middle and at the bottom widens, the levels of engagement with work, bosses and organizational strategy will reduce. This is a serious problem not just in terms of the impacts on the long term viability of a business but also socially and is something I will explore in more detail in Chapter 11.

A recent survey by Towers Perrin, the global professional services firm, found that only 11 per cent of European employees considered themselves to be highly engaged at work; some 22 per cent were disengaged and the remaining 67 per cent were moderately engaged.[31] Compared to the wider data, Europe comes out quite well as the Asia Pacific region has, surprisingly, a greater problem with engagement; compared to North and South America however, Europe lags considerably.[32] Engagement is important because it is the engaged employee who is willing to go the extra mile, who believes in the organization's mission and who believes what senior executives say. In short this 11 per cent are the people who believe they make a difference. Moreover they are less likely to leave or consider leaving if made a better offer by another employer – 65 per cent have no intention of leaving against the mere 15 per cent of disengaged workers.[33] Some of the problems associated with engagement can be put down to the psychological contract which still retains its importance despite the impacts of the business process reengineering zealots of the 1990s. It is well known that when employees feel that their boss or company has broken their expectations about work or career opportunities they typically feel less committed. When this happens, engagement dips, morale falls and the willingness to put in the extra effort that makes a difference vanishes.[34] We then end up with the issues raised by David Bolchover in his book the *Living Dead* – staff surfing the net, running businesses from their desks, emailing their friends and socializing with their work colleagues.[35] In fact doing everything else but work!

I believe that as commoditization strengthens its grip the problems associated with engagement and the psychological contract will increase. Presented with problems such as these, what is HR to do? Naturally focusing on the highly talented amongst the rank and file is important, but failing to address the motivational issues of the also rans, and those who although not destined for great things, are still critical to the success of the business is going to be fatal. So organizations are not only going to have to get smarter at winning the talent wars, but they are also going to have to get better at keeping the commoditized worker engaged. Both are important and both require an appropriate response, and HR will need to rise to the challenge.

Winning the talent wars

In a commoditized world, not everyone will be needed to take on the top positions within a company, but every organization needs some talent, otherwise it wouldn't survive. Corporations such as Wal-Mart, who pride themselves on maintaining a low cost workforce could not last long without employing a small cadre of smart people to work on their supply chain, build their sophisticated IT applications, innovate around the customer and address their strategic agenda. The same is true of Ryanair and every other commodity business. Of course, not everyone wants to work for low cost operators especially when there are global corporations that offer more interesting and varied careers, as well as better remuneration and benefits.

The war for talent, which following the collapse of the Dot Com boom conveniently went away is now coming back with a vengeance as the population ages and the number of new workers begins to fall short of the numbers required to run an efficient organization. Immigration may help but there are three reasons why this may not be the panacea that many, including politicians, believe it to be. First, despite the fact that immigration has helped to keep inflation low in much of the industrialized West, the ability to sustain this over the medium term is doubtful as it will require wave after wave of fresh immigrants.[36] Furthermore, immigration will not prevent populations from aging, as it is well known that immigrant communities will over time, drift to their host nation's birth rates.[37] So although they may prefer larger families on arrival, over time the number of live births regresses to the mean of the country to which they have emigrated. Second, many of the immigrants work at the low end of the economy and in entry level positions within organizations which may make them a valuable resource and may help to keep labour costs down, but it does not address the talent issues companies are facing at the strategic level. Finally, the qualified immigrants who have traditionally been attracted into the well paid positions are beginning to return home as their native economies expand and the opportunities for well paid employment and entrepreneurship increase.[38] For example in 1970, a fifth of Taiwanese graduates went abroad to complete their studies and once abroad the majority failed to return home – the economic benefits within countries such as the United States compared favourably with those in Taiwan. Today, graduates are drifting back and the brain drain is no longer such a pressing concern for the Taiwanese government. Those returning home do so with high levels of education and a superb understanding of Western business, particularly high technology. This has allowed Taiwan to accelerate the upgrading of technological infrastructure and build its equivalent of Silicon Valley – a region which extends from Taipei to the Hsinchu Science Park. This continues to benefit from the influx of thousands of United States educated engineers and software experts who have set up nearly 40 per cent of the 289 companies currently operating within this region.[39]

Addressing the talent war is therefore an issue for every company but is possibly a greater concern for those organizations within the commoditized zone because of the competition posed by those companies which require much larger numbers of talented staff. Such organizations are naturally more geared to providing them with the challenges, education and training and career trajectories necessary to keep them engaged (which as we saw above is critical if the company is to succeed). To win the war for talent, organizations need to do two things. The first is to really understand why talented people move on from their employers and the second is to define challenging and forward looking roles for their best staff. The first is the easy part, whilst the second may be a little harder. Irrespective of where the organization may sit along the commoditization continuum, attracting and retaining talent will be an essential component of the HR strategy.

When it comes to understanding why talented employees leave organizations we have a wealth of advice and research to draw upon. All you need to do is to read it and implement it, which of course most companies fail to do. It seems that few companies bring in sufficiently talented people, develop their people quickly and effectively enough to realize their latent talents, retain all their high performers or even know who they are.[40] The root of the problem is that many of the reasons why talent chooses to move on are hidden from view as employer and employee refuse to raise the issues before they become significant enough to lead to a prized employee leaving.

Before you can begin to manage your talent more diligently, it is a good idea to understand why they leave in the first place. The principal reasons are:[41]

- The job or workplace was not as expected, in other words there were unmet expectations on either side.
- Mismatch between job and person, where the role the talented employee was given provided limited opportunity to use skills and capabilities. This often happens when staff are sponsored to complete a post graduate qualification such as an MBA, only to return back to their old role when they finish their studies. In such instances, it's not long before they recognize the work is too limiting and decide to move on.
- Too little coaching and feedback without which it is impossible to keep your talent engaged with the organization's direction and their part in it.
- Too few growth and advancement opportunities which will, if left unchecked, leave the talented employee at best disengaged and at worst seriously thinking about moving on.
- Feeling devalued and unrecognized. Increasingly, the most obvious indication talented employees have of their value to their employer is their pay. When this appears inequitable or fails to reflect the going rate for someone of their capability, they will disengage and move on. This level of discontent is likely to increase as the full impacts of commoditization divides the workforce between the super talented and the rest (I will come back to this again in Chapter 11).
- Stress from overwork and work–life imbalance. As we shall see in the next chapter, some of the more enlightened organizations are already adopting practices to combat this. That said, stress levels are likely to increase as companies expect more from their most talented employees and reduce the span of control and scope of work for the remainder of their workforce; no one will be immune. Burn-out may become a real issue for the most talented and a significant number of employees are already complaining about their inability to maintain a healthy work life balance – 56 per cent according to one recent survey.[42]
- Loss of trust and confidence in senior leaders which appears to be a growing concern amongst many workforces. In Europe the single strongest influence on employee engagement is the belief that senior management aregenuinely interested in the wellbeing and satisfaction of their staff. In fact this is key to employees' passion, involvement and interest. Although critical, the bad news is that most employees believe senior management are not interested in them and fail to act in the best interests of the business.[43]

So what should organizations do to retain their high performing employees, and by high performing, I am not only referring to those destined for the very senior positions in the company. There are many talented people who work hard, deliver great results but are overlooked, mismanaged and leave, which costs businesses dear. The advice is thick and fast but most tends to boil down to a few hard and fast rules. The first is to talk to them and find out why they stay and what motivates them and what they want to do with their careers.[44] Obvious perhaps, but it is rare for senior executives to ask their subordinates why they turn up day after day. The next thing is to ensure that managers throughout the company take it upon themselves to look after their talented staff, something McKinsey call embracing the talent mindset.[45] This is important because it is the direct manager who has the greatest control and influence over employee perception.[46] This must be accompanied by meaningful discussions about career paths. Increasingly these discussions are not taking place which makes it very difficult for employees to understand what they need to be doing to progress (be that in terms of behaviour, next move, operational duties, training and so on). Talented employees may be left to go figure it out for themselves which is far from ideal. When such conversations take place they must consider the strengths the employee brings and these need to be both acknowledged and respected. One of the biggest problems in the corporate world today is the lip service paid to diversity, both in terms of skills and approaches to work. All too often companies promote clones and self-serving executives and leave those who have a different set of skills and talents behind. Although HR has done much to widen the awareness of the broad range of personality types through the application of profiling tools such as Belbin, Myers Briggs and others, they are rarely used in practice and few companies use them actively to get the best out of their staff. If talented people are to feel respected they have to be recognized and rewarded for what they bring, not penalized for what they lack. Focusing on their weaknesses will do little for their motivation, or levels of engagement. The remainder of the advice is standard fare and something that should be included within any decent HR strategy. Giving your talented staff the opportunity to grow, new experiences, new learning opportunities and being able to lead and make a difference are all critical components of any talent management approach. All this advice can be neatly summed up in the cycle of talent management[47] which consists of four quite obvious steps:

- attract
- select
- engage
- keep engaged.

In the end attracting and retaining the talent you need means adopting an active approach and building a value proposition that will keep as many as possible of your talented employees working for you rather than going to your competition. And when we cast our eyes back over the reasons why smart employees leave, most of them are under your control.

Keeping the commoditized worker engaged

As discussed above, the percentage of talented staff within a commoditized business is typically low as the business does not operate a model which requires vast numbers of them. In fact the business remains profitable by employing great armies of low cost employees and using a combination of outsourcing and offshoring to ensure its cost base remains as low as possible. However, just because there are fewer talented individuals within the organization it doesn't mean you should adopt a laissez faire attitude to the management and development of those that remain. In fact the opposite is true; it is comparatively easy to manage a small talent pool because the majority of those within it are motivated and self starters. Motivating low paid staff who may see working life as little more than just a succession of jobs is much, much harder. The problem is that as more companies come to depend on a commodity workforce the issues of associated motivation and commitment will become more significant.

As we saw above when we discussed the importance of engagement, all staff need to be engaged in their work if a company is to maximize its profits and remain viable over the long term. Failing in this respect can be costly. For example in the United States the costs associated with disengaged workers is in the region of $363 billion annually and this figure is almost entirely down to the loss of sales revenue caused by customers' disappointing interactions with disengaged employees.[48] The converse is true. Based on interviews with more than

65 000 US consumers, the University of Michigan demonstrated a clear link between customer satisfaction and financial success. Companies with high customer satisfaction out perform the S&P 500 by a wide margin. Unfortunately customer service is often one of the first things to falter when short-term financial pressure is placed on a business.[49] The other problem of not taking time to engage your lower level staff is the costs associated with unnecessarily high turnover. According to the Saratoga Institute the average cost of losing an employee is the equivalent to their annual salary[50] which may not be much in a commoditized business, but if turnover is high the costs can be significant and can be compounded if a rival has lower turnover. Comparing Wal-Mart's Sam's Club with CostCo highlights the significance of turnover on profitability. As arch rivals in the fiercely competitive low cost warehouse retailing arena they appear quite similar until you take a look at the way their labour practices impact their bottom line. As part of the Wal-Mart Empire, Sam's Club has adopted the aggressive control of employee wages and benefits familiar to every part of Wal-Mart. The pay of something in the region of $10 per hour is significantly less than at CostCo who pay an hourly rate of $17. In addition, most of CostCo's employees receive medical cover and pensions unlike Sam's Club where only around half receive such benefits. Although CostCo's employee related costs are higher than Sam's Club, they benefit from a much reduced turnover; 17 per cent against 44 per cent (which is close to the industry average). Assuming that it costs 60 per cent of an employee's salary to replace them it costs Sam's Club only $12 617 to replace each member of staff whilst at CostCo it costs $21 216. Although the individual costs may be higher the lower turnover at CostCo means that its annual costs are only $244 million compared to Sam's Club's $612 million. The loyalty which CostCo generates within its workforce clearly pays dividends.[51]

So what should organizations and the HR function more specifically be doing to address the challenges that the Wal-Mart – CostCo example highlight? Clearly the challenges are significant because commoditization can make for repetitive, restrictive and pressured work, but that should not stop organizations from being creative with their commodity workforce and looking after them (as we saw in Chapter 7). According to the authors of *The Enthusiastic Employee*, there are three primary sets of goals which people want from work – equity, achievement and camaraderie.[52] These three goals are consistent over time and vary little between different groups of workers and for the majority are more important than any other work based goals they might have. Let's look briefly at each of these three areas and consider what it means for the motivation, leadership and management of commodity workers. The first, equity, requires the organization to ensure their workers' physiological, economic and psychological needs are met. Providing a safe working environment, paying your staff a living wage and treating them with respect is a good place to start. Commodity workers, like all others, want to feel valued and if they don't all the issues associated with disengagement begin to appear and as we discussed earlier this can lead to serious problems with the bottom line. Next it is essential to give your staff a sense of achievement both in terms of their own contribution and daily work activities but also in the company as a whole. The factors which make a sense of achievement possible include:[53]

- challenge and stimulation;
- learning new skills and improving on those already acquired;
- the ability to perform which includes having as much control as possible over the execution of the work or the decisions required to support that work;
- recognition;

- adding value to the organization and its customers;
- collaboration and connection with others inside and outside of the organization.

The final element is camaraderie. The need to work with co-workers who are reasonable, competent and supportive is a basic requirement of most employees. When teams and groups work well they can deliver exceptional results. The converse is also true with dysfunctional work groups who can cause major barriers to the smooth running and harmony of an organization. For example, problems such as people not pulling their weight are common concerns amongst co-workers. As work becomes more commoditized the requirement to build a culture of support and camaraderie will become more important and it is down to HR to ensure that their commodity workforce remains motivated and engaged. As we will see in Chapter 9 those companies that go out of their way to engender a spirit of enthusiasm in their workers will be the winners in a commoditized world. Put into the wider context of the service profit chain[54] the engaged, motivated and enthusiastic employee can make all the difference between having high levels of customer loyalty, revenue growth and profits and having little or none of these. Because commoditized employees are increasing filling jobs which interface directly with the customer it is easy to see how disengagement and demotivation can impact the customer experience. Focusing on reducing turnover, improving morale and looking after your commodity resources should be as high a priority as looking after your stars, who will in the main, look after themselves.

Before we leave the issue of how to motivate the commodity worker, it is important to review the impact of the aging of the population on motivation and engagement. In Part I of the book I looked at how the combined effects of an aging workforce and the loss of key work-based benefits such as pensions will mean that fewer of us will be able to retire when we would ideally like to. This will mean that over the next decade the mix of Baby Boomers, Generation X'ers and Millennials will broaden the motivational needs of the workforce.[55] For the Baby Boomers who are beginning to reach retirement, work will take on a less important role, but for many it will still be necessary or something they wish to pursue on a more casual or part-time basis; flexibility is important to this cohort. Despite this, the mature worker still wants to contribute to the business and develop and apply new skills. The Generation X'ers tend to find themselves in a bottleneck with a range of issues affecting their motivation, including career stagnation, tensions in their work–life balance, skill attenuation, burnout and general disillusionment. For this cohort such things as having a comprehensive benefits package to help them through the demanding mid-life stage they are going through, and flexibility to allow them to meet their work and life commitments are important; but most of all they need stimulation, variety and a chance to reinvent themselves. The final cohort is possibly the most demanding but for different reasons than the Generation X'ers. They want flexibility, independence, to be treated individually, have flexible schedules and manage their own careers (the first generation to embrace this fully). They also want to be listened to, have regular feedback and expect to fit work around their social lives. As we saw in Chapter 7, this last cohort demonstrates the most extreme traits of self-absorption and believes that society is better off through individualistic not collective actions. A quote from some recent research highlights the impact this has on employers:

Baby boomers and members of Generation X were like dogs – treat them right and they will be loyal. But members of this latest generation, Generation Y, are more like cats: they just go where the money is. At recruitment fairs candidates used to try to stress what they could offer to a company, now it's the other way round.[56]

Table 8.5 Talent management focus across the continuum

Full commoditization	Partial commoditization	Limited or no commoditization
Critical It is essential to maintain a small and dedicated team of talented individuals who can address the innovation, project and strategic needs of the business. This should be comparatively straightforward to achieve. More critical, however, is to maintain a motivated, but highly commoditized workforce. Generating loyalty and minimizing turnover amongst this cohort is essential to profitability.	**Critical** Needs both an effective approach to attracting and retaining the talent they need (which will be in larger numbers than those companies within the commoditized zone, but fewer than those working fully outside the zone) and keeping hold of the commoditized workforce. It is necessary to guard against their talent drifting towards those companies which can offer more and also pay their commoditized workforce above what they could expect to get elsewhere.	**Critical** With innovation and uniqueness being core to a company operating in the limited or no commoditization end of the continuum, talent management must be top of their agenda. Attracting and retaining the best talent they can will be an essential strategy for survival especially as the ranks of the talented become fewer in number and as the pressures heaped upon them cause many to downshift to achieve a better work–life balance.

Innovation

According to the UK Treasury, innovation drives productivity growth in the short term and economic growth in the long run. They believe it encapsulates organizational change, adopting and adapting new technologies and the introduction of new goods and services. They also believe that it helps to explain the productivity gap between the UK and US. Comparing the UK against its major competitors suggests that as a nation it lags behind the US, France and Germany on even the most basic measures of innovation such as business enterprise, patents granted, gross domestic spend on research and development and the numbers of papers and citations per head of population.[57] Innovation is now a critical component at the national level, but what about for individual businesses?

A few years ago I was asked to edit a book on innovation for the London Business School.[58] The idea behind it was to highlight the importance of innovation to an organization's long term survival. What I found particularly interesting was the difficulty most organizations seem to have in harnessing the creative energy of their staff even though it is critical to their long term future. According to the London Business School, when faced with the challenge of engendering a spirit of innovation into a business, its leaders must answer the following key questions:

- How can you convince others that improving the organization's innovativeness is not only important but urgent?
- Where should the focus for innovation lie?
- Where are you going to find people who are good at innovation?
- How are you going to sustain the innovation process once it has started?[59]

These are not easy questions to answer and many CEOs admit they struggle with innovation. Despite this, the majority believe the ability to innovate is critical to their organization's future and most see their innovation encapsulating not just the traditional areas of focus such as product, market and service but increasingly including innovating around the business model itself.[60] This new focus recognizes just how easy it is for the status quo of an established business to change overnight as technology, commoditization and new entrants force the existing model into obsolescence. Take Eastman Kodak who in response to the shift away from traditional film media to digital have spent the past four years reengineering their business, and they are not finished yet. Such significant transformational investments are likely to become more frequent as the impacts of commoditization and its underlying drivers discussed in Part I affect a larger number of corporations. We can conclude that the ability to innovate is an increasingly important discipline especially as many companies are now finding themselves locked into the me-too hell of commoditization in which customers find it impossible to differentiate one company's products and services from another's. And although the focus of this innovation may vary considerably across the commoditization continuum it is still critical.

The lessons from the London Business School's Innovation Exchange point to a number of factors that have to be present if innovation is to be successfully harnessed. These are:[61]

- Innovation is a journey that will take time to achieve its objectives. This means staying the course and riding the ups and downs which come with taking this type of risk.
- You can't become innovative overnight and for those that wish to, it has to be treated like any other change programme.
- Innovation is a mind set which has to be embedded into the corporate DNA. Treating innovation as a fashion or the latest management fad which has to be followed will yield poor results and will certainly not allow you to escape the commoditization trap.
- Innovation requires different mindsets and behaviours and these can be very far from those prevalent within the organization. It was clear during the Dot Com boom that most companies struggled to cope with the very different attitudes and behaviours of those working within internal incubators. A sense of alienation and disconnection was common and political difficulties between the old and new schools soon erupted into turf wars.
- Innovation requires direction, support and active sponsorship from the board and the senior executives throughout the organization. It requires an effective and transparent process through which new ideas can be nurtured, developed, tested and launched. Such transparency is also critical in providing clear reasons (that is, not political ones) why a particular innovation will not be taken forward.
- Innovation necessitates a clear understanding of context (both internal and external) and strategic direction, otherwise it can become random and potentially destructive.

These are clearly important lessons which need to be addressed if innovation is to yield the much needed results organizations seek, but what is the best way to focus your innovation efforts? What is required is a strategy for innovation and according to Chartic[62] this can be achieved by combining the two principal elements of solution-based innovation (which involves introducing superior and highly defensible solutions to known market needs) and need-based innovation (which involves redefining market requirements based on fresh insights into the unspoken and more fundamental needs of the customer). Combining both is possibly the only way to avoid the me-too hell of commoditization. The two-by-two model which comes from combining these two critical dimensions is as follows:

- Where the solution is defensible and the market need well known, solution-based innovation is the best strategy to adopt. This is where the unmet, but known needs of the market can be targeted with superior solutions that are both cost effective and of significant value to the customer.
- Where the solution is defensible but the market need unspoken, then the approach should be one of changing the game. In this strategy the focus is on uncovering a fundamental market need and then developing highly defensible solutions to that need. To be successful requires a deep insight into the market and what drives it, which is what GE, Sony and others do very successfully.
- Where the solution is generic and the market need well known then you are in what Chartic terms, me-too hell. And as we saw at the start of the chapter there are a few strategies you can adopt. Most companies want to escape this commodity trap, but there are an increasing number who recognise that this is where they are likely to stay and plan accordingly. It is also clear from the research from the London Business School that switching on innovation is not an easy task and is highly dependent on the culture of the organization, but as we will see in the next chapter, some organizations have been able to escape the me-too hell either completely or partially through the effective harnessing of innovation.
- Where the solution is generic and the market need unspoken then the strategy is one of need based innovation which involves getting to the fundamental market need. This is never easy because it involves getting under the skin of the customer and really understanding what their needs are. This is one of the fundamental reasons why relationship based selling is so much in vogue, although I am yet to be convinced it will deliver in the long-term.

In responding to the impacts of commoditization and me-too hell, organizations are also turning to their customers to actively engage them in the process of innovation. Such outside innovation involves engaging directly with lead users and key customers to harness and commercialize their ideas and more importantly to co-design solutions that will better meet their needs.[63] This approach to innovation allows companies to avoid many of the problems that beset the traditional approaches, including creating products which have little connection with the customer's real problems, sales staff presenting solutions instead of uncovering needs and customer services failing to pick up some of the hidden problems that require solutions.[64] This last point has a significant read-across to some of the issues discussed earlier when addressing the commoditized workforce. When most of your commodity workforce sits in customer services, you had better start treating them well if you are going to be able to identify new areas for customer-based innovation. There are also some fundamental differences between traditional and outside innovation which have to be understood and embraced if it is to be successful. These include:

- customers not research and development lead the innovation effort;
- new products, services and business models are designed in the real world of the customer, not in the laboratory environment of research and development;
- customers scan the markets for you and help identify complementary solutions;
- customers actively promote new products and services for you thereby giving you a better hit rate when commercialising new ideas.[65]

The results can be significant, for example Lego® harnessed its customers to produce its most successful product of all time, Mindstorms®[66] and Staples engaged their customers to redesign processes and policies to make it easier for customers to buy their office supplies (the Easy Rebate program).[67]

With innovation taking centre stage in an increasingly commoditized world, the ability to both harness the internal talents of your staff and to engage your customers in developing products and solutions that will genuinely make a difference is becoming critical. Viewing innovation as a cornerstone of your response to the threats and opportunities posed by commoditization will go a long way to escaping me-too hell, if of course you want to.

Table 8.6 Innovation focus across the continuum

Full commoditization	Partial commoditization	Limited or no commoditization
Critical Even when operating in a fully commoditized environment, innovation is still critical. Although not typically focused on building brand new products or services, innovation is still needed to improve the customer experience and enhance the back office functions so that they cost less but add more value. Believing that innovation is not required is a mistake.	**Critical** Innovation is critical to organizations in this part of the continuum because without it there is a strong possibility of being dragged into a fully commoditized zone. Working a mixed model requires a broad focus on innovation which addresses the types of innovation required for commodity customers and markets as well as the high-end needs of customers who demand superior products and services. This can be a very difficult balance to manage, and may necessitate a change in business model to cope.	**Critical** Innovation should be a core and highly valued skill set within businesses at this end of the continuum. Employing the talented thinkers and designers as well as those who are capable of engaging with the customer is essential. Without constant innovation, it is unlikely that the organization could remain at this end of the continuum for very long.

Branding

Many years ago I attended one of these massive events hosted by the world-renowned Anthony Robbins. Like all such events the auditorium was packed with literally thousands of eager professionals desperate to hear how they could become very wealthy by merely believing they could. Whether any did of course is highly debatable and whether you believe the self-help movement is just snake oil designed to make those that peddle it rich is outside the scope of this book. However, there was some interesting content delivered at the event which may be relevant to how some companies choose to respond to the challenge that commoditization presents. And this is all about exclusivity. During the session we were informed about the different types of people in the world – well in fact there were four, but it was one in particular that was of special interest; the Achievers. The Achievers are those people who are at the top of their profession; earn significantly more than the average Joe and for whom exclusivity is the name of the game. They don't want to be like anyone else and they are willing to fork out whatever it takes to ensure they stand out from the crowd. Such people are willing to pay for those brands which tell everyone else around them that they have made it. Although focused on a small cohort of society, the message about branding is important because of the power which brands have to shortcut our decision making process when it comes to making purchases. In a commoditized and saturated world, branding is an increasingly important strategy to tackle the impacts of cost conscious buyers, be they part of the procurement function of your clients, or individual customers.

Although some believe that the brand has had its day (something we explored in Chapter 6) and consumers should be less concerned about brands than they used to be, the results of experiments by neuroscientists suggest that branding is still a very powerful force. When researchers scanned the brains of subjects exposed to images of brands they discovered that strong ones excited parts of the brain most associated with pleasure and reward. Other findings were equally intriguing, especially one which suggested that brain activity for an action seems to begin about half a second before a person decides to take the action. This suggests that we do not make decisions but become aware of a decision which has already been made.[68] All this has got the advertisers and brand management experts salivating because it means they might be able to control how consumers behave – the way *they* want them to.

Branding can also help to avoid some of the more obvious problems associated with commoditization, such as price sensitivity. Take salt for example. Salt is one of the most basic of commodities and is both abundant and cheap to purchase. Despite this, Morton, a US salt provider, is able to charge more for its salt than any of its competitors and has been able to increase its market share to 50 per cent. Successfully branding its salt, which comes in a blue canister with a girl with an umbrella on it and the promise that rain won't damage its pourability, has been key to its success.[69] The lesson here is that if it is possible to differentiate salt through branding then it ought to be possible to differentiate other products and services through branding too. In fact branding can turn small product and service differences into significant advantages, especially when coupled with a high sales volume. Companies such as Intel, Gillette and Campbell have all leveraged their brands and succeeded despite the highly competitive and commoditized markets in which they operate. Thus suggests that with the appropriate focus and investment in their brand a company can be extremely successful in a commoditized market where despite the competition, it can still be relatively simple to stand out from the crowd.

Just as it is possible to use the standard rules of branding and to follow the pack, it is also possible to do the opposite and succeed by taking a completely different direction. This often means going against the received wisdom, but it can pay off.[70] Scion, Toyota's youth-focused small car brand broke its 150 000 sales target in 2006 by 25 000. Instead of ramping up sales for 2007 they made the conscience decision to pare sales and production back to no more than 150 000 in order to keep the brand special, even though the belief was that they could have surpassed 250 000 cars without much problem. Not just that, but they are also reducing spend on advertising, already quite low by industry standards and may eliminate it altogether in a bid to create an 'underground' brand. They are also going one step further, as they will focus their marketing at the experiential level which will include branded entertainment following the success of the Scion music label for emerging artists and its own clothing line called Scion Release. As one dealer put it, 'Everybody is trying to be different, so it's important for Scion to not put too many cars out there, or they will be everywhere'.[71]

If we accept that branding is critical in the commoditized world, maintaining it is not always an easy ride, especially when there are others who are capable of taking your custom away. Ensuring excellence in service is one way commoditized brands can retain their customers, and damaging this in any way can be very harmful. JetBlue Airways the low cost US airline was recently criticized by congressional leaders after hundreds of its passengers were forced to sit aboard grounded airplanes for up to 10 hours because of bad weather in New York. The JetBlue president was forced to apologize for the unacceptable delays and offered each affected passenger full refunds and free return trips.[72] This move will save them a lawsuit and also go some way to protecting their brand. In the future, this type of action could become more common.

Table 8.7 Branding focus across the continuum

Full commoditization	Partial commoditization	Limited or no commoditization
Advisable/ critical Branding is a key area for a commoditized business. Small differences coupled with a strong brand can make all the difference between a me-too product destined to compete purely on price and one which is able to be priced at a premium.	**Critical** For those on the edge of commoditization, branding can be used as a strategic weapon to defend the product or service. Equally, seeking ways to shift the brand away from the commodity trap is also a possibility.	**Critical** Branding is essential for those companies working outside the commoditized zone. Brand associations, such as exclusivity or superior service have to be reinforced and backed up if the brand is to remain strong.

A final comment – the importance of organizational culture

We should never underestimate the power that culture, in all its forms, has over us. Whether we are talking about national culture or team culture, each will impact the way we behave and interact with other people and will define at least to some extent, our preferences.

Interest in culture in general and organizational culture specifically has gained ground within academic and business circles alike. However, for many employees and senior executives it still remains a mystery which is typically encapsulated in the phrase *the way we do things round here*. In contrast, for those who have taken the trouble to unravel it, it can be a powerful tool in the organization's arsenal. The reason why culture is so powerful is that it provides the necessary glue which keeps everyone aligned and engaged and it helps to build the norms of behaviour which make a company what it is. Although it is well known that a strong culture has a positive impact on performance, if it is too strong it can make it very difficult and indeed painful to adapt to changing circumstances. Before it had to transform itself, IBM had a very strong culture even down to the dress code – the ubiquitous white shirt and dark suit. This culture served it well and ensured IBM's image, reputation and brand were well known and relied upon. The problem, however, was that this created a degree of arrogance, which often happens with the market leaders, and prevented them from spotting the obvious changes in the way computers were being used. It took a lot of effort to change the culture so that the business was able to respond to the changing demands and expectations.

The lessons from IBM and others which have had to react to similar market conditions is that the culture of a corporation increasingly needs to be adaptive to the changes that will inevitably occur over the foreseeable future as commoditization takes on a greater significance. Such adaptability will necessitate a healthier attitude to change and being willing to recognize that the mix of skills, capabilities and competencies of the employees will need to adapt to the changing market and competitive conditions. This is not easy because it requires sensitivity and open communication so that every stakeholder is engaged in the process; and it requires a culture that is able to absorb change more effectively. The problem is that without an adaptive culture, change can be wrenching and it can take a long time for an organization to recover (as we saw with Kodak), if it recovers at all. When CEOs talk about innovating around their business models, what they really mean is a combination of changing their culture and how they approach their operational and market contexts. Addressing the cultural dimension of change lies firmly at the door of HR and it is up to these experts to create and nurture the ability to adapt – something few of us are really good at. Therefore, pursuing a broad strategy which includes many of the areas discussed in this chapter will require a real sensitivity to culture; ignore it at your peril.

Over the course of this chapter we have reviewed a number of areas which should form a response when addressing the challenge of commoditization. What is important amongst all this is that the response has to be consciously defined and cannot be entirely tactical. Naturally the choices you make will depend on whether you wish to operate within a commoditized environment or to avoid it as much as possible. It should also be remembered that there are already plenty of organizations that are very successful in operating in highly competitive, cost focused markets, which means avoidance may not always be the best strategy. It is also important to accept that commoditization is a continuous process so even if you are outside the commoditized zone now, you would be wise to address some of the areas discussed in this chapter in order to continue to thrive in an environment where you can avoid the issues associated with price-only decisions.

Before moving onto the responses individuals need to be making to protect themselves from the detrimental impacts which commoditization can have on their careers, it is worth highlighting a few companies which exemplify what it means to survive across the commoditization continuum. This is the focus of the next chapter.

References

1 Harvard Business School (1994) Beating the commodity magnet, 12 September, p. 1.
2 Pfundstein, D. (2004) Commoditization can explain the service economy, www.gclaw.com.
3 Towers Perrin (2006) Ten steps to creating an engaged workforce: key European findings, p. 2.
4 This quote from Walter Wriston, the former Chairman of Citicorp/Citibank, was taken from Sirota, D., et al. (2005) The Enthusiastic Employee, Upper Saddle River, New Jersey: Wharton School Publishing, p. 3.
5 This came up in a recent conversation about one particular organization that recognized that their ability to innovate was a little short of the mark.
6 www.chartic.com, avoiding the black hole of commoditization.
7 Chin, G. (2006) A way cool strategy: Toyota's Scion plans to sell fewer cars, The Wall Street Journal, 19 November, p. 2.
8 Kumar, N. (2006) Strategies to fight low-cost rivals, Harvard Business Review, December, p. 106.
9 Ibid., p. 109.
10 Ibid., p. 111.

11 Foote, N., et al. (2001) Making solutions the answer, *The McKinsey Quarterly*, Number 3.
12 *The Business* (2007) Dell needs a boy wonder, 10 February, p. 32.
13 Foote, N., et al. (2001) Making solutions the answer, *The McKinsey Quarterly*, Number 3, pp. 87–88.
14 PricewaterhouseCoopers (2001) Strange Days.
15 Jack, A. (2007) Downsizing Pfizer is setting the industry's agenda, *Financial Times*, 24 January, p. 22.
16 Agovino, T. (2007) Pfizer to cut 10,000 jobs, close plants, biz.yahoo.com.
17 Monden, Y. (1995) *Target Costing and Kaizen Costing*, Portland, Oregon: Productivity Press, p. 5.
18 Rogers, P. and Saenz, H. (2007) Make your back office an accelerator, *Harvard Business Review*, March, p. 30.
19 For the complete list of 20 ways to cut cost, see Stutely, R. (2003) *The Definitive Guide to Managing the Numbers*, Harlow: FT Prentice Hall, p. 379.
20 Johnson, A. (2006) Lean Cuisine: European airlines get stingy, *The Wall Street Journal*, Personal Journal, 8 November, p. D1.
21 These categories have been derived from a lecture delivered by Dr. Jeffery Sampler of Oxford University 7–9 March 2005.
22 McNeill, R. (2005) What is possible from offshore?, *Forrester Trends*, 15 March, p. 2.
23 Brown, R. and Karamouzis, F. (2005) Assess the 'Nearshore' advantages for business process outsourcing, *Gartner*, 12 September.
24 Marriott, I. (2005) Consider offshore options around the globe, *Gartner*, 13 June.
25 Lamming, R. (2001) *The Financial Times Handbook of Management* (second edition), London: Financial Times Prentice Hall, p. 398.
26 Lee, H. (2006) *The Triple-A Supply Chain, Harvard Business Review on Supply Chain Management*, Boston Massachusetts: Harvard Business School Publishing, p. 87.
27 Tyndall, G., et al. (1998) *Supercharging Supply Chains*, New York: John Wiley & Sons Inc., pp. 238–241.
28 For the full list of the 15 dimensions, see Tyndall, G., et al., (1998) *Supercharging Supply Chains*, New York: John Wiley & Sons Inc., p. 238.
29 Lee, H. (2006) *The Triple-A Supply Chain, Harvard Business Review on Supply Chain Management*, Boston Massachusetts: Harvard Business School Publishing, p. 88.
30 Albrecht, K. and McIntyre, L. (2005) *Spychips*, Nashville Tennessee: Nelson Current.
31 Ibid., p. 4.
32 Ibid., p. 5.
33 Ibid., p. 10.
34 CIPD (2002) Sustaining success in difficult times, p. 1.
35 Bolchover, D. (2005) *The Living Dead: Switched Off, Zoned Out the Shocking Truth About Office Life*, Chichester: Capstone.
36 Searjeant, G. (2006) Immigrants help to hold down interest rates, Bank report says, *The Times*, 11 December, p. 34.
37 Wagstyl, S. (2007) An important test of tolerance, The world in 2007, *Financial Times*, 24 January, p. 8.
38 Wonacott., P. (2006) Indian scientists return home as economy moves a step up, *The Wall Street Journal*, pp. A1 and A12.
39 Legrain, P. (2006) *Immigrants: Your Country Needs Them*, London: Little, Brown, p. 196.
40 Michaels, E., et al. (2001) *The War for Talent*, Boston Massachusetts: Harvard Business School Press, p. 9.
41 Branham, L. (2005) *The 7 Hidden Reasons Employees Leave*, New York: AMACOM, pp. 31–194.
42 Diromualdo, T. and Winter, J. (2005) Manifesto for the new agile workforce, Career innovations (Executive summary).
43 Towers Perrin (2006) Ten steps to creating an engaged workforce: key European findings, p. 8.
44 Kaye, B. and Jordan-Evans, S. (1999) *Love 'em or Lose 'em: Getting Good People to Stay*, San Francisco: Berrett-Koehler Publishers, pp. 1–8.
45 Michaels, E., et al. (2001) *The war for talent*, Boston Massachusetts: Harvard Business School Press, pp. 19–39.
46 Kaye, B. and Jordan-Evans, S. (1999) *Love 'em or Lose 'em: Getting Good People to Stay*, San Francisco: Berrett-Koehler Publishers, p. 9.
47 Branham, L. (2005) *The 7 Hidden Reasons Employees Leave*, New York: AMACOM, p. 208.
48 Ibid.
49 Hart, C. (2007) Beating the market with customer satisfaction, *Harvard Business Review*, March, pp. 30–32.
50 Branham, L. (2005) *The 7 Hidden Reasons Employees Leave*, New York: AMACOM, pp. 3&4.
51 Cascio, W. (2006) The high costs of low wages, *Harvard Business Review*, December, p. 23.
52 Sirota, D., et al. (2005) *The Enthusiastic Employee*, Upper Saddle River, New Jersey: Wharton School Publishing, p. 9.

53 These factors are pretty common – see Sirota, D., et al. (2005) *The Enthusiastic Employee*, Upper Saddle River, New Jersey: Wharton School Publishing, p.15 and Dychtwald, K., et al. (2006) *Workforce Crisis*, Boston Massachusetts: Harvard Business School Press, pp. 207–208.

54 Heskett, J., et al. (1994) Putting the service-profit chain to work, *Harvard Business Review*, March–April.

55 For a detailed discussion on the needs of each cohort see Dychtwald, K., et al. (2006) *Workforce Crisis*, Boston Massachusetts: Harvard Business School Press, pp. 35–134.

56 Booth, R. (2007) Generation Y speaks: it's all me, me, me, *Sunday Times*, 4 February, p. 5.

57 HM Treasury (2005) The 2005 productivity and competitiveness indicators, URN 05/1955 pp. 8–9.

58 Von Stamm, B. (2003) *The Innovation Wave*, Chichester: John Wiley & Sons.

59 Ibid., p. 2.

60 IBM Global Business Services (2006) Expanding the innovation horizon: The global CEO survey 2006, p. 11.

61 Von Stamm, B. (2003) *The Innovation Wave*, Chichester: John Wiley & Sons, p. 31.

62 www.chartic.com, Avoiding the black hole of commoditization.

63 Seybold, P. (2006) *Outside Innovation: How Your Customers Will Co-design Your Company's Future*, New York: Collins, p. 3.

64 Thull, J. (2005) Value creation: the new core competency, www.marketingProfs.com.

65 Seybold, P. (2006) *Outside Innovation: How Your Customers Will Co-design Your Company's Future*, New York: Collins, p. 5.

66 Ibid., pp. 30–50.

67 Ibid., pp. 80–99.

68 Mitchell, A. (2007) Advertisers turn to science to get inside consumers' heads, *Financial Times*, 5 January, p. 10.

69 Surowiecki, J. (1998) The commoditization conundrum, www.slate.com.

70 Ries, A. and Ries, L. (2004) *The Origin of Brands*, New York: HarperCollins, p. 139.

71 Chin, G. (2006) A way cool strategy: Toyota's Scion plans to sell fewer cars, *The Wall Street Journal*, 19 November, pp. 1–2.

72 Frank, T. and Stone, A. (2007) Fliers' misery stings JetBlue, *USA Today*, 16–18 February, p. 1.

9 *Surviving in a Commoditized World*

The entry of Wal-Mart will be like an economic Tsunami.[1]

Marx labelled the ruling ideology of capitalism – the displacement of human relations by commodity exchange – commodity fetishism.[2]

It is clear from the last chapter that organizations have a wide range of responses to choose from when addressing the opportunities and threats posed by commoditization. Some may choose to focus on their cost base, whilst others may focus on innovation. Whatever strategy is adopted, it will be driven by a range of factors including the market or markets in which the organization operates, the nature of its competition and how easy it is for them to become commoditized. One of the things that is often helpful when weighing up the various options is to consider what other companies have done, or are doing. The purpose of this chapter is therefore to present a number of vignettes which highlight how different organizations have approached the challenge of commoditization. We will see that for some it has involved the complete reengineering of the business whilst for others it has been to concentrate on their workforce so that the benefits of full engagement can be realized. What we can conclude from these is that there are many different ways to tackle commoditization and that many do so successfully. This is helpful because it demonstrates that it is possible to work very effectively within commoditized markets. For those organizations which are comfortably outside the commoditized zone, it will give them some insights on what to do should the risk of commoditization increase to a point where action is necessary. The companies selected cover a range of industries, many of whom are global or have global ambitions. But what is particularly interesting is that for a number of the companies mentioned in this chapter the option of moving outside the commoditized zone was a real one. Therefore, just because you may find yourself trapped in a me-too commodity market, it does not mean you have to remain there.

Best Buy – smashing the clock[3]

Like all other companies in the retail sector, Best Buy, the United States' leading electronics retailer, is under immense pressure to maintain its margins. Working within the fully commoditized end of the continuum they have to contend with significant competitive pressures from companies which include Wal-Mart and Target as well as customers who expect more product for less outlay. The workforce is fairly typical of a low cost operator with the work being tightly defined and controlled with significant pressures on employees to hit targets and make sales. Although moving into services through the introduction of Geek Squad and a customer centricity programme in which the sales force become technology consultants, Best Buy found that it was afflicted by high levels of stress, burnout and a significant increase in staff turnover. To combat this local managers, with the help of a couple of far sighted people from HR, introduced a results only work environment (ROWE) in which staff can work the hours and schedules they like so long as they deliver the results expected of them. It wasn't long before things started to change and ROWE spread across Best Buy's head office. Staff can now turn up to the office when they want to, leave early to pursue their outside interests and hobbies and deal with the needs of their families which so often suffer when hours are long and demands are high. There are no mandatory meetings, schedules or any requirement to maintain face time in the office. Although currently concentrated within Best Buy's head office, the results speak for themselves: increased employee satisfaction, engagement and productivity (up by 35 per cent) and a significant reduction in voluntary turnover. The clockless office is also proving to be a major pull for new recruits and Best Buy is also seeking to exploit its experience and create new revenue streams by working with other organizations who want to achieve something similar. So not only have they been able to improve the level of employee engagement, which is often difficult within a commoditized business, but they have also identified a new area for the company to exploit which, as yet at least, is outside the commoditized zone. Although many organizations currently employ some form of flexible working no one has done it so resolutely as Best Buy. And in the commoditized zone you need to look after all your employees; high turnover hits profits as we saw with Wal-Mart's Sam's Club in the previous chapter.

Ryanair – moving from high to low cost provider

Ryanair is a perfect example of how an organization is capable of transforming itself from a high to a low cost provider. It also demonstrates how radical such a transformation has to be if it is to succeed and how it is possible to change consumer behaviour to allow the organization to expand and take market share from its established rivals.

Ryanair was started in 1985 by the Ryan family and at that time operated a single aircraft from Waterford (Ireland) to Gatwick (England) and had a staff of just 25. By year end some 5000 people had flown with them and their staff had grown to 51. Over the next four years it expanded rapidly acquiring new planes and opening new routes, including some regular services into continental Europe. By the end of 1989 they had 477 staff and some 644 000 people had flown on their aircraft. Then the crunch came as the level of investment combined with the intense competition and pricing strategies of its principal competitors, British Airways and Aer Lingus, started to unravel the business. Although passenger and staff numbers rose slightly, the firm accumulated £20 million in losses. The initial strategy of undercutting its rivals by up to 50 per cent was only successful in the short term as both British Airways and Aer Lingus cut their high fares in response. If it was to survive it had to remodel itself and undergo a significant transformation. Basing itself on Southwest Airlines, the successful United States low cost airline, Ryanair brought in Michael O'Leary to turn the business around.

O'Leary recognized that if Ryanair was to be successful it had to be up to 90 per cent cheaper than its established rivals, as it would be impossible for them to match such low fares. Cutting fares alone would not make the company profitable however, so O'Leary completely remodelled the basis of travel to allow low fares to drive profitable growth. The key changes he introduced included:

- Standardizing the fleet on Boeing 737s and thereby simplifying the engineering and maintenance needs of the airline. The existing fleet consisted of 14 different aircraft which made the ongoing maintenance unnecessarily expensive.
- Operating from secondary cities rather than secondary airports around primary cities.
- Eliminating indirect and manual booking by first moving to shared service centres to book over the telephone and then to the Internet so that all booking was direct with the customer.
- Concentrating purely on economy and leisure travellers and eliminating business class from the aircraft.
- Ceasing the serving of free meals and drinks to passengers, instead offering a limited range of simple snacks and beverages for sale which saved three cabin staff.
- Increasing the turnaround of aircraft through the elimination of assigned seating and carrying freight.
- Simplifying ground operations and aircraft maintenance to allow it to outsource both.

The result of this transformation speaks for itself. By 1995 they overtook Aer Lingus and British Airways to become the largest passenger airline on the Dublin–London route and transported over two million passengers and by 2002 became Europe's number one airline for customer service beating all other European airlines for punctuality, fewer cancellations and the least lost bags. By the end of 2006 Ryanair carried a record 42.5 million passengers (an increase of 22 per cent) on 436 routes across 24 countries, had 100 Boeing 737-800s in its fleet and followed its established rivals such as easyJet and British Airways by introducing online check-in. In 2007 it became the world's largest international airline in terms of passenger numbers.[4]

Ryanair continues to innovate and change at both the back and front ends of its business. For example it will be enticing its passengers to carry hand baggage only by charging for bags which are carried in the hold of the aircraft and it continues to cut costs, which in 2006 were reduced by 6 per cent. As an exemplar of how to survive within the commoditized zone Ryanair has demonstrated how it can be done.

Wal-Mart – supply chain par excellence

When Sam Walton established Wal-Mart in Bentonville in 1962 he founded the company on the principle of providing everyday low prices to his customers. To achieve this he focused on improving sales, reducing costs, implementing efficient distribution and logistics processes and applying technology innovatively. Most important however was his belief that any savings should be passed directly to his customers, rather than increasing the profits of the company. And it was this that set Wal-Mart aside from its competitors. Nothing has changed since the early days of Wal-Mart except its size; it is now the largest retailer in the world. In 2005, Wal-Mart reported a net income of $10.3 billion from earnings of $285 billion.[5]

One of the principal reasons why Wal-Mart has achieved this pre-eminence is because of its highly efficient supply chain management practices. Today Wal-Mart is able to offer a vast range of products at the lowest cost in the shortest possible times through its highly automated distribution centres and its inventory system which has reduced shipping times and costs and speeded up the checking out time and recording of transactions.[6] Unwrapping this further allows us to identify some of the factors which make Wal-Mart's supply chain management one of the best there is. First, when it comes to procurement Wal-Mart negotiates directly with its suppliers, cutting out all intermediaries. It also spends time with them to understand and improve their cost base so that they (Wal-Mart) can be assured they are getting the lowest price possible. Second, with respect to distribution Wal-Mart retains control over this by using its own warehouses so that it is capable of supplying 85 per cent of its inventory. This allows it to replenish stock within two days and keep its shipping costs to around 3 per cent,[7] which is much lower than its rivals. Each distribution centre uses integrated barcode technologies and increasingly RFID (Radio Frequency Identification) to pick and track the products as they move from warehouse to store. Third, in terms of logistics Wal-Mart exercises its usual tight control by employing dedicated drivers with over 300 000 accident free miles to operate the 3500 company owned trucks.[8] The operating principles under which the drivers work are explicit, monitored and reinforced and this helps to establish a smooth supply of goods from the distribution centres to the stores. In addition Wal-Mart exploited the cross-docking technique which involves the finished goods from the manufacturers being sorted and supplied direct to the customer thereby reducing the handling and storage requirements. Requisitions from individual stores are converted into purchase orders and sent direct to the manufacturers who confirm their ability to meet the deadlines associated with the order. This has led to changes in the way Wal-Mart has managed its supply chain as cross-docking made the process far more customer pull than retailer push, which in turn has reduced the need for centralized control. The final aspect is associated with inventory management which is where Wal-Mart has probably invested the most in IT. Their inventory system is able to track sales and merchandise in its stores across the United States and can even inform staff in individual stores where products are in the supply chain (in the distribution centre, being loaded onto a truck or on their way to the store). It is also able to reduce unproductive inventory by allowing individual stores to manage their own stock levels and most critically by using a retail link system which connects Wal-Mart to the thousands of suppliers, allowing suppliers to monitor the sales of their goods and replenish inventories as their products are sold.[9]

Of course to be successful Wal-Mart has had to engage with its suppliers. The earliest example of this was the alliance established with Proctor & Gamble which incorporated vendor-managed inventory, category management and other inter-company innovations. Proctor & Gamble even opened an office next to Wal-Mart's head office in Bentonville so that a dedicated team which represented their key functions such as sales and marketing, distribution and supply chain management and IT were on site ready to improve and enhance the service provided to their most significant customer.[10] This relationship became the basis from which Wal-Mart redesigned and computerized its dealings with all its major suppliers.[11] Today there are around 400 Proctor & Gamble employees on the Bentonville site and they have been joined by 500 of Wal-Mart's largest suppliers who like Proctor & Gamble have opened offices in northwest Arkansas to be close to their principal source of income.[12]

More recently and in order to overcome the inconsistent supply chain language used across its supplier base, Wal-Mart has initiated a programme to ensure all its suppliers understand the roles, processes and metrics associated with the retail supply chain. They have partnered with Accenture's Supply Chain Academy and the Retail Industry Leaders Association to produce and market a Retail Supply Chain Certification programme.[13] The benefits of the certification are clear, and especially so to Wal-Mart, as it standardizes the language used between trading partners which reduces the time spent debating inventory policy definitions, forecasts and other technical details. It also establishes the basis for building and rewarding supply chain expertise. And finally it will allow supply chain staff to concentrate on the forward thinking elements of effective supply chain management, such as demand-driven supply networks, demand forecasting and inventory optimization.[14]

Geely Group – growing off the back of outsourcing

The Chinese company Geely Group has been able to exploit the upside of outsourcing by leveraging the increased levels of process knowledge that have come with the offshoring of the manufacturing and design of automobiles. When the first cars rolled off the production line six years ago they were crude and the annual production was very small at around 5000. Today that number has increased to 180 000 per annum and Geely now makes sports cars and sedans, exports to Latin America, the Middle East and Russia and is supplying the Black Cabs you see around London's narrow medieval streets. According to Li Shufu, Geely's chairman, how to make cars is no longer a big secret because the technology and processes to design and manufacture automobiles are now common and widely available. In fact it has been the shift to outsourcing nearly everything associated with the car industry that has allowed this to happen. Today pretty much everything has been outsourced – from the initial design through to component manufacture – and this is making it far easier for companies such as Geely to join the ranks of the major car manufacturers. So in many ways cars have become a commodity, but as Bill Ford, Ford's chairman commented recently, 'It's easy to build a car; it's harder to build a brand'.[15] And as we saw in the previous chapter brand is a key factor in fighting the commodity magnet. That said, it is clear that the American car giants such as General Motors and Ford are struggling to compete with their more nimble competitors.

Starbucks – extending the coffee experience into a brand

As we saw in Chapter 2, it is remarkable how coffee, one of the most basic of commodities, has been transformed into a lifestyle product that seemingly few of us can do without. And none have done this quite so well as Starbucks. Starting out in Seattle, Washington, in 1971 its dream was to transform the coffee drinking experience of the average American, by combining high quality coffee with the charm and romance of the European coffee house.[16] Starbucks' success speaks for itself; since 1992 its stock price has increased by 5000 per cent, the number of people employed by them has grown from 100 in 1987 to 100 000 in 2006[17] and today it sells four million coffee drinks every day in the US alone. There are a number of factors which have allowed Starbucks to achieve such a remarkable and sustainable track record and one of the most prominent is the way it treats its staff. Apart from allowing them to share in the wealth of the business, they provide extensive training in product knowledge, guiding principles for success, personal empowerment and building great customer experiences. They also ensure that staff understand the link between their efforts, the customer experience and the profitability of the company. New partners are given a 104 page booklet that they complete within their first 90 days of employment. This includes a map of the coffee growing regions of the world, information on farming, roasting and brewing and the range of flavours that Starbucks offers their customers. Partners are also expected to complete verified tastings twice a year and each is given a pound of coffee each week to continue to develop their knowledge of the coffees which Starbucks sells. Over time, they are also given the opportunity to become coffee masters – true experts in their field. Such attention to developing a consistent approach to the delivery of their product and ensuring their staff are knowledgeable is one of the ways Starbucks develops a strong corporate identity. And this pays significant dividends for the business especially in terms of retention and building strong relationships with existing as well as new customers. Turnover is 120 per cent lower than the industry average for those working in the quick-service restaurant sector.[18] But there is more to Starbucks than this, as despite being within a commoditized market, they take time to innovate. Such innovations may not be massive, or indeed require major investment, but they are critical to the brand. Such things as the ubiquitous recycled cardboard sleeve (aped by many of their competitors) and the introduction of the gift card are just two examples. In many respects Starbucks has made drinking coffee into a social phenomenon, which they now want to leverage.

Not content with changing the way we drink, and how and where we work, Starbucks wants to become a global corporation to rival McDonalds. Unlike McDonalds, however, Starbucks intends to influence pop culture from what music we listen to, what books we choose to read and what films we watch. Considering their influence so far, they have been able to:

- make it acceptable to pay $4 for a cup of coffee;
- raise the quality and taste of the coffee we buy, forcing McDonalds and Burger King to follow suit;
- introduce mass customization into the ordering process, giving the consumer total choice in how they want their coffee configured;
- make healthy food fashionable through the introduction of a range of food which is better for their customers;
- create an environment where people can meet, socialize and conduct their business – following in the footsteps of the coffee house which was at the centre of the emerging financial and insurance industries in 17th century England. Everything the company does is designed to create and reinforce a positive experience while buying and consuming their food and beverages;[19]
- bring the awareness of social and environmental issues to the wider population, by means ranging from using Fair Trade coffee growers to the use of recycled material. For example, they are replacing 5 per cent of the energy used in their US stores with wind energy, reducing their carbon emissions by 2 per cent and have set a goal of providing $10 million to water projects in developing countries in the next five years.[20]

With such an influence, it's no wonder that Starbucks wants to take this further and use its influence elsewhere. For example, two years ago they established Starbucks Entertainment, which they wish to use as a vehicle through which their name can be associated with music, films and books. So far they have promoted the Ray Charles Genius Loves Company CD (of which their stores have sold 835 000 copies – about 25 per cent of the total) and the Akeelah and the Bee movie (which has been less successful). It is also looking to promote books and provide entertainment downloads by improving the wi-fi networks already in its stores. With five more stores opening every day worldwide, its long term goal is to have 30 000 globally. By reaching into normal peoples' lives and changing the way individuals eat, drink and perceive the world around them, Starbucks is likely to become the pop culture guru it wants to be.

However, there is no room for complacency as even a brand such as Starbucks is at risk of being viewed and treated as a commodity by its customers. A recent memo from the Chairman, Howard Shultz[21] outlines the risks of commoditization and the need to remain vigilant. In his memo he questions some of the decisions made by Starbucks as it has expanded over the last ten years and believes some of them have watered down or commoditized the brand. He claims that although many of the decisions were right at the time, it has been their cumulative effect which has resulted in the dilution of the Starbucks experience. For example swapping out the old espresso machines for ones which are automated may have solved the issue of efficiency, but it has reduced the romance and intimacy of watching the coffee being made by the barista. In another example, he cites how the move to flavour locked packaging (needed to supply the thousands of stores across the USA and every international market) has reduced the aroma that is part of the attraction. The biggest issue he believes has been the loss of the store's soul and neighbourhood feel, primarily due to the need to streamline store design and satisfy the financial side of the business. Indeed according to his memo, customers are viewing the stores as sterile and no longer reflecting the passion the partners feel about Starbucks coffee. He believes all of this has allowed the competition to steal market share and he feels this loss of competitive advantage should be eradicated by returning to the core of what made Starbucks what it is – the heritage, tradition and passion that is central to the Starbucks experience.

Avon – focusing on costs; benefiting its representatives

Avon has been selling cosmetics through its network of representatives for over 120 years and up until very recently it has always done well no matter what the political or economic environments were doing. Since it started in 1886, more than 40 million women have sold its products and today the business has 5 million representatives operating in 120 countries with annual sales of $9 billion.[22] As the world's largest seller of beauty products it is under increasing pressure from other direct sales companies such as Nu Skin Enterprises and Mary Kay as well as the mass market businesses such as Proctor & Gamble. In order to address both the competition and a decline in profits, Avon is aiming to transform itself over a period of three years, the result of which will save at least $300 million. But it is not a purely cost driven initiative, as Avon intends to double its advertising spend, recruit stars including Salma Hayek and the Hollywood makeup artist Jillian Dempsey, focus its research and development resources on product innovation and make its brand more competitive. Most importantly it will be recruiting and aiming to retain a larger pool of representatives – the lifeblood of the organization and without whom there would be no Avon. To support this they have launched a $340 million advertising campaign called Hello Tomorrow. In particular Avon will be improving the commission rates which tier representatives earn. The Avon Lady has moved on, with many now selling their products over the Internet, in shopping malls and even shops created in their own homes. Making the proposition attractive to the representatives has also meant moving outside the traditional cosmetics market. They have established a men's catalogue and are now offering everything from children's books to fitness- and health-focused products. They are also positioning themselves as being central to the promotion of women's issues and rights and are currently looking into such areas as domestic violence, economic empowerment, literacy and micro-lending.[23] The CEO Andrea Jung believes this is essential to distinguishing Avon from their competition. Avon is more than just an organization that sells cosmetics.

The Avon model is certainly not broken – women continue to feel very comfortable buying from their friends; it just needs to maintain its pre-eminence, addressing the challenge posed by new channels and competitors by leveraging what is core to its success – the representative.

Toyota – mastering innovation

A number of years ago Toyota and General Motors were both pursuing the development of a hybrid car that was capable of running on electricity as well as gasoline. Although General Motors was slightly ahead of Toyota at the time, having developed a prototype, the huge cost associated with its development put them off. They were not interested in selling the hybrids at a loss, so they decided to concentrate on building the gasoline cars they always had in the past. Toyota on the other hand decided to proceed and developed the Prius which is only just turning a profit after selling at a loss for a number of years.[24] The risk paid off as the Prius is now the hottest hybrid on the market and has given Toyota a significant advantage over its rivals especially in terms of the environment. Whilst their rivals still roll off 'gas-guzzlers' from their production lines, Toyota is doing their bit to reduce emissions. Whilst General Motors are losing money and closing plants, Toyota is doing the opposite, having announced the building of a $1.3 billion assembly plant in Tupelo Mississippi; its eighth in the US.[25]

Of course, Toyota was not always as well known and no one would have believed that it could rival the mighty General Motors. Fifty years ago when it entered the US market with the 60-horsepower Toyopet Crown it was a bit player in the global automobile market. From its beginning Toyota has focused on innovation, invested heavily in advanced technology and maintained a philosophy of continuous improvement.[26] Today its highly effective manufacturing method which relentlessly roots out waste and enhances quality has allowed it to sell more cars in the United States than it does in Japan and make record profits of $13 billion. Mathew May, the senior advisor to the University of Toyota, has distilled what he terms Toyota's elegant solution for mastering innovation into three principles and ten practices.[27] The three principles are:

- The art of ingenuity. Toyota sees innovation as the matter of removing organizational barriers in order to release the talents and creativity of their people. In adopting this attitude Toyota have been able to amongst otherthings, introduce ground breaking supply chain management techniques. Central to this has been their ability to engage their staff at a level at which they can understand the underlying purpose of their job. So staff see themselves as protecting families as they travel, not just as operators of machinery.[28]
- The pursuit of perfection. For Toyota there is no other choice but perfection. This sets them aside from their competition and makes it hard to replicate their success. When you consider that Toyota's workers on the factory floor might implement up to a dozen ideas on every shift and managers may well spend 50 per cent of their time on a range of ideas you can see why it is near impossible for anyone observing to absorb or replicate what is going on.[29] Toyota pursues this perfection by starting with the ideal outcome and working backwards, so instead of looking at what can be improved they start with understanding what could block perfection (the ideal) and then do their best to remove those blocks. This is exactly what they did to create the luxury Lexus brand of automobile. Starting with the ideal of besting BMW and Mercedes they worked tirelessly to establish what is now the de facto standard for luxury motoring.[30]
- The rhythm of fit. Toyota learned early on the importance of fit when the Toyopet Crown failed to make any real headway into the Los Angeles market; the little car simply did not fit with the sprawling highways of the city and was prone to overheating and severe shaking, consumed excessive amounts of gas and oil and could not even accommodate the average sized American.[31] Developing their cars in isolation and away from their markets

was no longer viable but viewing them as part of a wider system was, and it would be eight years before Toyota would re-enter the US car market.

The ten practices are:

1. Let learning lead. Toyota believes learning is central to their success and this has helped them to be one of the prime examples of a learning organization. By integrating learning into the day-to-day job and supporting this through the Toyota university, technical training centres and knowledge management systems, they have ensured learning is part and parcel of their culture.[32]

2. Learn to see. Toyota practices the outside-in innovation approach discussed in the previous chapter and takes it to the point where they will immerse themselves into their customers' lifestyles in order to design cars which will be successful. For example, when designing the Lexus, staff actually lived the life of luxury for a period of time so that they could understand how a car could best meet the comfort and exclusivity needs of the wealthy.[33]

3. Design for today. Toyota is careful to develop their range of cars for real needs, not those which might be perceived or which attempt to second guess the market. In many respects this is a bit like the shift towards selling solutions instead of products mentioned in the last chapter. Toyota calls this approach market-in and this involves them understanding what wider factors are playing out now which could develop new opportunities in the future. Using this approach they were able to influence the market into accepting the hybrid automobile (the Prius) and build a car for the upcoming generation Y cohort (the Scion, mentioned in the previous chapter).[34]

4. Think in pictures. Building a picture of the future is one way in which Toyota is able to bring their product strategies to life and was central to the development of the Lexus. Early on in this process they used a multimedia educational immersion experience to ensure that every associate understood the new brand and its strategic direction. As a result the ideas were more readily accepted and the relationships between the underlying concepts and the practical realities of the car easily understood.[35] And the principle of making it visual and alive was used to great success when the concept of the Scion was presented to the board.[36]

5. Capture the intangible. If all Toyota did was sell cars they might be in the same position as many of their rivals. However, they don't. Toyota recognizes that people buy their cars for a variety of reasons, many of which are emotional in nature. Whilst those who buy the Lexus want it to say something about their lifestyle and status, those that drive the Scion want to look youthful and cool. These intangibles are significant factors in the design of all Toyota models and are something that sets them aside from their competitors.

6. Leverage the limits. It is too tempting to allow budgets, the workforce and inventory to grow as a company grows, but some of the things which may have made it successful in its early years can be lost as the organization gets fat and complacent. Indeed, it may even lead to its downfall. Within Toyota, the reverse is true. They constantly strive to improve by setting powerful limits on resources to ensure they apply their ingenuity and creativity to come up with solutions which both work and provide value for money. Using this approach they were able to reduce the running costs of the North American Parts Operation by $100 million, take out $90 million from their inventory and improve customer satisfaction by 35 per cent and all within three years – which at the time was thought to be impossible.[37]

7. Master the tension. Toyota use what they term dynamic tension to ensure that the obvious solutions to a problem are not automatically selected and to ensure that success requires different thinking. It is this that is credited with helping to arrive at the Lexus and Prius and with the creation of their Competitive Design Strategy.[38]
8. Run the numbers. Innovation is not just an art and at the heart of the Toyota approach is the discipline of numbers, data and facts, as without it there could be no true breakthrough. They do not fall into the classic either/or problems associated with innovation – either driven too much by hard numbers or left to the creative geniuses of research and development. For Toyota it is both.
9. Make Kaizen mandatory. Kaizen is the Japanese word for continuous improvement and this is what makes Toyota what it is today. Few companies have embraced continuous improvement in quite the same way as Toyota and it helps them to maintain one of the best records for reliability. It also ensures that they continue to innovate on a daily basis and that new ideas come from everyone across the business day after day.
10. Keep it lean. The final element to Toyota's approach to innovation involves minimizing complexity as much as possible. Whether this is within their supply chain or in their university, keeping things simplified ensures new ideas flow more effectively; and if they do, innovation will follow.

Tesco – building and leveraging customer loyalty

Tesco is not only the UK's number one retailer, it is also the world's most successful Internet supermarket, and Europe's fastest growing financial services provider. Central to Tesco's continued success is their singular focus on building and leveraging customer loyalty. If you wander into the headquarters of Tesco in Cheshunt in the UK, you will see the centrality of customer loyalty enshrined within their mission statement on a plaque on the wall. It states that the company's core purpose is to *create value for customers and to earn their lifetime loyalty*. Central to Tesco's dominance of the UK's retail market has been the continued success of its Clubcard loyalty card programme. The card was piloted in 1993 and rolled out nationally in 1994 in the belief that it could deliver more than a boost to like-for-like sales. Tesco were looking for an increase in customer goodwill and ultimately loyalty.[39] In a highly competitive market in which the price of goods is the most significant factor in the average consumer's choice, Tesco knew that if they could create a powerful following through the Clubcard they could keep their existing customers coming through their doors and could grow market share.

Tesco had not always been so focused or indeed lucky with its loyalty campaigns. Although it was a great proponent of Green Shield Stamps, which were awarded to its customers from 1963, they did not achieve the loyalty Tesco expected and by 1977 the programme was costing the company too much (£20 million per annum) at a time when customers were losing interest in Tesco, which they believed was too expensive. The Green Shield Stamp programme was cancelled.[40] This marked the beginning of the transformation of Tesco that took it to the development of the Clubcard. Key to being able to make the Clubcard work and to locking-in their existing customers was linking spending patterns to real people so that the reward vouchers could be sent directly to the customer's home address. This made the Clubcard more powerful than any discount scheme because it personalized it and ensured that it kept their customers interested. This was in sharp contrast to Sainsbury's rival scheme which depended on customers taking their rewards on demand (which meant as they were paying for their shopping at the checkout). The early results were better than the board could have hoped for; over 80 per cent of the daily sales were coming from Clubcard members. And over the next 18 months, Tesco adapted and advanced the Clubcard concept in terms of how it rewarded its customers, how it turned customer data into valuable customer knowledge and how the card and its benefits were marketed. By May 2006 over £80 million was paid to Tesco customers every quarter, significantly more than the £14 million that was paid out when it was launched in 1995.[41] Today this money can be spent on a whole range of food and non-food items, which includes books and magazines, holidays, days out, theme parks, film hire and so on. Over the course of a year, the rewards add up to be quite significant and can for example allow a family of four to travel on the Eurostar to Paris or Brussels for £100 in Clubcard vouchers. The usual price would be £400.

What has made Tesco's Clubcard programme so successful and its sustained growth so profound has been the creation of a strong bond between their customers and the brand. This customer-Tesco contract has five steps and neatly encapsulates how they have established a virtuous cycle which continues to pay dividends in a highly competitive and commoditized market:[42]

1.   Identify individual customers.
2.   Reward involvement, spend, consolidation of spend.
3.   Build dynamic customer knowledge.
4.   Create accurate segmentation for marketing efficiency.
5.   Enable more personal, relevant service to customers.

Clubcard has provided Tesco with a number of real options, but the most significant has been their launch into the e-commerce space. At the very outset Tesco decided to integrate Clubcard with Tesco.com and in this way was able to lock the customer in to the point where 93.9 per cent of purchasers shop loyally. Moreover, because it already had the details and shopping habits of its customers this made the transition to the online environment a lot smoother and much less costly than many of the online stores found during the Dot Com boom; all that was needed was the Clubcard number. Using a combination of the offline data collected from Clubcard customers in-store and that accumulated online Tesco was also able to eliminate many of the other problems associated with the early forays into online food stores, such as the willingness to purchase fresh food. The centrality of data continues to provide dividends and increase the number of regular shoppers who are willing to become loyal customers of Tesco. For example, they are using customer profiling to understand which categories of shopper are likely to use the online store and combining this with outside customer data to attract new customers using a combination of targeted mail shots and email to entice them onto the site and from this into their stores.[43] This is proving to be a significant untapped growth area for the company. The continued power of the Tesco brand lies in its ability to connect with the customer, give them what they want, when they want it and through this generate the value and the lifetime loyalty, which is gold dust in the commoditized world.

GE – dominating markets and adapting to changing environment

GE has been in business for over 126 years and yet it is probably not the same business it was when it was founded by Thomas Edison in 1879. Its leaders have come and gone and some have been more iconic than others, with Jack Welch being the most prominent. GE's success has been put down to a number of factors, including leadership, talent, influence (over a whole range of stakeholders which includes government bodies through to unions) and management systems (indeed today we use many of the techniques developed by GE), but it is their adaptability that is possibly the most significant factor in their continued success.[44]

GE's roots lie within the electricity industry, which in the late 19th century was still in its infancy. Edison understood the need to adapt and even drive this new market and he did this by bringing his inventor's discipline and vision to the organizational setting. Instead of dismissing other peoples' ideas and failures, Edison was willing to experiment, adapt and build upon others' work and then exploit this for financial gain. He supported this by protecting his patents and copyrighting everything; he had over 1000 approved patents. More important, however, was Edison's desire to dominate the markets in which he operated. He did this through a combination of equity ownership, licensing, partnerships and helping his customers by taking an equity position in their businesses. In that way, they were able to leverage and build on the Edison name and he was able to maintain a stake in their companies.[45] In addition to dominating the markets in which they operated, GE also began to adapt. As the emerging electricity and utility industry expanded, they recognized that they could no longer continue to finance the nascent companies on their own, so GE established EBASCO (the Electric Bond and Share Company) to finance the electric utilities and this not only stabilized the industry, but it also provided the basis for negotiating with state regulators.

During the 1920s and 1930s, when the management of GE passed over to Swope and Young, the focus on maintaining the company's position remained powerful. In order to do this they used a variety of approaches, including franchising, controlling retail prices and relationship selling.[46] Although important, it was the application of the benign cycle strategy that allowed GE to maintain its market dominance. By building and marketing an increasing number of electrical products across all of its markets it would stimulate greater demand for electricity which would require the utility industry to upgrade its systems, which GE would supply.[47] This strategy allowed GE to remain profitable throughout the Depression. And in the same way they dominated the electricity industry they managed to dominate the emerging radio and broadcasting industries.

During the next phase of their evolution GE became heavily involved with the US war effort and were able to apply their know-how to the requirements of the military. During this period, the focus of GE shifted away from consumers as they took direction from the military. The most significant dividend from this was diversification which ensured the company was well positioned for the consumer boom which followed the end of the war. The other principle benefit which this brought was recognition that growth could be achieved through internal means and talent rather than through acquisition or merger. And to achieve this, GE took the trouble to identify and nurture its talent and professionalize its management. This theme of being in the vanguard of many of the management techniques that we now take for granted was something that would continue as GE was guided under the direction of Jack Welch, who was the unexpected winner from the leadership race that preceded the retirement of the then CEO Reg Jones.[48] Welch's selection was another indication of GE's core strength of adaptability because Jones recognized that the company needed a leader with new ideas and a different style.[49]

One of the first things that Welch did was to address the sacred cows within GE. He believed that if the company was to continue to be successful each business had to either grow and lead its chosen markets or be sold off. In the first two years of his tenure Welch sold off 71 product lines and completed 188 deals.[50] Part of his success was down to his willingness to allow the GE logo to be sold off with each of the businesses – just one of the many sacred cows. In many respects Welch epitomized GE's adaptability which he encapsulated within his six rules.[51]

1. Face reality as it is, not as it was or as you wish it were.
2. Be candid with everyone.
3. Don't manage; lead.
4. Change before you have to.
5. If you don't have competitive advantage, don't compete.
6. Control your destiny, or someone else will.

Of these it is the fourth and sixth which are focused on adaptation and the third and fifth which focus on dominating their chosen markets. Not satisfied with applying this to the portfolio of businesses, Welch also applied it to his managers and leaders so that only the best were rewarded and those at the bottom of the performance scale were sacked. Brutal perhaps, but Welch knew that the ability to adapt to dominate their chosen markets required managers and leaders who could do the same. Welch was willing to seek out and apply any techniques and tools that would satisfy the objectives of the company and many companies watch what GE does before following suit. Jeff Immelt who succeeded Neutron Jack in 2001 has continued to grow the firm, despite the belief that Jack Welch *was* GE.

Dell – standardization and selling direct to the customer[52]

Dell started out a little over three years after the first IBM PC hit the market in 1981 and today it is the largest PC sales company in the US and the world.[53] Its success can be put down to a number of things, but the three most important elements are: cutting out the middleman, pursuing a strategy of component-based standardization and keeping its inventory as low as possible. When the company started, PCs were largely sold through retailers. Although this model worked, Dell believed that a more efficient model was possible by eliminating the middle man and selling direct to the customer. This allowed them to sell their computers at a lower price than the competition, which saved the company between 25 and 45 per cent of the mark up typically made on computers sold through the retailers.[54] However, although Dell was successful in cutting out the middleman and driving down costs, it was the focus on component standardization that allowed it to truly thrive. And in the same way that Ryanair was able to change the focus of the airline industry, Dell has done the same within the computer hardware industry.

Dell applies the principals of commoditization extremely well and does so by initially watching what the market does. When new technology arrives, such as the PC, it tends to be proprietary in that the hardware tends to be created in its entirety by the manufacturer. This restricts competition and allows the manufacturer to capture market share through the first mover advantage, and to keep its margins high. This continues until others enter the market which leads to increased competition and a standardization of the technology. This is used by Dell as a key indicator of potential market returns and this is when they take action. Their aim is to both undercut and outperform the existing suppliers by building machines using less expensive, off-the-shelf, standardized parts.[55] Once Dell has entered the market it becomes almost impossible for the incumbents to force their customer base back to proprietary hardware; HP and IBM have both tried to do this and both have been unable to reverse the trend. Apart from the price sensitivity, it is also due to the customers' refusal to limit their choice to one supplier who has the power to charge what it likes. The final element of Dell's success has been the focus on its inventory and taking its build-to-order process to the extreme. In 2000 Dell had about six days worth of inventory and by 2005 it had reduced this as low as two hours in some of its plants. Dell has placed the onus on its suppliers to deliver the components it needs to build PCs and other hardware just in time and in order to do this many have co-located their factories next to Dell's. It is able to fund this by billing customers as soon as they make an order and then paying its suppliers between 30 and 45 days later. Other factors that have made this possible include reducing its supplier base, letting the suppliers hold the inventory, and only taking delivery of the components when it needs to.[56]

Semco – respecting staff and reaping the dividends

The Brazilian company Semco has no official structure, no organizational chart, no business plan and no strategy. It has no mission statement, no budget, no fixed CEO, no vice presidents, no standards or practices and no HR department. There are no job descriptions, career plans or contracts.[57] And yet Semco is a very successful company which has grown significantly since 1995 when the founder's son, Ricardo Semler, took over the company and executed what could only be described as radical change. During this time the company has grown from a $35 million turnover business with 350 employees to a $160 million company with 3000 staff.

The focus of the company is broad and diverse and includes machinery, new business start-ups, real estate and industrial products. Each of the business units within the company operates under three principles. First, they must be addressing a complex business requirement and if there is not a high complexity barrier to entry then Semco will not enter the market. Second, they have to be the premium player within that market and offer a high-end product. In this way they are often the most expensive and can stretch what the customer will pay. And third, they must be a niche player as they want to be in a position where, if they left, there would be a major outcry from their customers.[58] But it is not what it does that makes Semco special, it's the way it goes about it.

Like any other organization that works in competitive markets, establishing high-end products and niches is critical and an effective way to beat off the competition. But it is how Semco addresses the people issues that sets it aside from many of its competitors. When Semler first took over the company from his father it was a traditional company in every respect with a typical pyramid structure, with rules, regulations, standards and procedures.[59] All this has changed because of Semler's guiding principle of trusting his employees. He does not believe them to be mindless slaves who are paid to do what they are told, but instead considers each and every one of them to be responsible for the cooperative effort required to make products and the company a success.[60] Semco has made employees central to the organization's successes, so rather than being treated as a commodity, they are viewed as strategically important and highly valued. Examples of how Semco achieves this include:

1. Profit sharing is democratic with employees deciding how the 25 per cent allocated each year is distributed.
2. When new employees are being brought into the company, their potential work colleagues and supervisor all have a chance to interview them. This allows everyone to understand the strengths and capabilities of the new hires and in turn accelerates their induction into the business.
3. Workers can organize how they and their local team work, which extends to the design and functioning of the working environment. Factory workers can come into work anytime between 07:00 and 09:00; employees can paint machinery, add plants and generally make the environment their own. There are no rules or restrictions.
4. Whenever the company is considering taking over another business, everyone has the opportunity to discuss the appropriateness of the acquisition. This may even entail the company shutting down for a day to allow everyone to engage in the process and the associated discussion. If they decide that the new business is not right for them, then it will not be acquired.
5. Once a worker has been with the company for three years they cannot be dismissed without passing through a series of approvals. This is designed to increase job security but also to ensure that people are let go for the right reasons. This does not of course mean that Semco will hold onto staff who are not effective; they are as commercial as any other business.
6. Job rotation, job enrichment and job enlargement are built into the company ethos so that each employee is expected to move to another part of the business every couple of years and new employees are expected to work in 12 departments in their first 12 months with the company. This approach ensures that staff remain motivated for longer. And by continuously learning new skills they develop a broader appreciation and understanding of the business and the contribution others bring.

The dividends which this approach has delivered are the envy of most other companies and many visit Semco's headquarters every year. Profits have risen fivefold, productivity is up sevenfold and they have one of the lowest staff turnover rates on record. It is the company in Brazil that graduates and talent want to work for, which speaks volumes about just how effective Semler has been in his transformation.

Lafarge's cement division – segmenting the customer base to escape the commodity market[61]

Lafarge's cement division is one of the world's largest producers of cement and yet it only holds 6 per cent of the market share, which demonstrates the fragmented and commoditized nature of the market in which they operate. Against this setting the focus was on sales, not marketing, and protecting market share without setting off a price war. Things like differentiation or developing a value proposition were never going to be on the radar. All this was going to change when François Jacques took over as the Senior Vice President for marketing in 2002. The transformation took some four years to complete and involved putting marketing rather than sales in the driving seat and more importantly changing the commodity mindset which was prevalent within the cement division. By focusing on customer segmentation Lafarge was able to see that they were selling to different groups that required different products. In many cases the product could be sold at a higher price than the existing commodity price which they were wedded to. Changing this mindset meant talking to customers to uncover their needs (see also the previous chapter where I discussed the shift from a product to a solution mindset), redesigning the supply chain and changing the offerings to meet a range of customer requirements. Over time this increased the value to both Lafarge and their customers and led to the creation of a customer relation management tool which Lafarge uses to protect prices without compromising sales volume. The results speak for themselves; in 2003, the first year of operation Jacques' work contributed $6 million to the bottom line and as of today the contribution totals $150 million, which is the equivalent of a 2 per cent price increase. This is expected to rise even further in 2008 to $260 million, which will be equivalent to a 3.5 per cent price increase. Achieving this was not easy, but there are some key lessons from Lafarge's experience that can be applied to those who feel trapped within commodity markets.

1. Make lots of friends – like any top down driven initiative its success depended on both gaining the support from the senior stakeholders within the Lafarge business and more critically the general managers of the cement division, without whom the initiative would fail; they were the ones that had to shine, not marketing. This required a number of things; including acknowledging and addressing some of the past initiatives that failed to improve the cement division's commodity mindset; remaining in the background and being patient. Eventually in late 2005 when the 900 cement executives convened for their five yearly get together marketing took up a third of the agenda and none of the presentations were by marketing – a true sign that things had changed.
2. Begin with the basics – as with many functional specialisms, people do not necessarily understand the basics despite using the terms quite freely. Focusing on generating a consistent understanding of what a customer segment was (defined by their purchasing behaviour and the sophistication of their business) and then standardizing the use of marketing terms, supported by a toolkit, ensured Lafarge were able to build the consistency it needed in the way unit managers approached the marketing-planning process. Since 2003, all 45 business units have been posting three-year marketing plans in a common format for the division-wide global marketing plan.
3. Win early, win often – creating momentum through early wins was an essential component of the initiative and this was possible through the selection of four pilots, which were designed to demonstrate that the approach would be valid everywhere. Four pilots were chosen that gave the right mix and geographic spread and these represented 16 per cent of the division's revenues. Using the early results of the segmentation identified some quick wins, as it highlighted how the same types of customer around the world were paying very different prices for the same product and how they were missing out on the opportunities presented by differentiating their product. By the end of 2003, the pilots had improved the bottom line of the division by 0.1 per cent, or $6 million.
4. Measure, measure, measure – creating a measurement system from the very start was essential, even though it was imperfect. Without this it would have been difficult to connect the efforts to the bottom line and to gain commitment from the general managers. Seeking input from the customers and especially in those instances where prices were rising allowed the quid pro quo of the changes to be identified. For example, the Romanian

customers were happy to pay more, so long as the ordering and delivery processes were improved. The experience with Romania formed the basis of a global index which is used in combination with a standard customer satisfaction survey to link customer perceptions with those of Lafarge's. Still evolving, the index includes measures on innovation and the price-premium that Lafarge has over its competitors, both key to understanding how marketing is adding value to the business.

5. Share, share, share – engendering a spirit of organizational learning so that new ideas could be surfaced and pursued if valuable was key if the initiative was to have life beyond its project boundaries. Therefore building opportunities which allowed ideas to be shared and tested as part of the day-to-day business was important. This was achieved by establishing peer-to-peer forums comprising each business unit's senior marketing and sales managers who meet six times a year. Each meeting involves visiting a problem customer and exploring the causes of the problem and generating solutions. In addition Lafarge has paired the marketing and sales staff from the higher performing units with those which need improvement, which is helping to facilitate the direct transfer of knowledge and improve overall performance.

6. Stake out your territory – as the success of the initiative grew, other business units wanted to get involved and wanted to build their own marketing units. This may have been successful, but it was believed that maintaining a central marketing division would be the best approach, although this was resisted by many. To address this, a temporary task force was created with the role of bringing consistent marketing approaches to the 15 business units which delivered two thirds of the revenue. This temporary approach allowed the divisions to become familiar with an independent marketing function which by 2005 had become a permanent feature and has nearly 20 per cent of the division's high potential employees, another success for the function.

7. Find your place – integrating the new function into the existing business was not easy, but it was critical. This was achieved by securing marketing a place at the strategic and performance planning meetings that took place every year; ensuring they were included within the budgeting round so that projections attributable to marketing were included; keeping them on the agenda of each and every executive visit and placing them at the heart of Lafarge's career planning and development efforts.

Each of the vignettes covered in this chapter illustrate how organizations can tackle the commoditization of their business. Some, like Semco and Best Buy have focused on their human capital, whilst others like Wal-Mart and Ryanair have concentrated on their key business processes and especially their back offices. Each approach has yielded dividends; some greater than others, but it is important to recognize that the response developed will be contingent on a variety of factors which range from those which are market driven to those which can be considered to be entirely internal to the company. There is no one best way and it is essential to remember this when developing your own response.

Having reviewed what organizations can do and indeed are already doing to address the challenge of commoditization, we can now move onto the final chapter in this part of the book which looks at what individuals can do to survive in an increasingly commoditized working environment.

References

1 Vandana Shiva, owner of a local organic food business on Wal-Mart's arrival in India, *MoneyWeek*, 10 December 2006, p. 22.
2 Desai, M. (2002) *Marx's Revenge*, London: Verso, p. 211.
3 Conlin, M. (2006) Smashing the clock, *Businessweek* Online.
4 Robertson, D. (2007) Fewer passengers, falling profits, sliding shares – time for a price war, says Ryanair, *The Times*, 6 June, p. 51.
5 Ryan, J. (2006) Wal-Mart and China: boon or bane for American interest, *European Business School*, p. 1.
6 Richmond, B. (2003) Wal-Mart's supply chain management practices, ICFAI Center for Management Research (ICMR), p. 3.
7 Ibid., p. 4.
8 Ibid., p. 5.
9 Ibid., p. 7.
10 Byrnes, J. (2003) Supply chain management in a Wal-Mart world, Harvard Business School, *Working Knowledge*, p. 1.
11 Bianco, A. (2006) *The Bully of Bentonville: How the High Cost of Wal-Mart's Everyday Low Prices is Hurting America*, New York: Currency Doubleday, p. 180.
12 Ibid., p. 178.
13 Langdoc, S. (2005) Wal-Mart, Accenture, RILA team to bring common language to retail supply chain, AMR Research Alert.
14 Ibid.
15 Fairclough, G. (2006) As barriers fall in auto business, China jumps in, *The Wall Street Journal*, 7 November, p. 1.
16 Michelli, J. (2007) *The Starbucks Experience*, New York: McGraw-Hill, p. 2.
17 Ibid., p. 14.
18 Ibid., pp. 8–9.
19 Ibid., p. 11.
20 Ibid., p. 31.
21 This memo was picked up on the Starbucks Gossip website – http://starbucksgossip.typepad.com/_/2007/02/starbucks_chair_2.html.
22 Rushe, D. (2007) Avon lady sets out her calling, *The Sunday Times*, 11 March, pp.3–13.
23 Ibid.
24 Naughton, K. and Sloan, A. (2007) Comin' Through, *Newsweek*, 12 March, p. 42.
25 Ibid.
26 Ibid., p. 43.
27 May, M. (2007) *The Elegant Solution*, New York: Free Press.
28 Ibid., p. 25.
29 Ibid., p. 41.
30 Ibid., pp. 42–47.
31 Ibid., p. 54.
32 Ibid., pp. 71–72.
33 Ibid., pp. 86–87.
34 Ibid., pp. 99–104.
35 Ibid., p. 111.
36 Ibid., p. 119.
37 Ibid., pp. 136–142.
38 Ibid., pp. 146–151.
39 Ibid., p. 37.
40 Ibid., pp. 40–42.
41 Ibid., p. 71.
42 Ibid., p. 69.
43 Ibid., pp. 231–232.
44 Ibid., p. vi.
45 Ibid., p. 17.
46 Ibid., pp. 57–58.
47 Ibid., pp. 58–59.
48 Ibid., pp. 183–185.

49 Ibid., p. 189.
50 Ibid., p. 194.
51 Ibid., p. 208.
52 Holzner, S. (2006) *How Dell Does IT*, New York: McGraw-Hill.
53 Ibid., pp. 1–2.
54 Ibid., pp. 5–6.
55 Ibid., p. 64.
56 Ibid., pp. 85–106.
57 Semler, R. (2003) *The Seven Day Weekend*, London: Century, p. 3.
58 Ibid., p. 15.
59 Semler, R. (1999) *Maverick!*, London: Random House, p. 1.
60 2Witty (2005) History of Semco – Business Management Essay, www.freeonlineresearchpapers.com.
61 Jacques, M. (2007) Even commodities have customers, *Harvard Business Review*, May, pp. 110–119.

10 *Individual Responses*

The ability to knit together information from disparate sources into a coherent whole is vital today.[1]

Tacit interactions demand that employees make judgements based on experience and be comfortable with ambiguity. Those who undertake these interactions, such as salespeople and managers, command higher salaries and have a disproportionate impact on the organization.[2]

Instead of competitive individualism it could be a time of varied individualism. We may decide to be different from, rather than better than, our fellows.[3]

The world of work is undoubtedly changing as it has done many times over. The dynamics of aging populations, immigration and the rise of the super-educated means that anyone wishing to pursue a typical middle class career will need to be far more adaptable than ever before. At the same time organizations are beginning to respond to the pressures of an aging workforce and the rise of low cost competition by hollowing out their workforces and seeking new ways to differentiate themselves in the market. As we saw in the last chapter, corporations have a wide range of options to pursue and some of them, but by no means all, will require a workforce which is adaptable, flexible and able to turn on a dime.

The real challenge for us all is how we go about upgrading and transforming our skills to maintain our employability throughout our careers. People with outdated skills and attitudes will find it increasingly difficult to maintain a reasonable income, or in some cases, any income at all. As we have discussed throughout this book, we are already witnessing the gradual decline in benefits, pay and quality of work for a growing proportion of white-collar workers and if we are to believe the increasing number of studies, this is expected to become a greater issue over the next decade or so. It is clear that new jobs demanding old skills will not materialize; new jobs require new skills and many of the old jobs will change as they become less content rich and more technology driven. The same is true of offshoring, which although its leads to the creation of new jobs in the countries which offshore, these rarely require the same skills which have been destroyed in the process.[4] With governments and organizations generally slow to respond to these issues, it is up to individuals to ensure that they are appropriately skilled throughout their careers. Although skills are clearly important, the white-collar workers of the future will also have to face issues such as downward mobility, income stagnation and limited career prospects. All of this will test their ability to navigate through a productive and successful career.

Avoiding the risks which commoditization poses to you and your career requires a degree of discipline and ownership that many of us have had the good fortune to avoid over the course of our working lives. However, as many of the trends outlined in the earlier chapters play out, the need to become more aware of what's going on around you and be more actively engaged in defining your future will increase. So what can you do to maintain a productive career? Well the good news is that there is quite a lot you can do but before you can take any action, however, you will need to embrace a few ground rules,[5] which I have set out below:

- You have to accept that you are a free agent and that you have choices which you can exercise. Believing that you have no control over your working life or career will leave you at the mercy of the worst effects of commoditization. By the same token, you cannot afford to rely on your employer to do it for you either. Employers are focused on broader issues which might encapsulate your career if you happen to be on their talent radar. However, in the majority of instances, it is unlikely that it will and in any case, they will be looking to exploit the skills they need today, not necessarily those which you need tomorrow.

- Hope for the best, but expect the worst. Being optimistic is an essential trait so long as you are not viewing the world through rose-tinted spectacles (seeing the world how you would like to see it, rather than how it is). As we saw in Chapter 7, one of the biggest problems confronting the upcoming generation of workers is the mismatch between what they have been told their future will hold and what it will actually turn out to be. The need to maintain a high self-esteem in order to bolster their fragile egos is leading them to believe that everything will be just fine and that they are destined for great things. The unfortunate thing is that this mindset is both incredibly näive and psychologically damaging. A far better approach is to be a defensive pessimist, which involves anticipating potential problems and taking steps to avoid them.[6] This can be very successful because it reduces the disappointment when things go wrong, which is usually very high in those who are overly optimistic.

- Don't be scared of examining your failures as much as your successes when determining what you can do next. Again, one of the problems with the pop psychology fed to us through the millions of self-help books is that it accentuates the positive and avoids any discussion of the negative (the opposite is true in some companies, most notably the large multi-disciplined professional firms who only focus on the negative aspects of performance which they euphemistically call development points. This is of course equally problematic). Improving your performance and creating broader career options requires an assessment of what went wrong as well as what went right.

- Embrace complexity and tolerate contradictions. The ambiguity created by complexity is present in most aspects of our society and increasingly in the workplace. The problem is that most people and especially those who live in the West struggle because they have been brought up expecting to come up with the right answer, but as the level of complexity grows it is becoming much harder to arrive at what could be considered as anything nearing the right answer. This has to change and if you are going to cope with the ambiguity associated with the world of work, you are just going to have to get used to admitting (to yourself at least) that you just don't have all the answers.

Strategic and tactical approaches to tackling commoditization

When considering the actions you can take it is best to view them at both the strategic and tactical levels. The strategic actions are associated with future-proofing your career and provide you with the bedrock you will need to continue to earn a decent living as you move through your 30s, 40s, 50s, and perhaps well beyond this, especially if you have no choice but to keep on working. It won't be long before giving up work in your 60s will be classified as early retirement.[7] There are four elements to consider:

- Developing the right approach to learning and thinking to allow you to both adapt to the changing dynamics of the workplace and keep you marketable in as broad a sense as possible for as long as possible.
- Embracing lifelong learning which means taking a far more active stance when it comes to the learning process.
- Establishing the foundations for a portfolio career. Becoming multi-skilled and multi-disciplined will ensure you have options during your mid to late career, as this is when stagnation becomes very tough to deal with.
- Developing a long-term strategy which entails understanding what skills and capabilities you have, what knowledge you need and how best to reach your career goals.

The tactical actions, which will allow you to be effective on a day-to-day basis and help to insulate you in the short-term against commoditization include:

- Being an adaptive specialist which means applying your skills in both a deep and a broad sense. Specialism is of course important, but the ability to connect it to a broader context is increasingly necessary (we will see this shortly when we discuss the mindsets that will be essential in the future).
- Actively planning your career through cycles of experience which are geared towards gaining specific skills and capabilities.
- Working locally and in high touch jobs. As a deeply tactical move and in order to avoid becoming a target for offshoring this can be highly effective.

Strategic actions

Many of us are poor at projecting our working lives much beyond perhaps one or two years. Sure we often start out our careers with grandiose plans of what we would like to do and where we would like to end up, but few of us ever continue with this level of enthusiasm as our careers take shape. Irrespective of why this might be, the ability to take the long view is a skill many of us now need to develop. The simple reason for this is that if we don't then the future will define us, and this may be an uncomfortable prospect to deal with, especially if it results in downward mobility as our earning power diminishes over the course of our careers. This lack of career planning is something that has been highlighted by a recent survey which suggested that many of the UK's managers are ignoring its importance, which is exacerbated by the changes in employment law which force companies to focus on skills rather than experience when recruiting.[8] So just because you may be young, hungry for success and have boundless energy, if there is someone with more relevant experience than you, you will lose out. That's one of the things that has had to change with an aging workforce. So if you have yet to think about your future career, then now might be a good time to start.

Key mindsets for the future

Alvin Toffler discussed the concept of future shock in 1970, a term for the psychological state of individuals and entire societies when too much change happens over too short a time. Toffler argued that society, at the time he wrote the book *Future Shock*, was undergoing enormous structural change, and a revolution from an industrial society to a 'super-industrial society'. This change was overwhelming people because of the accelerated rate of technological and social change and leaving them disconnected, suffering from 'shattering stress and disorientation', in other words, future shocked. Toffler's view of how change can leave many of us overwhelmed is as relevant today as it was when he wrote his seminal work, and when we project commoditization forward, as we will in the final chapter, it is conceivable that many of us will be left future shocked. Therefore addressing, or perhaps coping with the problems that future shock presents is something that we are all going to have to become expert at and there are a couple of strategies that will allow us to both cope with the future a little bit more readily and develop the capabilities that will be needed a few years from now.

COPING WITH THE FUTURE

One of the best ways to adopt the right attitude to change is to use the principles and techniques of Neuro Linguistic Programming (NLP). NLP was derived from research into the transference of therapy skills between counsellors and since then it has been adopted by business coaches and others who are interested in helping people reach their peak performance. The neuro (N) component states that our behaviour stems from the way we experience the world around us through our five senses. It also relates to our physiological reactions to the things we sense. The linguistic (L) element relates to the language we use to order our thoughts and behaviour, and the way we communicate with those around us. Finally, the programming (P) aspect refers to the way in which we, as individuals, choose to respond to the conditions around us.

There are two elements to NLP that are of particular relevance to commoditization; understanding and changing beliefs and maintaining peak motivation and performance. The former is about updating our belief system in order to become more effective. As individuals we all have barriers to personal growth that are embedded in the way we view ourselves and these can restrict our capabilities and abilities. NLP provides the basis for reframing our self beliefs to become more successful by focusing on how we can adjust to the world around us more effectively. It provides some tools with which to do this including modelling and visualizing success, reframing failure as an opportunity to learn, and understanding and adjusting our personal values. All of these are important tools which we can use as we grapple with the impacts of commoditization.

The second element is associated with maintaining peak motivation and performance using our physiology. This essentially means identifying physical feelings, body posture and mental images associated with success, achievement and high performance and replicating these time after time. This was, after all, how Roger Bannister was able to break the four minute mile, despite the received wisdom of the medical profession at the time believing it to be impossible and potentially life threatening. More importantly, it means recognizing the physiology associated with low performance and either avoiding it, or having recognized it, switching into a more positive, high performing state. This plays on the well known fact that the brain's ability to process information is far greater when a person is in a high performing state than when in a low performing or anxious state. It also means that, when in a high performing state, an individual is more resourceful and more able to overcome significant obstacles. It is worth taking a course on NLP because if nothing else it will provide you with some new techniques which you can use to approach your career and face the inevitable challenges more positively.

DEVELOPING THE MINDSETS THAT WILL INSULATE YOU FROM COMMODITIZATION

Howard Gardner, professor of cognition and education at Harvard Business School, recently published the book *Five Minds for the Future*[9] in which he outlines the cognitive abilities that will command a premium in the coming decades. He believes that the combination of globalization, increasing amounts of information and the domination and penetration of technology necessitates a new way of thinking in education and business circles. Although Gardner does not explicitly mention the commoditization of work, it is clear that the mindsets he introduces are possible ways to avoid the trap of commoditization because if you adopt them you will be able to work at a level of complexity that will, at least for the medium term, be difficult to commoditize. The five mindsets are:

- The disciplined mind.[10] Gardner makes the distinction between knowing facts and being able to regurgitate these when required and disciplined thinking. Whilst the former allows people to give the impression of having deep knowledge, it often fails them because they see information as an end in itself. What makes information useful and indeed the employee invaluable is the ability to use a combination of the wider context within which the information sits and the means to better-informed practice. In other words, Gardener is recommending that we understand our disciplines, be they accounting, marketing or information technology very well rather than superficially. And he believes that once you delve deeply into a subject, you will naturally want to find out more thus creating a virtuous cycle of learning, development and practice.
- The synthesizing mind.[11] The ability to knit together information from a wide range of sources is increasingly important in today's workplace. And as the amount of information continues to double every two or so years, this mindset will be the one that will command the highest premium and will be the one that insulates you the most from the coming commoditization of white-collar work. Unfortunately it is also one of the hardest to master especially as it requires you to apply the disciplined mindset to multiple subject areas and to see the connections between them. It is also a mindset that is not generally recognized or rewarded in most organizations; yet.
- The creating mind.[12] Corporations everywhere talk of the need to harness the creativity and the innovative capabilities of their employees (something we have touched on in a number of the chapters), yet few seem to be able to do it successfully. The problem is that creative people tend to stand out from the rest of their colleagues (which they usually enjoy), are generally dissatisfied with the status quo and are willing to question and challenge convention. This creates problems for the organization which requires order, discipline and functional experts. Those who stick out are often marginalized, or in extreme cases fired. Ironically, as commoditization pushes further and further into the heart of many businesses, the need to embrace the creative mindset will be an essential foundation to breaking out of the me-too hell which accompanies it.
- The respectful mind.[13] This may not appear, on face value at least, to be a mindset that will help you to avoid the trap of commoditization. But on a second look, developing it could

serve you well. Remembering the wider context in which the world of work is changing: the aging of the West, increased levels of immigration; globalization; intense cost-focused competition; outsourcing and offshoring, the need to work effectively with people from different cultures, with diverse life experiences and with different skills and capabilities from yours will be critical to your survival in the workplace. Therefore, respecting other people both for what they are and for what they bring will be essential if you are going to be respected yourself.

- The ethical mind.[14] Acting in an ethical way is the bedrock of trust and trust in the workplace is important if an organization's position in the market is to be maintained. One only needs to look back a few years to see how quickly trust can unravel when the leaders of an organization turn out to be unethical. The demise of Enron, WorldCom, Andersen and the many others who were caught up in the accounting scandals of the early 2000s is testament to the need to remain ethical; markets and authorities are far less forgiving than they used to be. So if you are considered to be ethical, trustworthy and professional you are more likely to be perceived to be a valuable member of any organization.

Although we could argue that it is possible to get by without the need for developing all of the mindsets Gardner believes are critical, he makes his case for them very strongly when he outlines the downside of not developing them:[15]

- For those who fail to develop one or more of the five disciplines the future will be bleak, as they will be unable to cope with the demanding nature of the workplace and will, instead, be restricted to menial tasks and be ideal targets for commoditization.
- Those without the synthesizing capabilities will struggle to deal with the ever increasing amounts of information and data. They will be overwhelmed with information and will be unable to make effective decisions both in their professional and private lives.
- For those who lack the ability to create, the future will be one of commoditization with computers replacing their role in the workplace. They will also drive away those amongst their ranks who have the creative abilities, which will compound the problems for the broader workplace especially when the premium on innovation will be much higher than it is today.
- Those without respect will not be worthy of the same and will infect and destroy the workplace.
- Those without ethics will create a workplace devoid of decent workers and will over time fail.

Embracing lifelong learning

The concept of lifelong learning is not necessarily new, but the need for it to be fully embraced perhaps is. One of the most striking things I see time and time again in my professional life is the lack of interest people have in learning. Many assume that their learning stops as soon as they leave school or once they have finished university or graduate school. Although this kind of thinking might still be very common, it is increasingly ill conceived and does little to protect you against the effects of commoditization. Of the five mindsets which will command a premium in the future, it is the disciplined, synthesizing and creative mindsets that will depend on your ability to continuously learn. It is clear that if you are unwilling to embrace lifelong learning in its fullest sense you cannot expect to have much earning power in the mid to latter stages of your career. So it is important to develop a bias towards learning, and if you are going to do this, it helps to understand the four factors which underpin a culture of learning:[16]

- Aspiration and motivation. If you are going to embrace lifelong learning then you have to understand the economic benefits which this brings and be encouraged (by your employer) and motivated (through your own intrinsic curiosity) to do so. The economic upside at worst will be a static or moderately increasing income, protected from the ravages of commoditization and at best will be significant because it will allow you to differentiate yourself from the many individuals who can't be bothered.
- Fully informed. You must be both fully informed and impartially advised of how best to improve your skills and capabilities to maximize your economic advantage. Whilst the former is possible by keeping track of such things the salaries commanded by certain jobs, the latter is less straightforward. Employers are not always good at providing you with impartial advice with respect to the skills you may need in the future, especially if you are very competent at your job. In fact they are more than happy for you to continue to perform the same work until it is no longer required.
- Choice. Opportunities for learning are, of course, all around you, but the focus here is on the opportunities for structured learning provided through such things as classroom based learning as well as the remote learning that is increasingly available. The essential thing is tailoring the learning you need to your short and long term goals and to your preferred style of learning (for more on this I would recommend the Kolb learning model[17]).
- Appropriate financial support. The final element to learning is the provision of financial support, as if you cannot afford to learn then it is highly likely that you won't. As we saw in Parts I and II people are often unwilling to invest in the learning they require when their working lives are volatile; it presents too great a risk in the short term. Ultimately of course not doing it presents an even greater risk in the longer term. The issue we all face is that commoditization will increase the levels of volatility which will mean we will need to take greater risks when developing our skills.

I believe lifelong learning will take on a greater significance over the next few years and especially when organizations begin to realize that without a workforce that is adaptable and able to turn on a dime, their future will be somewhat bleak. Those organizations which adopt a learning culture will be the winners in the medium term as they will be able to recruit and more importantly develop and retain the talent that will keep them viable. By the same token, those amongst us who are willing to continuously learn will be able to adapt to the changing needs of the workplace more readily than those who don't.

Building the foundations of a portfolio career

One of the things that Charles Handy wrote about in his book, *The Empty Raincoat* was the portfolio career.[18] Unlike the typical career path that many of us are familiar with and which served the baby boomers particularly well, the portfolio career is geared towards pursuing a mix of employment opportunities simultaneously. Advances in technology, the shift towards knowledge work and the greater emphasis placed on outputs means that portfolio careers are much easier to pursue today than when Handy wrote his book in 1994. But despite this, being successful depends on whether your skills, capabilities and knowledge are considered valuable on the open market. It's a sad fact that many people move into portfolio careers because they have to; they may have been made redundant or find their careers cut short through mergers, acquisitions or other shock events. In such instances, moving to this mode of working may be an uncomfortable prospect because those forced into it may have given little thought to what it means in practice. However, those who have adopted the portfolio approach as a deliberate strategy can be very successful and often manage to regain the balance between their working and non-working lives that is increasingly being lost.

I am currently a portfolio worker, and indeed many consultants often are because they tend to have had a career that has spanned many disciplines, companies and sectors. I have a range of clients where I apply a broad range of capabilities, I write a couple of books a year and I pursue my academic interests. The beauty of the model is that I can mix the work I need to do along with that which I want to do and this keeps it interesting, allows me to develop new capabilities and satisfies my curiosity. Being a successful portfolio worker requires a combination of employability (that mix of skills, capabilities, knowledge, attitudes and behaviours which makes you attractive to potential clients), having a vendor mindset and having the necessary resilience to cope with the fluid nature of the model.[19]

When looking into the future of work and the likely impacts of commoditization, it is clear that possessing a range of skills and expertise ought to be capable of protecting you from the dangers of being a one trick pony. Viewing the five mindsets through the lens of the portfolio career demonstrates the value which comes from combining the disciplined and synthesizing minds. Within the portfolio career the ability to exhibit deep knowledge across a range of disciplines allows you to engage with a mix of clients across a number of quite different agendas, both technically and functionally. What will really make you invaluable, however, is the ability to connect these together as this is where most organizations struggle. So when thinking about your future it is sensible to consider building the foundations for a portfolio career so that if the time should come when you have to fend for yourself, you will be in a strong position to do so. With this and the other strategic options discussed so far we can now turn to the crux of your strategic response and that's building your career strategy.

Building your career strategy – avoiding commodity skills

Key to avoiding the trap of commoditization is to make sure the skills and capabilities you have are not only current and in demand, but ideally difficult to replicate. In the past this was a lot simpler for two reasons. First, the number of people who may have had similar skills and capabilities to yours was probably lower than it is today or certainly than it will be in the future. Second, many of the skills and capabilities which are now considered commoditizable were unlikely to have been so in the past. As we have seen, the ability to codify work is now a lot simpler and there is nothing to suggest that this process of codification will slow in the foreseeable future. To succeed in the future workplace, where many of the skills and capabilities which we use now will have become commoditizable activities, we will need to have a sustained understanding of what skills are important and what skills we both have and need.

One of the best ways to develop your strategy is to follow the GROW model. This model is designed to draw out what you want to achieve and how you are going to achieve it by stepping through four stages:

• Stage 1 is about defining your goals both in relation to your career and in terms of what you need to learn.

- Stage 2 is focused on understanding what is happening now in relation to these goals by assessing what you currently know and what you need to know.
- Stage 3 helps to explore the variety of options you could take to implement your strategy.
- Stage 4 is about taking action. In other words making it happen.

The model is both simple and effective and I will walk you through each stage in turn.

STAGE 1 – INDENTIFY YOUR GOALS (THE G OF THE GROW MODEL)

We all have goals in life. Some are well articulated, whilst others appear fanciful. Many are hidden from view, not just from our employers, but from ourselves too. The important thing about goals is to make them explicit by writing them down. The very process of committing them to paper will create an association in your brain and hence make them more likely to occur. However, setting goals without establishing a course of action to meet them will, in the main, ensure that they remain on paper. The first step is to understand what your career goals are over the next few years and answer the following questions:

- Where do you see yourself three, five and ten years from now?
- How will you know when you have achieved your goal?
- What will you see, hear and feel, having achieved your goal?
- What will you know when you have reached this goal?
- How much personal control do you have over your goal?
- What resources do you need to accomplish this goal?
- How will you have avoided becoming a commodity worker?

These questions will help you visualize the completion of the goal and help you make it appear real rather than abstract. This visualization is one of NLP's techniques discussed above. The questions will also help you to assess how you will get there and what kind of support from those around you (including your employer) you will need to succeed. In answering these questions you might want to consider what sort of career you wish to have and whether work and achievement are more important than having a full life that is not dominated by the office, email or your BlackBerry. It is also necessary to determine whether you want to follow a generalist or specialist career (more on this later, when we talk about the tactical actions you can take) and how you intend to keep ahead of the white-collar wave of commoditization. Whatever your choice, it is necessary to know what your medium term goals are, as otherwise it is likely that you will drift from one job to another without gaining as much as you can from the experiences (again, more on this later when we discuss cycles of experience). The other consideration you need to give some thought to as you develop your goals is to think about who can help you achieve them; after all you are not an island. It is also necessary to consider the needs of those who currently employ you (or will in the future). This is the sweet spot,[20] which brings together: what you want to do, what your employer wants to do and what you can actually do. This will help to ensure that your strategy is congruent with your employer's. If you don't know what your employer's strategy is, you ought to ask. And if you find that your goals are incongruent with your employer's, that will help you to decide where you need to take your career.

STAGE 2 – UNDERSTAND REALITY AND WHAT NEEDS TO CHANGE (THE R OF THE GROW MODEL)

Having defined your career goals, it is necessary to establish where you currently sit in relation to these. In essence it is about doing a knowledge and learning stock take. The purpose of this stage of the GROW model is to answer the following questions:

- What do you know at the moment (in the widest sense)?
- What is missing from this?
- What skills and knowledge do you need to develop (based upon the goals you have set yourself)?
- What skills and knowledge do you need to drop?
- What skills and knowledge do you have which you are not currently using, and hence which you can refresh and exploit?

This stage consists of four steps:

1. Current state assessment, which involves understanding what skills you currently have.
2. Blind spot analysis, which entails taking a hard look at the gaps in your knowledge.
3. Future profile assessment, which requires you to identify your future skill needs.
4. Skill categorization, which involves you assessing those skills and knowledge that will yield the most value.

Current state assessment

This first step is very important as it creates the baseline from which you can then assess your blind spots and develop your future profile. Understanding reality should start by assessing your skill/knowledge levels (low and high, or somewhere in between). As a starting position you could consider your ability in the following areas: team working; analytical thinking; leadership; self development; people management; project management; strategy; information technology; coaching and mentoring; business development; negotiation and risk management; there are of course many others and you might want to see if you have developed any of the future mindsets discussed earlier in the chapter. Make a note of all your skills, both soft and hard, and take a view on how deep these skills are. Developing a disciplined mind as we saw above will be critical for long-term employability so it is essential to develop a strategy that builds deep capabilities, which may involve enhancing the ones you already have as well as acquiring new ones.

Blind spot analysis

Once complete, the next thing to do is to assess your knowledge and use this to help identify your most significant blind spots. This can be done using the knowledge grid of Figure 10.1. The grid's four quadrants are:

- Explicit knowledge. These are the things that you know that you know. You can discuss them in detail and you are comfortable in their application. It is also easy for you to write them down and explain them to other people. In essence they are at the forefront of your mind and are easy to recall. These are probably the things you are known for in your work

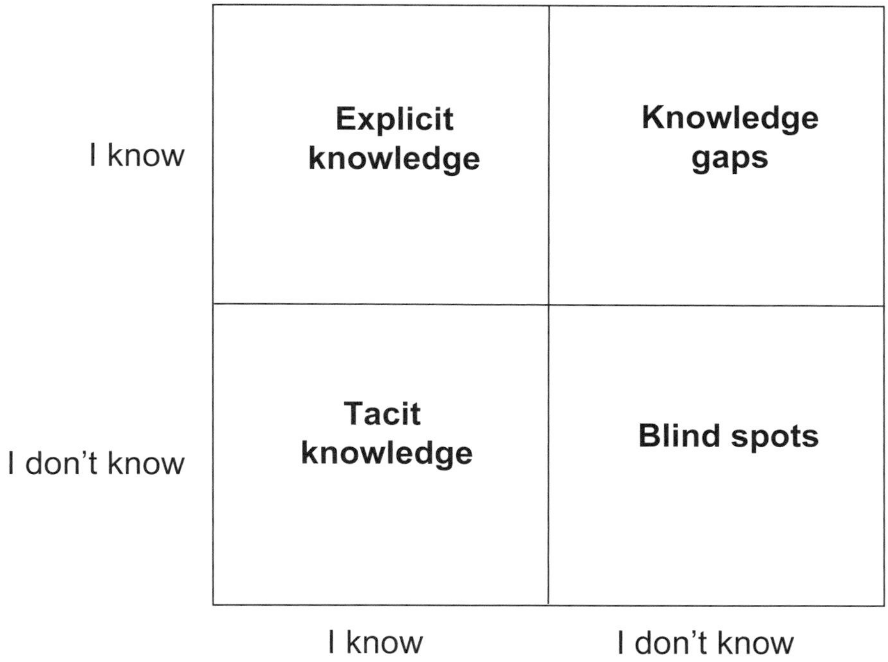

Figure 10.1 columns (bottom): I know | I don't know

Rows (left): I know | I don't know

Quadrants: Explicit knowledge | Knowledge gaps | Tacit knowledge | Blind spots

Figure 10.1 The knowledge grid

and are likely to be functional in nature; they may even form the basis of your profession, honed through years of professional training (the disciplined mind). This knowledge sits well and truly in your comfort zone.

- Tacit knowledge. Here you don't know that you know something. Very often you will perform tasks or apply knowledge automatically. Sometimes such knowledge can be 'lost' and if only occasionally applied can be difficult to regain without some refresher training. This of course may be because the knowledge is no longer relevant or is so commonly applied that it requires little thought; in essence a commodity skill which is easily transferable. However it is still worth checking it out before you finally discard it just to make sure it is no longer serving you the way it once did.
- Knowledge gaps. You may already know where the gaps in your knowledge lie and indeed may be actively trying to plug them. Some will be obvious, such as the functional skills you need to acquire and develop in order to progress in your career. Others may fall out from your career strategy, as these may be things you may have never considered as important to learn until you identified them as a gap. Identifying the gaps in your knowledge is crucial because it is these that will drive your strategy in the short and medium term and that will help you capture those aspects of your strategy which can protect you from commoditization.
- Blind spots. These are those things you have yet to identify as being necessary for your working life and you will probably be oblivious to them. We do have to be careful about blind spots because we all have them to a greater or lesser extent. Very often they may be pointed out to us by a third party which makes them all the more difficult to accept, especially if this happens to be your boss. This is where a coach and/or mentor can prove to be very helpful because they will help to identify your blind spots before they derail your

career. Blind spots are often behavioural rather than technical in nature and will relate to how you are perceived by your peers, subordinates and superiors (in an organizational, not intellectual sense), and this is the reason why they are often so difficult to deal with. Once again, it is worth remembering Gardner's mindsets, especially the respectful and ethical ones.

At the end of this assessment you will have:

- captured your current skill and knowledge profile;
- assessed your levels of explicit and implicit knowledge;
- highlighted your knowledge gaps;
- identified some and if you are lucky, all of your blind spots.

Future profile assessment

Having completed your current state assessment it is now a good idea to develop a future profile which identifies the depth and breadth of skills, attitudes and behaviours you need in the future. When creating this second profile it will be necessary to revisit your goals to ensure this new profile matches your career objectives as well as addressing the threats posed by commoditization. These two stages can be iterative and therefore you should be prepared to pass through these at least twice. If you cannot stabilize your profile after three or four iterations then it might be necessary to seek out some professional career advice or seek input from your coach/ mentor if you have one. Once you have a defined set of goals and a target knowledge profile, it is useful to compare this profile with the one produced during the current state assessment. If they look almost identical then you are either not being honest with yourself, or your skills are precisely what is needed in the future, although I would doubt that very much given that commoditization is likely to change your skill profile over time. More likely is that you will see some major differences between the two profiles. Some of the skills may have gone entirely, or moved from low to high (or vice versa) and new ones may have appeared.

Skill categorization

The final part to this stage of developing your strategy should focus on categorizing the types of skills and knowledge you need in the future using the following categorization:[21]

- **Commodity skills**   These are skills that are general to any role or business. They can be picked up quickly by most people and are increasingly easy to codify. They include following processes, as well as other types of skill, such as technical maintenance and machine minding (such as in a factory), call centre work, reviewing x-rays, and most forms of transaction processing such as accounts payable or auditing. We all need commodity skills, as do organizations, but to maximize our earnings throughout our careers and to gain the most satisfaction we need to move beyond these. Furthermore, if we look at where the major impact of globalization has been, it has been in the area of commodity skills, because these are easy to automate and offshore. This, as we have seen throughout Part I, helps to explain why so much blue-collar activity has been exported overseas and why we are now witnessing the same thing happening to white-collar work. Commodity skills do not command a big income now and they certainly won't in the future.

- **Leveraged skills** These are skills that are non-company specific, more complex and typically have a higher value attached to them and may be considered more valuable to some companies than others. The ability to synthesize would fall into this category for example. The best way to think about this category of skill is how much value you can derive from it externally (away from your existing employer). Consultancies provide a good model because they have a wealth of intellectual capital which they can sell to their clients. The breadth and depth of the skills and expertise available, together with the ability to bring in other cross-sector experiences is how the consultancies add value. Although many organizations may have similar skills internally, they are often unable to brigade them when required, plus they are not always able to break through the barriers to change such as politics and resistance. This is why clients are willing to pay such high fees to consultants (although consultancy is also becoming more of a commodity service which is facing the same drop in margins as many other businesses). Similarly, there will be skills within a company that are highly valued and highly rewarded. Understanding which skills these are and whether you have them (or need them) is very useful.
- **Proprietary skills** These are the skills and knowledge that are company specific and which a company will pay a premium for because they translate into the wider company brand. Think of Coca-Cola, Disney, Mercedes Benz and similar companies. Each develops and utilizes its unique blend of skills to create products and services that command respect and loyalty amongst their customers. In a similar vein, there are skills and knowledge which are valued in the workplace which you possess and which you can command a premium for. It is important, however, to recognize that such skills are company specific, and although this does not mean they are not portable, they do have to be repackaged to suit a new employer. This is principally because each organization has its own way of doing things defined by its culture and in order to fit in you will need to make the effort to adapt to the new environment, otherwise you may not be as successful as you'd expect.

This categorization helps you to identify which of your skills:

- add significant value but are easy to replace;
- add little value and are easy to replace;
- add little value and are difficult to replace;
- add significant value and are difficult to replace.

Ideally you should be aiming to have knowledge that has a lot of value and is difficult to replace. The more value adding skills you have that are in demand, the more secure your future will be. But key to exploiting the knowledge you have is to understand where it is and how to exploit it. Similarly, the five mindsets defined above are also key to creating a secure future hopefully untouched by commoditization.

STAGE 3 – DETERMINE YOUR OPTIONS (THE O OF THE GROW MODEL)

Now that you have completed Stages 1 and 2, the next thing to do is to determine what you need to do to close the gap between the current and future states. But, rather than jumping straight to action, it is better to explore the wider options first. This stage is therefore designed to answer the following questions:

- What could you do to move from where you are now to where you want to be (as defined by your goals)?

- What alternatives are available?
- What approaches have you seen used in similar circumstances?
- Who might be able to help?
- What constraints do you have to work within (time, money etc.)?
- If the constraints were removed, what would you do?
- Which of the options interest you?

During this stage it is necessary to take an objective view of the options rather than going for the most obvious or the most attractive. Sometimes it means taking a risk and placing yourself out on a limb. Moving outside your comfort zone is uncomfortable but it does accelerate learning considerably and may be necessary if you are going to avoid downward mobility.

STAGE 4 – ACTION PLANNING (WRAP UP, THE W OF THE GROW MODEL)

This final stage is about action planning. You will have created the basis of your strategy in the previous three stages, and now it is time to assess how you are going to implement it by deciding on which of the options you looked at in the previous stage you are going to take. Action planning is designed to answer the following questions:

- What are the next steps?
- Will these address your goals?
- When will you take them?
- What might get in the way?
- How will you ensure that the next steps are taken?
- Who needs to know?
- How will you get the support you need?

Like any form of planning, it is worth spending sufficient time on this to ensure that your plan is capable of delivering your strategy. It is best to draw up a short document that summarizes your strategy and this should cover:

- your career goals over the next two to three years;
- your skill, capability and learning objectives over the same period;
- your strategy for achieving each of these (for example, change job, go back to university, and so on);
- what specific actions you will take;
- when you will take these actions (which could be monthly, six monthly or perhaps annually);
- how you will know you have achieved what you set out. Such measures of success are vital as they prevent you from deluding yourself that you have succeeded when you haven't, and stop you from making excuses.

The GROW model and its principal steps should help you clarify what you want to achieve in your career and more importantly take the necessary dispassionate look at your skills and capabilities. If you can commit to this process and to repeating it every two to three years you will be able to assess where you are along your journey and update it as required. More importantly, it will allow you to keep a weather eye on how commoditization is changing the working dynamic, what skills are likely to be in vogue and which ones are likely to become commoditized in the future.

Tactical actions

Within the military there is a clear distinction between strategy and tactics but both are inexorably linked. Strategy without tactics is as useless as tactics without strategy. Although there are a number of tactical actions you could take to address the challenge of commoditization these need to be placed into the context of your medium to long term strategy, which is why we discussed it first. However, if you want to go completely tactical then I would recommend you think seriously about working in a career or job that requires a local presence and which needs a high degree of personal contact (more on this shortly).

So what tactical actions would I recommend? Well, there are three:

- becoming an adaptive specialist in which you are expert at mixing your specialist and generalist skills;
- following cycles of experience which are designed to build the capabilities you will need to meet your strategy;
- pursuing jobs which are both high touch and which need a local presence to be successful.

Becoming an adaptive specialist

Naturally, the breadth and depth of knowledge you need to accumulate over a lifetime of work depends on your chosen career path. It is clear that some professions require deep levels of expertise and hence for those that follow them, acquiring specialist knowledge is more important than acquiring general business skills. For example, there would be little point in physicians developing generalist skills when their ability to perform their job depends on the skill of diagnosing and curing disease. Furthermore, their ability to advance in their profession requires them to continue with their specialist education in order to maintain the currency of their knowledge. If we are to look at the job of a physician the knowledge content of the work has increased dramatically. When compared to the doctor of 100 years ago, the modern day physician has to understand microsurgery, antibiotics, ultrasound, x-rays and increasingly genetics. All of this requires continuous learning albeit within a specialist context.

Even for those who follow a generalist path, some degree of specialist knowledge is still required, especially in the early stages of their careers. If nothing else this provides a route into an organization and provides a selling point to a prospective employer. However, having established a foundation, the need to expand skills into other business areas is important and is usually expected by an employer. Therefore for the majority of people the requirement to follow a single specialism throughout their career is less important than collecting a whole range of different capabilities. Indeed holding onto specialist skills for too long may actually become a hindrance to long-term career prospects and of course may make you a prime target for commoditization, especially if your skills happen to fall into the easily codifiable category.

Whatever mix of specialist and generalist skills you decide you need, it is important to recognize that both require effort to develop. Whereas we might understand the commitment required to become an expert in a particular field, we often underestimate how much effort is needed to follow a more generalist path. Consider how long it takes to become a doctor, dentist, architect or engineer. Having spent between three and seven years at university, further study and professional exams are also required, which can take up to a further two to three years to complete. Even after that, reaching the pinnacle of a chosen profession requires continuous professional development and constant learning, often monitored by a professional body. Although this may sound like a long slog, the advantages of following a single vocation is that the path to the top is well defined and the learning needed to achieve success is well established. Also, for those who follow the major vocations such as medicine, dentistry and teaching there is unlikely to be any need to change tack, assuming of course nothing dramatic happens.

From a general perspective adopting a generalist career would appear to be a much safer and easier path. But this requires more planning and the acquisition of a wider range of skills, as well as dropping those skills that become outdated. Think about your career so far. You have probably worked for a small number of organizations, worked in different functions and been involved with various projects. All of this has required you to adapt and learn new skills and capabilities. In a generalist career it is more important to have skills and capabilities that cover a variety of disciplines coupled with one or two that are more specialized in nature; that combination of the disciplined and synthesizing mindsets again. This has long been the view taken by consultancies who attempt to develop 'T' shaped consultants who have a particular specialism, for example supply chain, augmented by more general skills, such as project management, problem solving, business development, and so on. The same principle should apply to your career. Having skills that are more general in nature ensures that you can adapt more readily to the changes around you. Many people get caught out when the skills they have acquired and used over many years are no longer useful, have been commoditized or are no longer capable of commanding a decent income.

I believe there is some advantage in becoming an adaptive specialist, in other words mixing the specialist and generalist skill sets together so that you are able to bring the specialist skills to bear when you need to but continue to work in a broad sense. This type of tactical action will keep you interesting to any employer or client and more importantly, allow you to adjust more readily to a sudden change in circumstances.

Cycles of experience

When I look back on my career so far it occurs to me that I have passed through a number of quite distinct cycles of experiences. These experiences were usually associated with developing and mastering a new skill, moving business sectors, or changing employers. All of them were quite deliberate and have broadened and deepened my skills and capabilities as well as my overall experience. For example, when I decided that I needed to gain some IT expertise, I left my first employer to gain the experience I felt was missing at the time and it took two moves to build up my knowledge to a point where I felt I was sufficiently expert. Of course, I did other things too, such as undertake a masters degree, learn project management and so on. So I guess there are cycles within cycles. I am sure if you look back on your own career you may well see similar patterns even if you have only worked for a single employer. Such cycles of experience are increasingly critical to us all and as we saw above, possessing a portfolio of specialist and generalist skills is one way you can maintain a productive and engaging career.

The best way to make cycles of experience an active process rather than something to look back on is to follow a few simple steps. The first is to focus on what you want to learn, or gain expertise in. You can use some of the strategic actions discussed earlier in this chapter to help you with this. Once you have decided on what you want to achieve, set yourself some objectives which might be associated with a specific experience, like running a large project, a skill you want to acquire through a training course or perhaps a combination of both. You then need to think about how you are going to achieve them which may, of course involve changing jobs, functions or even careers, but that's the beauty of making it an active process, it forces you to take control. As you pass through the experience you might want to use an After Action Review (AAR) every now and then to assess how well you are doing against your targets. The AAR originated during the Vietnam War, where the soldiers in the field knew more than those at headquarters. It allows people to learn immediately after an event, irrespective of whether it was a success or failure. To get the best out of it, you need to answer the following questions:

- What should have happened?
- What actually happened?
- What were the differences between what should have, and what actually happened?
- What lessons can be drawn from the experience and how can any strengths revealed be built upon, and any weaknesses reduced or eliminated?

I find this really helps to track how well you are doing against the objectives you set yourself and provides you with the basis for making adjustments. Once you have achieved your objectives you can then decide on what your next cycle of experience is going to be. I have found cycles can last from as little as a few months to as much as a few years and the amount of time they take will depend on the nature of the objectives you set yourself. However long it takes, it is a great way to remain fresh and actively engaged in your career.

Working locally and in high-touch jobs

One thing is clear about commoditization and that is that any job that has to be performed locally and which can be considered to be high-touch will be largely immune from its worst effects (at least for the foreseeable future). This does not mean that you will be well paid or that your job is safe from being carried out by someone who is willing to do it for a lower income, but it may allow you to continue in steady employment without the threat of commoditization hanging over you. There are of course other risks you might have to face down the line, such as the long-term impacts of technological change, so there is no room for complacency.

As we saw in Chapter 7, up to 29 per cent of all United States jobs could be offshorable and hence commoditizable. This is a sizable percentage of the workforce but don't forget that this leaves 71 per cent of jobs which are relatively safe and this majority covers some 607 occupations.[22] So if you are especially concerned about the possibility of your job being commoditized or offshored, then you might want to consider working in an occupation that includes a significant amount of face-to-face time and which requires a degree of locality. The types of jobs that fall into this category include broadcast technicians, sound engineering technicians, secretaries, customer service representatives, producers and directors, purchasing managers, nuclear technicians, astronomers, sales managers, business operations specialists and advertising sales agents.[23] This is only a fraction of the jobs that could be considered to be safe from commoditization, so all is not lost.

The tactical actions covered here should help you concentrate on the short-term activities you can begin to apply, and undertaking these within the umbrella of your strategic plan should provide a comprehensive approach to keeping ahead of commoditization.

This completes Part III of the book, which leaves us with the final part in which I will attempt to look into the future of commoditization and how it will continue to affect us all. I think once you have read this, you will understand just how important career planning is going to become for many of us.

References

1 Gardner, H. (2006) *Five Minds for the Future*, Boston, Massachusetts: Harvard Business School Press, p. 46.
2 *McKinsey Quarterly* (2007) Interacting for competitive advantage, *The McKinsey Quarterly Chart Focus Newsletter*, January p. 1.
3 Handy, C. (2001) *The Elephant and the Flea*, London: Hutchinson, p. 206.
4 OECD (2007) Employment outlook 2007, p. 107.
5 James, O. (2007) *Affluenza*, London: Vermilion, pp. 101–102.
6 Segerstrom, S. (2006) *Breaking Murphy's Law*, New York: The Guildford Press, pp. 138–141.
7 Chapman, J. (2007) Quitting in your 60s is 'early retirement'. *Daily Mail*, 19 June, p. 17.
8 Eglin, R. (2007) Ignore strategy at your peril, *The Sunday Times*, 25 February, pp. 4–8.
9 Gardner, H. (2006) *Five Minds for the Future*, Boston Massachusetts: Harvard Business School Press.
10 Ibid., pp. 21–44.
11 Ibid., pp. 45–76.
12 Ibid., pp. 77–101.
13 Ibid., pp. 103–125.
14 Ibid., pp. 127–151.
15 Ibid., pp. 18–19.
16 Leitch, S. (2006) *Prosperity For all in the Global Economy – World Class Skills*, Norwich: HMSO, pp.105–106.
17 For more on the Kolb learning styles, see Holmes, A. (2003) *Lifelong Learning*, Oxford: Capstone Publishing, pp. 112–113.
18 Handy, C. (1994) *The Empty Raincoat*, London: Hutchinson, pp. 175–179.
19 Bridges, W. (1996) *Jobshift*, London: Nicolas Brealey, p. 57.
20 See Stumpf, S. and DeLuca, J. (1994) *Learning to Use What You Already Know*, San Francisco: Barrett-Koehler Publishers, pp. 107–115.
21 Stewart, T. (1997) *Intellectual Capital: The New Wealth of Nations*, New York: Currency-Doubleday, p. 89.
22 Blinder, A. (2007) *How Many Jobs Might Be Offshorable?* Princeton University, CEPS Working Paper No. 142, March 2007, p. 19.
23 Ibid., pp. 42–43.

IV The Future of Commoditization

Sometimes it takes an outsider to speak the unpalatable truth that everyone knows but is unwilling to acknowledge outright.[1]

This is, then, a story of a decline in social capital caused by economic changes – in this case, changes that dramatically increased economic individualism and widened income differences.[2]

In an attempt to draw the book to some kind of a conclusion, there is merit in taking a punt at what the future may hold. It is clear from my research that commoditization is a double edged sword. On the one hand, it provides significant benefits to us as consumers and for society at large. Without it we may never have progressed beyond an economy reliant on agriculture, the vagaries of the weather and hard labour. The advancement of the past civilizations was at least in part dependent upon building a smooth and efficient basis on which to run; and to achieve this required a degree of standardization. Then the great innovators of the 17th, 18th, 19th and 20th centuries created the basis for entire new industries, competencies and products and services. To succeed, the innovators' ideas had to be understood, unravelled and harnessed in order to make them accessible to the masses. To do this required the commercial and political leaders of the time to codify, systematize and commoditize the underlying processes, technologies and activities that supported the emerging industries. This allowed the products and services created by these industries to be delivered at a price that was acceptable to the broader population and ensured the industries expanded. I believe the need to understand, codify and make efficient is a trait of the human condition which is central to the commoditization debate and will continue to push it into new directions.

On the other hand, there is another side to commoditization which is less positive. The process results in the elimination of skills and expertise through the combination of common standards, processes and new technology. It is also making work more demanding, as we saw in Chapter 7. As the nature of a particular skill set becomes well understood and codified, the deep expertise required during the early stages following its emergence is no longer needed. This makes it easier for others to perform the same role despite having fewer skills and for technology to subsume it because it has become sufficiently codified and systematized. For those who find themselves without the necessary skills to maintain an effective position in the workplace, the choices become stark; downward mobility and an inability to rise back up the ranks of the employed, plus the social consequences of underemployment and unemployment.

Commoditization also makes industries and companies less profitable and they too can face a long slow slide to collapse. It is becoming easier to mimic the competition and for industries to converge so that they end up occupying and fighting it out in the same markets with the same customers. A significant number of organizations, some well known, and others less so, have found that it is at best difficult and at worst impossible to enjoy outstanding commercial success when in a commodity business. This is because it becomes much harder for them to provide unique offerings to their customers and tough to attract the talent they need to drive the business forward and innovate.[3] And once in this kind of death spiral the only way is down.

With this backdrop in mind, we can move onto the final chapter of the book which looks at where technology and demographic change might take us, what the impacts of increased income inequalities could be and whether or not commoditization will eventually touch us all.

References

1 Waters, R. (2006) Microsoft sees the beginning of the end for the PCs, *Financial Times*, 29–30 July, p. 8.
2 Wilkinson, R. (2005) *The Impact of Inequality: How to Make Sick Societies Healthier*, New York: The Free Press, p. 207.
3 Hax, A. (2005) Overcome the dangers of commoditization, *Strategic Finance*, July (http://goliath.ecnext.com).

11 *Where Will Commoditization Take Us?*

In a few years when this is ultimately perfected, we start losing jobs, and I helped.[1]

But today's public anxieties are both broader and more intense. In exit polls last week, 40% of voters said they expect the next generation of Americans to have a lower standard of living.[2]

The shift to an ideology of personal responsibility for education coupled with an increase in the number of highly skilled, college educated workers both inside and outside the United States has helped create the current liquidity of intellectual labour. Central to the ability of corporations to offshore that labor is the appearance of global, digital communications networks that enable oversight-at-a-distance. Without this communications network, there could be no off-shoring of intellectual labour.[3]

By treating yourself and others as commodities, you are deprived of volition. Being bought and sold, you begin to experience yourself not as a person but as a powerless entity whose value is wholly determined by the market, something that is ultimately beyond your control.[4]

A new aristocracy of talent is retreating into golden ghettos and running the global economy in their own interests.[5]

On the one hand we have Wal-Mart's low prices, the endless variety of products made in China and access to all the information we desire on the internet. On the other hand, we have started to turn a screw that is pushing the great majority of people downwards. When prices are low, wages are also low. When wages are lower, we are more dependent on lower prices.[6]

Predicting the future is an imprecise science, and something that should always be carried out carefully and the results should be taken with a pinch of salt. That said it is sensible to assume that most of the drivers of commoditization are likely to remain in force for the foreseeable future. So unlike the futurologists who attempt to predict how society and technology will change over the next 50 years, I am only going to look a few years ahead, which is a more sensible time horizon. History is not always a good predictor of the future, but in the case of commoditization I think it is. It is clear that when we look back in time we can see how the process of commoditization has subsumed great tranches of industry, eliminated significant numbers of manual labourers and increased the general efficiency and effectiveness of society. In many respects we could argue that it was important to the advancement of the industrialized economies of the West. In projecting forward from this point, we should expect commoditization to continue to expand its footprint into areas which we currently think are outside the realms of possibility. After all, no one would have expected the IT industry to have become so commoditized when it first emerged during the 1940s. And in the same way that white collar workers were caught out when they believed they were immune from the initial waves of downsizing and offshoring that affected the manufacturing sector, others at the mid- and high-end of the workforce may also be caught out sometime in the future. And as commoditization continues to advance it will touch on many more peoples' lives and livelihoods.

When we look into the future and how commoditization might play out we can see a variety of potential changes in the nature of work and employment and in some of the wider processes which govern and define society. For the purposes of this brief peek into the future, I will focus on:

- Technology and how it will continue to eliminate work at the low, mid and high end of the employment spectrum.
- The emergence of the extreme worker at one end and the disenfranchised jobber at the other and the inevitable rise of a wider labour war which will no longer be focused on just the most talented in society.
- The widening gap between the winners and losers within the workplace and the impact the subsequent inequality in income has on the health and wellbeing of all concerned.
- The emergence of a vicious cycle which may be impossible (for most of us) to break out of.
- The rise of protectionist behaviour to combat the worst impacts of commoditization.

There may of course be a number of other changes which could be less or more significant than those I am about to explore. Some of them might be disruptive and unpredictable, but in the end we can only see what the future holds once it arrives. What we can do however, is to prepare for it as much as we can.

Technology – squeezing work at every level

Sophisticated computer software now has the capability to write basic code, eliminating the need for many programmers to do this routine work.[7]

There can be little doubt that the micro chip will continue to advance and this is likely to allow activity which currently requires high-touch or significant intelligence and brain power to complete to become subsumed within the next generations of computer systems. The recent launch of Nvidia's GeForce 8800 chip is perhaps just the beginning. Nvidia invested over $400 million and four years perfecting the chip, which involved a fundamental redesign of the circuitry so that instead of handling one task at a time, it is now capable of handling more varied and parallel jobs. The launch of the new chip was accompanied by an image of an actress which was so lifelike that it looked as though it had been generated by a camera not a computer. Capturing the image involved gluing reflective dots over the actress' body and taking hundreds of pictures of her movements (which took some five hours to complete). The result was, however, dramatic, in that it was possible to see her shoulder blades move beneath her skin, facial expressions and even individual pores on her face. Apart from the obvious application within the gaming industry, Nvidia believes the GeForce 8800 will be used in special purpose computing applications and accelerator devices to take on jobs such as weather forecasting, financial simulations, rendering images from medical scanning equipment and more importantly in opening up a whole new class of computing. As we saw in Chapter 3 when we reviewed the commoditization of the IT industry, the capability of chip technology continues to advance at such a progressive rate that we should expect the GeForce chip to be surpassed in the not too distant future even though it has around 681 million transistors packed onto its surface; double the number on the current generation of chips and significantly more than Intel's Core 2 Duo Microprocessor which has only 291 million.[8] And it seems that this not too distant future is already upon us with the announcement from Intel and IBM that they have made possibly the biggest and most significant breakthrough in chip technology in 40 years. Both claim that Hafnium, a metal used in the manufacture of nuclear reactors, could soon replace the silicon chip and with it, its limitations on power and speed.[9] Intel believes that it will be possible to double the density of transistors packed onto the chip thereby making computers more powerful and faster and reducing the cost of powering the transistors by one third.[10] We have yet to feel the full impact of this or indeed the future generation of microprocessors that will inevitably follow over the coming years, but even now the reality of avatars replacing actors and newsreaders is fast becoming a reality. Such high-touch employment could go the same way as the typing pool and we may not require the services of the highly paid newscasters reading from an autocue for much longer.

Although it might take time before high-end work is fully commoditized, the same cannot be said of the mid and low end activities of the workplace. In fact we should expect the routine work undertaken by the average white collar worker to be squeezed out of existence, or reduced to the bare minimum required to ensure that people are on hand to deal with the occasional crisis. As we saw in Chapters 4 and 5, this process of commoditization is being driven by a combination of process standardization, improved interconnectivity between IT applications and the availability of a cheaper workforce overseas. Although standardizing process and having a cheap and capable labour force are important, key to the changes we are witnessing is the capability of technology, as without effective and connected systems it would be almost impossible to move any work offshore or take advantage of the capabilities of workers from different geographies. The relationship between technology and the elimination and offshoring of work is also circular; as technologies improve through the intellectual efforts applied by those that develop and advance them, it becomes easier to move the location of that labour to other locations across the world, something not lost on the IT industry. Moreover, as technology improves it leads to a greater instability in the working environment and increases the level of uncertainty for both physical labour (as we witnessed in the Industrial Revolution and more recently with the manufacturing sector) and knowledge-based labour (as we started to see in the 1990s and of course now).[11] Indeed such uncertainty and the insecurity it brings is believed to be broader, more insidious and more damaging to workers' morale than in the past. This uncertainty is largely driven by the recognition that no one is free from the risk of a sudden change in fortune and income, no matter how well trained or educated. Such rapid changes can occur both when the economy is booming and when it is contracting. Moreover, the level of uncertainty seems to be growing as more of our economies become dependent upon the knowledge and service sectors.[12]

Today it is possible for the transactional activities of an organization to be performed by technology and moved to outsource service providers and increasingly offshore. Over time the focus of technology will shift away from the most obvious targets associated with transactional activity to, first, the removal of process intensive activities (as soon as they have been standardized and simplified – see Chapter 8) and finally to the non-critical decision making activities which can be aided by effective data mining and business intelligence software (Figure 11.1). The embedded intelligence within technology is creating smart systems that over time will become more efficient and cost effective in eliminating the low end activities which are narrowly defined such as customer support (queries, order processing etc.).

The logical extension of the continued improvements in technology is for all labour to become a commodity. In the same way that blue collar labour has become commoditized and offshored, white collar work will become a commodity as organizations continually shift labour from country to country in order to exploit the differences in labour costs.[13] The smarter technology becomes, the higher up the food chain commoditization goes. And as long as we have scientists and technologists pushing the envelope of technology, this process will continue. For example in approximately five years from now, computers will be able to read and tag the news stories and information emanating from the myriad of newspapers and agencies across the globe. So what, you might ask, but this is the same information that is currently used by the highly paid traders in stock exchanges throughout the world and if this technology is as good as they believe it will be it could potentially make them obsolete, saving their employers literally billions in salaries, bonuses and share options. In a commoditized world, anyone whose job is defined by or involves a significant use of computers is at risk of downward mobility.[14] Reuters is building the technology that will allow the information fed from its systems to be machine readable by trading applications and heralds a time when human intervention will be increasingly replaced by sophisticated computer algorithms capable of making the same judgements currently made by traders. To allow this the feeder systems will upload pricing information up to 23 000 times per second.[15] Given time it will be possible to replace even the most cost-effective and productive white collar worker, just like the machine operators of the Industrial Revolution or the production line workers of the automobile industry.

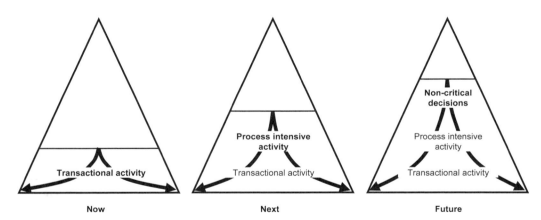

Figure 11.1 The shifting focus of technology

Even now with computer technology not as advanced as it could be, organizations are seeking to reduce and potentially eliminate the work undertaken by the professionals working in their back office functions such as finance, HR and IT. The work they undertake is perceived as being at best a necessary evil which reflects the complexities of the business model, and at worst an unnecessary and expensive overhead. Increasingly back office activities and those performing them will be under intense scrutiny as low cost providers force the less nimble organizations to seek savings wherever they can by eliminating complexity from their business models and the fat from their workforces. Today's tentative moves to offshore such work will pick up in speed as the capability of technology increases and the ability to virtualize work allows it to be delivered more efficiently. As a result many of the current barriers, bar the political ones, will fade away. There are already a few examples of such work being completely offshored and this will increase once those organizations in the vanguard have proved the concept. As soon as other organizations recognize that there is no real requirement to maintain an expensive back office, the commoditization of white collar work will accelerate and much of the work undertaken by today's well paid professionals will disappear. And once this has fully played out, the focus will turn to the process intensive activities and then work which entails non-critical decisions.

Where it will end is a question that is on an increasing number of workers' lips and surely there will be some work that can avoid the commoditization trap. Work which requires innovation and high intellect may be safe, as removing this from the core of the organization may be a step too far. But this will not stop companies from attempting to reduce the reliance on expensive resources and eliminating the need for human contact through the use of new technologies; it's inevitable in an increasingly commoditized economy. And this is already happening. For example, Proctor & Gamble (P&G) is currently employing *cave technology* to accelerate their market research. The technology allows P&G to create a virtual reality store in which their clients and customers can walk through and explore their products. The cave recreates the stores of their customers, such as Tesco, Sainsbury and Boots, in every detail and provides an environment in which customers and clients can walk through the store, handle the merchandise and even buy products. P&G is using the reactions of customers to test alternative store layouts, displays and packaging. The cave allows them to dramatically accelerate the pace of innovation and cut costs whilst working to win over powerful retail clients. The process, which used to take up to two years to complete and was often fraught with difficulties, can now be completed within three months. We can only speculate what this might mean for the armies of skilled market research professionals, but if history is anything to go by, the writing might be on the wall for the majority.[16]

The extreme and disenfranchised worker and the emerging war for labour

There are a few books in my library which discuss in some considerable detail why employees leave their jobs and what employers should be doing to retain their best staff. The messages they contain are very important and we mentioned some of these in Chapter 8 when we looked at how organizations should be responding to both the threat of the upcoming shortages of talented staff as well as the general impacts of commoditization on their workers. As time marches on, the local pools of talented staff on which organizations depend are expected to dry up because of the aging of the population and the constraints (political, as well as physical) imposed on immigrant labour. For those with the skills in demand the future is bright and it may not be long before we begin to see job auctions emerging in which the most talented in society open themselves up to the highest bidder.[17] Indeed we are already witnessing the growth in the income share which is accruing to the top 0.1 per cent of workers. According to the OECD this reflects the effects of globalization which is creating opportunities for a small elite cohort of workers.[18] Being the most talented will bring some very high rewards, which for some can mean calling the shots and enjoying a lifestyle that will be increasingly out of reach for the majority. But at a personal level such high incomes won't come cheaply. Extreme jobs in which employees are required to work exceptionally long hours whilst juggling immense and conflicting responsibilities in order to both justify their high incomes and to service their global clients may not be new. After all we all know of workaholics who will literally sacrifice their entire life for their careers, but such jobs may well become the norm for those with talent who wish to stay on the top of the career ladder. And if you think this is bad, just consider the lengths many middle class people will go to, to ensure their offspring end up in these positions. In China parents are able to send their very young children to the Early MBA programme, an American-inspired course for three to six-year-olds, described as 'enrichment education for tomorrow's leaders'. The subjects taught to these toddlers (after all that is what they are) include mathematics, economics, astronomy and team-building.[19] Forcing children into a pattern of work at such an early age is nothing short of insane, but the sad truth is that such courses and parental pressures will probably increase over the next decade or so as the intensity of competition for top jobs increases. In a similar vein, competition among graduates for jobs is already so fierce that career coaches have started to emerge who charge up to £5000 to help those willing to pay for a step onto the career ladder.[20] With three graduates chasing each graduate level job, it is no longer enough to have a good degree (as we saw in Chapter 5), and as graduates and their parents become more desperate to secure good jobs, such services are likely to be in high demand. Cynical though the purveyors of such advice are and although success cannot be guaranteed, it is likely that their ranks will increase over time. At least with greater numbers their services will become commoditized, so the £5000 charged today will undoubtedly drop.

Extreme jobs may entail 100-plus-hour work weeks often spanning the weekends. We see this today within the investment banking community. Fresh-faced graduates enter their banking career by putting in 100-plus-hour weeks for at least 24 months.[21] The same is true of the legal profession, which continues to be associated with gruelling schedules, fairly dull work and little work life balance.[22] Some of the reasons why we will see an increasing number of extreme jobs include.[23]

- The intensification of competition. Over time the number of promotion opportunities for staff will diminish as hierarchies flatten, the impact of mergers and acquisitions eliminates senior roles, new workers (often immigrants) who are willing to put in inhuman hours to get on, join the workforce and work is offshored to save costs. We discussed the impacts of changing ownership, one of the most significant drivers of this, in Chapter 7.
- The cult of the extreme. It can be very difficult for executives to demonstrate their worth to themselves or those around them without some outward evidence of their long hours, much of which remains invisible. So in order to increase the visibility of the sacrifice they make, extreme workers are increasingly being equated to sports superstars; investment bankers will brag about the deal they have just pulled off against all the odds and at massive personal cost in the same way a base jumper will after completing a particularly dangerous leap. Extreme workers will tell anyone who is interested about how demanding their roles are and how they have no time for anything else. They get their rush from working incredibly long hours, under immense pressure and rarely having any time to relax. For them, it's their badge of honour and they, of all people don't need or even want a life.
- The impact of technology. As we have already seen, technology is a significant factor in the intensification of work. Increased connectivity between client and service provider

and boss and subordinate means that those in extreme positions will rarely escape the office. In fact they will become the office, always accessible no matter where they are or what time of day it is.

- Work replacing home as the new social centre. The loss of social capital because of the increasing hours spent in the office means that, for many at the high end of their professions, work will be their social life; it's where they build the majority of their relationships (albeit superficial and one-dimensional) and where the few friends (or perhaps acquaintances) they have reside. Many extreme professionals prefer to be at work than at home, where they feel alien and unneeded and generally unsettled. I know of one senior executive who will arrive late into the office, usually at the end of a normal working day, to avoid any contact with his wife or children and I know of one chief executive who never spends any time with her children, mainly because she is only interested in her very important role and the wealth and status it brings. Such people do not value traditional relationships unless they are work related.
- The shift to knowledge work. In the past it was possible to down tools at the end of a shift and pick up your social life. In the modern corporation which employs brains not brawn this is no longer the case. And unlike manual labour, knowledge work is never done because there is often no physical product at the end of it.
- Globalization. The most successful organizations are those which can attract the best and brightest talent and very often these are the global players who have the necessary complexity required to keep the extreme worker focused, engaged and busy. Addressing the challenges presented by overseeing global operations spanning multiple time zones requires long hours and being on call for 24 hours a day; just what the extreme worker enjoys.

But there is a cost and this can be significant, as a recent survey of extreme workers by the Centre for Work-Life Policy found. The survey found that 45 per cent of executives were extreme workers putting in more than 60 hours a week and meeting five other criteria which included being on call 24 hours a day, facing demands from several time zones and meeting ever more demanding deadlines. Some 65 per cent of men said that their work stopped them from having a strong relationship with their children; 33 per cent of women executives said the same. Intimate relationships also suffered with many dual-income families referring to 'four in a bed' relationships – two people and two BlackBerrys (now euphemistically called crackberrys). And at the end of the day, 45 per cent of all respondents said they were too tired to say anything at all to their partners.[24] Extreme work takes its toll on workers' health, relationships, marriages and many other aspects of their non-working lives. Issues such as lack of sleep, burnout, depression, lack of exercise, alcohol and substance abuse and marriage breakdown are increasingly common amongst this cohort of the working population.[25] And although there are plenty of people who thrive on this mode of working, there are many who believe it to be unsustainable in the long term and most do not see themselves in such extreme positions for much more than a year.[26] No wonder then that even now many workers want to quit the rat race and pursue what is labelled 'zenployment' in which fulfilment overrides the need to earn ever increasing amounts of money (not that they will of course in a commoditized world). According to one recent survey, one in two British employees would be happy to earn less if the role made them feel better about themselves. Many wanted to become yoga teachers or animal welfare officers or counsellors.[27] Another survey, this time of lawyers, suggested that, despite record pay – some charge £1 000 per hour – many are unhappy with their lot in life. As one lawyer stated, the hours are relentless, the people dismal and the work very dull.[28] Many wind up divorced and there is a joke making its rounds that it is only after the second divorce that a partner can claim to be truly committed to the firm.[29]

The extreme position is encapsulated by the ½ x 2 x 3 formula described by Handy in which there will be half as many people in the core of the company, paid twice as well and producing three times as much.[30] In an increasingly fragmented working world such extreme positions will grow in number as the nature of work continues to favour the winner takes all mode of employment and as more work lower down the organization is commoditized and reduced to little more than machine minding.

However, there is more to staffing than just talent. And despite the current focus on the war for talent, which is of course critical and something we discussed in Chapter 8, what is missing is a similar emphasis on those workers who are required to perform the more routine duties and who very often are expected to act as the interface between the business and the customer, something else we focused on in Chapter 8. The current emphasis on trawling the world for employees who are culturally aware, strong on innovation, comfortable with the demands of a global business and able to deal with high levels of complexity is important but may turn out to be short-sighted. Indeed, a recent survey suggests that things like agility, customer service and innovation are far more important than talent management.[31] Furthermore, the demanding and exciting roles are not exactly plentiful in any organization and will undoubtedly reduce over time. There is also plenty of other work that needs to be carried out if the corporation is to remain viable in the medium to long term. As the impact of commoditization reaches deeper into the rank and file of the white collar worker, more and more people will be expected to undertake less demanding and interesting roles. The problem with this is that if the work isn't interesting there is little to keep the employee engaged in the company or its strategies apart from a pay cheque which may be somewhat stagnant and may even be reducing in real terms. The possibility of an unfulfilling working life as part of the many living dead frequenting the workplace is very real and we should all take David Bolchover's view of office existence very seriously.[32] When this happens, staff turnover and absenteeism will undoubtedly increase and levels of motivation and commitment decrease as the swelling ranks of the underemployed lose their work ethic. The problem of course is that this will impact the bottom line, as staff lose their focus on what's important to the organization and what matters to the customer. Therefore it may become difficult to maintain service levels and institutional knowledge. Such problems already beset call centres and the low end service economy jobs, where staff will move to another employer at the drop of the hat especially if it involves more money. They will also be off sick more often and have a poorer attitude to work than their extreme worker colleagues. Instead of working at the top of Maslow's needs hierarchy they work towards the bottom, where the basic needs take on a greater significance. With work holding little or no interest and employers focused on their most talented these workers will move to whoever will pay them the most. Loyalty is lost and the ability to maintain a cohesive and high performing organization becomes increasingly difficult. Organizations that fail to look after their low level employees will lose ground to those that do. What is needed is a renewed interest in these employees and although they may not have the same opportunities as the most talented, they still need to be looked after, challenged, led and motivated. The emergence of a labour war is something to guard against and with an appropriate focus on all employees, not just the cream of the crop, organizations will be able to address the challenges commoditization presents more effectively.

Increasing income inequality and its effects

Inequality, it is said, is the price that has to be paid for economic efficiency.[33]

Work and the workplace have always been unequal. No matter what the pundits, Human Resources or academics might say about meritocracies they rarely exist in their pure form. Whenever an organization is stripped bare, unless it is within government, you will find significant variations in what employees are paid even within the same grade or job role. We are already seeing the highly educated workers pulling further and further ahead and the less educated falling further and further behind, but this hides the true fact that it is only the top 10 per cent of the employment pool who are truly excelling and enjoying significant wage gains.

It is clear that income inequality is rising between skilled workers as much as between the skilled and unskilled cohorts of the workplace.[34] Indeed, inequality is even increasing between those knowledge workers with similar skills and capabilities. As we move towards a high skill, low wage economy the process through which this happens will not be uniform in that those who find themselves in senior positions and who are able to sell their knowledge and insights to global businesses will be highly rewarded, even when those with the same expertise come under the wage pressures familiar with the lower end of the service economy.[35] So whilst many knowledge workers will prosper, many will not. But before we look at the impact that such income inequalities have on people and particularly their health, it is worth reiterating why income inequality is likely to increase over the coming years. As we saw in Chapters 5 and 7 stagnating salaries and actual drops in income (downward mobility) are very real and are already affecting an increasing number of white collar and professional employees. We also saw in Chapter 6 how companies in response to the threat of commoditization and increased competition are hollowing out as they routinize work and then eliminate it using a combination of technology, outsourcing and offshoring. This trend will undoubtedly continue and as it does so the incomes of those who undertake such work will drop either because the role no longer offers a premium salary (because it requires less skill, is less complex and has been suitably codified to allow others with less knowledge and expertise to perform the work instead) or because they are forced further down the service economy's hierarchy as the good jobs dry up. Not everyone will find work and despite the current belief that it is the undereducated that are suffering the most, it appears that the contrary may be true, with a greater proportion of well educated and professional employees finding their earning power severely eroded.[36] This should come as no surprise because as more graduates enter the global employment market their average income will continue to go down. In essence the law of diminishing returns affects labour as it does everything else and includes the positional advantage of higher education, which will decline domestically as well as globally.[37] Again it should come as no surprise that the well educated middle classes are experiencing major swings in their incomes, so although the inequality in family incomes is changing, it is not changing as fast as the instability of their incomes and this see-sawing is making it harder for the middle classes to see a future in which their wealth and standard of living will keep on rising in the same way in which that of the Boomer generation did.[38] As we saw in Chapter 7, at least some of this is due to the increasing levels of personal responsibility everyone, and particularly the middle classes, has to cope with. Increasingly it will be the middle classes who share the economic pain and a few, perhaps no more than 20 per cent of the workforce will continue their upwardly mobile path.[39] As most of the safety nets disappear the future of today's and tomorrow's workers will become increasingly precarious. The other problem that the well educated professional classes have to contend with is the fact that many of the skills they need to excel in today's workplace are increasingly risky investments. Although necessary and often costly to develop they can become obsolete almost overnight as the economy and the job families on which it depends shift leaving those with outdated skills with few opportunities for applying them elsewhere.[40] This makes some of the strategies introduced in Chapter 10 all the more critical. As income distribution bifurcates between the minority who are highly paid and the majority who are not, the impacts of inequality will be more widely felt and especially amongst today's middle and professional classes. What is also interesting about income inequality is that in those countries where it is higher, there tend to be longer working hours.[41] One can only guess that this is to make up for lost ground, or to show the boss that you are truly committed to your job. The other point to make here is that growth in countries with high income inequality is slower than in those with lower levels of income inequality.[42] So even from a simple economic standpoint such variations in income seem to inhibit rather than accelerate economic growth.

Will Hutton wrote the book *The State We're In* in 1986. Although aimed at exploring the economic problems caused by the United Kingdom's then conservative government, many of the issues he raised then are still prevalent today. One of the most interesting parts of the book is where he describes how Richard Wilkinson had illustrated the income distribution of UK employees by using height as a way of showing how the term 'average salary' masks major differences in income between the lowest and highest paid employees. Back in 1998, if all the employees of the UK were to walk past you in one hour it would take 37 minutes before someone of average height (that is, average income) would walk past. Indeed, for the first 15 minutes you might have problems seeing them at all because they would be dwarves. At 57 minutes you would see people who were twice the average height and in the last few seconds you would see giants of such height that you wouldn't be able to see much above their shins.[43] If this exercise were to be repeated today and in light of the enormous sums CEOs, their boards and certain sectors of the economy, such as investment banking, command, the time it takes to reach average height may be quite a bit longer than 37 minutes and the height of the giants would be significantly greater than before. There will also be many more dwarfs. Repeat it again in 20 years from now and I am sure that the time taken to see someone of average height will be even longer. Of course things may well change as the need to ensure companies remain competitive may well lead to a reduction in the incomes of the most highly paid. Take Infosys, the Indian outsourcing giant who pay their chairman and chief executive $100 000 each and their highest performing executive $250 000. Not bad, but when you consider that Accenture pays their top executive $6.1 million and EDS $8.7 million and their share prices are doing significantly worse than Infosys one has to ask where is the return on management. There are those who believe that firms such as EDS and Accenture could save as much by sending 100 top management positions to India as by eliminating 10 000 staff.[44] Whether this would actually happen is an entirely different matter of course. Although this might be unlikely, all CEOs should be concerned with the impact their enormous salaries has on their staff. According to some latest research, huge salary imbalances between CEOs and their employees weaken loyalty, erode the talent pool and increase turnover.[45] All of the above is interesting because it illustrates just how much variation exists across the income scale and it is the impacts of such inequality that we will need to be increasingly concerned about.

The effects of income inequality have been studied for a long time and are well documented. Richard Wilkinson has written extensively on the subject and details the effects in his book, *The Impact of Inequality*.[46] He found that higher levels of inequality within a society are accompanied by increased levels of mistrust, social exclusion, crime, homicides, insecurity, poor educational attainment, teenage pregnancies, mental illness and many other social, physical and psychological ills. The reverse is true for societies with lower income inequalities, which are healthier, happier and generally more stable places to be, with a perfect example of this being Denmark, where income inequality is kept to a minimum through a combination of high marginal tax (which can be high as 72 per cent for some workers) and high value added tax (at 25 per cent) rates coupled with an effective social economy where everyone is looked after. Once tax has been taken into account the highest paid earns no more than five or six times the lowest and only 6 per cent of the population live off less than half the average income.[47] In contrast, the United States and United Kingdom, nations which have some of the highest levels of inequality, have the most trouble with the list above, but so do many of the other capitalist nations; a World Health Organization study into emotional health and income inequality showed that, as one would expect, the United States had the highest incidences of emotional distress of all market driven countries. That said, New Zealand, the United Kingdom, Australia, France, Singapore and the Netherlands were not far behind.[48] At the individual level, those on the lowest incomes suffer the most in terms of health. No matter what type of illness you choose to look at, it is those on the lowest incomes that display the highest levels of the diseases under the spotlight. In fact a health gradient exists along the entire income scale, with those earning even slightly less than someone above them in the hierarchy suffering more of life's ills and diseases. Even small variations matter, but where the differential between the lowest and highest paid is low, society and the health of the citizens within it benefit.

A good illustration of what could happen as commoditization continues to erode the incomes of the ranks of well paid white collar professions and as the levels of inequality increase between the highly paid extreme workers at one end and the commoditized workers at the other is the case of Russia and Eastern Europe following the changes to communism during the 1970s and 1980s and especially since the collapse of the Soviet Union following the fall of the Berlin Wall in 1989. In the 1960s many of the countries that fell under the Soviet Union's control had better life expectancy than many of the richer countries of the West and this was despite their lower per capita income. This was due to a more even income distribution that relied on a collective system of employment and a centrally driven economy. However when market reforms were introduced during the 1970s and 1980s in response to the uprisings that took place during the 1960s as the Eastern European satellite states pushed back against the Soviet model, a greater emphasis was placed upon individual economic incentives. As these reforms took hold, the ideals that had previously held the Eastern Bloc together started to unravel, especially when Soviet society became more individualistic. Over time life expectancy dropped as death rates increased dramatically, crime and alcoholism climbed significantly higher and income differentials enlarged appreciably as people could no longer rely on the state to provide employment or a steady income.[49] All the social issues identified by Wilkinson surged as inequality increased.

The collapse of the communist regime is a prime example of how an increase in economic individualism not only leads to a widening of income differences but also a rise in the wider problems of society, such as crime, illness and social exclusion. It should come as no surprise that we are already seeing some of these impacts as the early effects of commoditization begin to play out across the industrialized economies of the West. Of course, such changes are not only affecting the West as some of these effects are now being visited on the growing economies of India and China where the gap between the highly paid and the average worker is widening. Many amongst the middle and professional classes of the West are finding it difficult to stand still, let alone improve their lot in life and a significant minority have been borrowing against the value of their real estate in an attempt to maintain their lifestyles. Over time we should expect these problems to increase as the winner takes all meets the loser gets none economy. The question is of course, what to do about it. These are macro issues which require national interventions, but in a market economy, governments do not have the appetite to address the problems of those further down the income scale. And because such people lack the skills needed in the workplace they can be easily abused and pushed around; over time a greater number will opt out of the economy and society altogether because they see no future ahead of them. This is especially the case amongst the young. For example, in the United Kingdom there are currently 1.24 million people aged between 15 and 24 who are not in education, work or a training scheme, a 15 per cent increase since 1997. This sets up a cycle of deprivation that can be near impossible to escape from.[50] Furthermore it is not only those at the bottom of the income scale who will suffer (as they do now), but it will be large numbers of the middle classes who will be finding themselves gradually pushed towards the edges of the economy as their lives become more uncertain and insecure. Unfortunately, the sad truth is that insecure workers tend to under-invest in their skills, are more reluctant to change jobs and try to minimize their sense of job commitment to insulate themselves from the psychological loss when the work dries up,[51] which further compounds the problems of inequality.

We should of course be very concerned about the long-term implications of widening inequality. If it gets too large you tend to end up with revolutions which could be peaceful or extremely bloody. One only needs to look to history, both ancient and modern to see how once great civilizations collapsed under the weight of high levels of inequality; Ancient Egypt, Mesopotamia, Rome, India, China and Europe have all been affected and there is nothing to suggest that the same won't happen here as the rich pull further and further away from the rest of society.

The emergence of the vicious cycle

With the backdrop of widening income inequalities and an increasing number of previously well paid employees finding their income falling it is easy to see how commoditization can create a vicious cycle which may be difficult to break.

Figure 11.2 illustrates this cycle as it affects goods, services and the pay and benefits of the workforce. It is clear that we are now living in a society that expects to purchase goods and services at ever cheaper rates; whatever we buy these days, unless it is over priced luxury goods or perhaps property, we assume the price will drop year on year whilst expecting the quality to improve. Price deflation is a very real phenomenon and affects a wide range of consumer products. Between 2000 and 2006 price deflation has affected used cars (down 3.6 per cent per year), IT equipment (down 20 per cent per year), photographic equipment (8 per cent per year), clothing (6 per cent per year), toys (5 per cent per year) and new cars (2 per cent per year).[52] Although such changes are due to the redeployment of Chinese peasants to industrial towns where they are employed as low-waged factory hands, and to the technological advances of computer technology, these are not the only reasons. The internet is also having an effect through the increasing number of websites which provide price comparisons. This has increased transparency and pushed down prices.[53] I wonder how many of us stop and think about the wider implications of this?

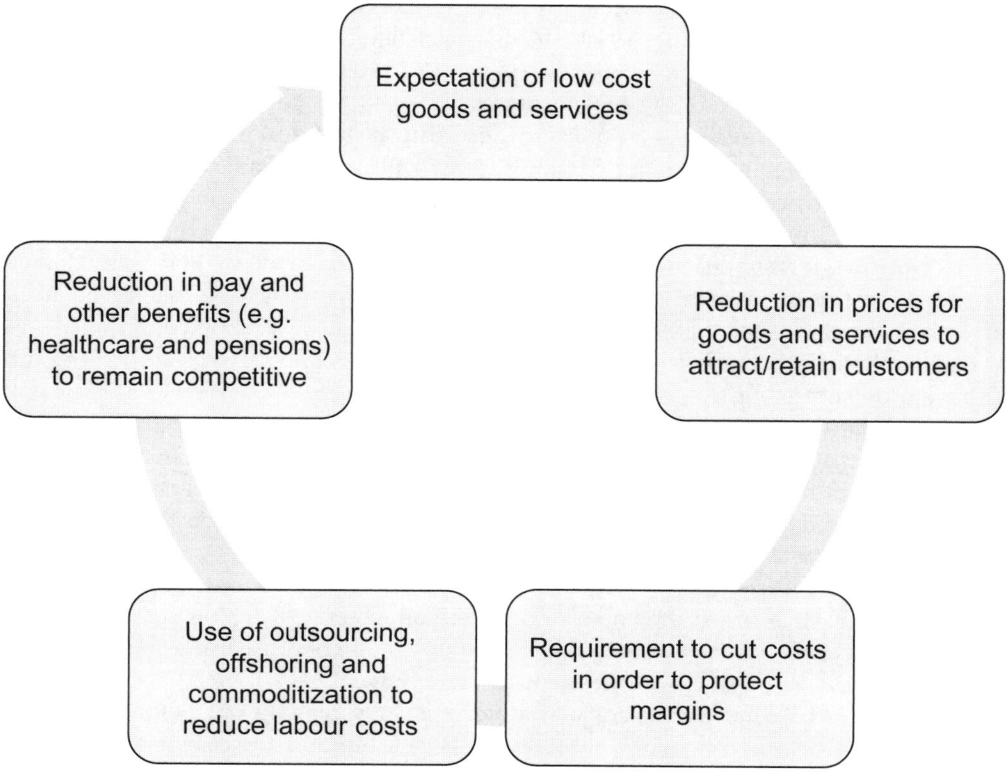

Figure 11.2 The vicious cycle

As we can see from this simple model, companies which have to reduce their prices (in real terms) in order to attract new customers and retain their existing ones have to recoup their lost margins elsewhere. This is typically achieved in one of three ways: they can increase the productivity of their staff so that they produce more for the same cost, they can create internal efficiencies using a mix of process redesign, technology and restructuring, or they can use outsourcing and offshoring to lock in lower costs and in this way treat their staff as a commodity. Although the first two options are often pursued by most organizations, there is a tendency for the costs to creep back up again, especially if management lacks the cost focused disciplines of the low cost operators as we saw in Chapter 8. This makes the third option more attractive and once this has been chosen it becomes much simpler both to move additional work overseas and to shift where the work is executed as new opportunities to shave their costs and hence improve margins materialize.

Over time the number of organizations exploring and opting for this third option will increase with the continued advances of technology especially in terms of its ability to connect remote workers. This shift to the outsourced and offshored model generates a downward pressure on the pay and benefits of staff because the very threat is enough for people to hold back on their pay demands. There is mounting evidence to suggest that increased volatility in labour demand is leading to moderation in the bargaining power of workers.[54] Many employers are using the threat of offshoring to gain agreement to such reductions which not only include limiting salary increases and reducing pay, but also targeted reductions in headcount and benefits such as pensions. We have seen this strategy successfully applied in the recent past by a number of the United States airlines who have struggled to exit Chapter 11. Most have used a combination of staff cuts, changes to pension provisions and the lowering of salaries to ensure they emerge from Chapter 11 as viable businesses.

Left with limited choices, especially for those who lack the transferable skills required to adapt to the changing workplace demands, most will cave in under the pressure; better to have a reduced income than no income at all. We can see this in action with Wal-Mart who drive their Chinese suppliers very hard to produce their products at the lowest possible price (see below). If a supplier is unable to meet the demands made by Wal-Mart, they will lose the business and in such a cut-throat environment, many have no choice but to cut workers' incomes, increase their hours and make them work in sweatshop conditions.[55] With less disposable income employees will expect cheaper goods and services and in the main will have little choice but to seek them out. If retailers and service providers put their prices up, the consumer will hold out for price reductions or find someone else that matches their price expectations which these days will undoubtedly include the internet. In fact as peoples' incomes go down the demand for cheaper goods and services goes up, which of course adds to the pressure to reduce costs. With the modern economy dependent on the service sector and consumers for its smooth running, it is easy to see how the vicious cycle of Figure 11.2 is perpetuated. Once locked into the cycle it takes a brave company to buck the system and as we saw in Chapter 8, there are limited options open to you when battling low cost competition. One thing seems to be clear, especially if you listen to commentators such as David Bosshart, author of *Cheap?*,[56] and that is that the cycle is here to stay.

A microcosm of what the future may hold is already playing out before our eyes in the shape of Wal-Mart. Although Wal-Mart can be held up as an excellent example of an organization that thrives within the commoditized zone (something we discussed in Chapter 9), one of the biggest complaints laid at its door is its unwillingness to pay a living wage to its employees and provide suitable medical cover. For example the Wake Up Wal-Mart campaign, funded by the United Food and Commercial Workers Union is aimed at mobilizing protests against the retailer in order to force them to begin to pay staff a decent wage.[57] In the late 1960s the biggest employer in the United States was General Motors and they paid their staff on average $29 000 (in today's terms) together with generous pension contributions, health care and other benefits. Today Wal-Mart is the biggest employer and they pay their staff $17 000 on average with few if any benefits. When staff are paid near or below the minimum wage, they can only afford to spend their hard earned cash at Wal-Mart or the other retailers who mimic them; they just can't afford to shop elsewhere. Other companies are increasingly finding that they have to follow Wal-Mart's lead in that the benchmark 'China price' has to be beaten by those at home if they are to stand any chance of avoiding work going overseas. When you consider that this China price means producing something at between 30 and 50 per cent of what it normally costs, it is easy to see the pressures this creates. Wal-Mart and companies like it exert such extreme pricing pressures on their suppliers that the vicious cycle ends up spilling over into the wider economy as executives of the organizations affected face the stark choices of shrink, close, or move to China.[58] For example, the RCA television plant in Circleville, Ohio, USA had to close because it could no longer supply Wal-Mart with the televisions it required at the price expected. Rather than lose all its revenue to other Chinese suppliers, it closed the plant and moved its operations to China. The result was a loss of 600 jobs.[59] This hollowing out of the economic heart of communities across the United States and elsewhere is all too common. And as the effects of commoditization spread, the vicious cycle will grip more than just the manufacturers, IT organizations and the back office functions which are currently in the throes of dealing with the impacts this has on their profits, people and futures. The danger of significant portions of the economy ending up locked within this cycle is an increasingly real one.

The temptation of protectionist behaviour – the return to mercantilism

If we think that the competition from emerging economies such as China and India is simply about low wages and manufacturing, then we are kidding ourselves. These countries are also competing with us in high-tech, high-skilled sectors because they are investing more and more in research and innovation.[60]

The transition to an environment where jobs are being increasingly commoditized will be a painful one and will generate significant amounts of noise from pressure groups and political parties alike. Such noise is nothing new as we witnessed similar outbursts in the past from the Luddites in the 19th century who destroyed factory machinery in response to the loss of work; the union workers smashing up Toyotas in Detroit in response to surging Japanese imports and the anti-globalization protestors running amok through Seattle at the 1999 World Trade Organization summit.[61] The noise was tempered by the governments at the time reassuring their citizens that globalization of the manufacturing processes would allow their countries to move into the knowledge economy, where the future employment would be. They were also told that this future was more secure because countries (most notably China) would never be in a position to compete in the knowledge economy; they just didn't have the skills. However, having spent two decades hollowing out the West's manufacturing industry; China now wants to spend the next two moving from 'Made in China' to 'Invented in China'.[62] In fact China is now only second to the United States when it comes to the amount spent on research and development and in the last decade this has more than doubled as a share of the country's gross domestic product.[63] Multinationals are lining up to establish research capabilities in China where scientists and engineers can undertake the work for only for 20 per cent of the labour costs.[64] China is also demonstrating its ability to use its strength in low-cost, low-end manufacturing to expand into the world's most sophisticated high technology businesses. For example, Intel's $2.5 billion integrated circuit manufacturing plant in the north eastern port city of Dalian has been approved by the Chinese administration.[65] This and many other examples are evidence of how easy China is finding it to transition from a low-wage economy making cheap goods to a (comparatively) high-wage economy producing valuable ones.[66]

So now that knowledge work is also being offshored, these promises look somewhat empty and people are becoming uneasy about their employability once more. As the noise gets louder the potential for protectionist behaviour to increase in order to stem the reduction in income and loss of jobs overseas is highly likely and may be politically necessary for the administrations in power if they are to retain popular support. For example, as the Democrats become increasingly optimistic about winning the 2008 United States election, especially on the back of seizing the House of Representatives and the House of Senate in the 2006 mid-term elections, they are beginning to play the protectionist card. Some amongst their ranks are calling for the renegotiation of the North American Free Trade Agreement (NAFTA) and trade ties with China to ensure they include protection for United States labour.[67] There are also increasing calls to limit the offshoring of American jobs and several states have passed laws that prohibit the export of public sector jobs. In addition, the Senate passed a law in 2004 which prevents private sector companies from using offshore workers in order to compete against government workers when bidding for new contracts.[68] Similar views are emerging within the European Union, where it is now recognized that the comparative advantage associated with the knowledge economy is beginning to unravel as China and India continue to develop their expertise in the high-skilled, high-tech sectors.[69] Even amongst the typically pro-globalization community of industrialists and bankers in the United Kingdom there are those who are beginning to question the commitment to open markets, especially in light of the increasing number of British companies falling into foreign ownership. The same is true in Italy where the Italian motorway group Autostrade called off its merger with Spain's Albertis after intense political pressure.[70] Ben Bernanke, chairman of the Federal Reserve recently commented when addressing an audience on the history of economic integration, *'the social and political opposition to openness can be strong. Although this opposition has many sources...much of it arises because changes in the patterns of production are likely to threaten the livelihoods of some workers and the profits of some firms, even when these changes lead to greater productivity and output overall'.*[71] These words may not reassure the increasing numbers of middle and professional class employees who will be looking to their governments to provide them with some protection against the onslaught of white collar commoditization. If governments are unwilling to provide a suitable safety net through the subsidising of retraining or unemployment benefit then the electorate will expect them to look towards protectionist barriers which will allow them as much as possible to maintain their current lifestyles and economic longevity. For example United States politicians are currently trying to block Evraz, a Russian steel company, from buying a small US based rival.[72] It is likely that the calls for the World Trade Organization to abandon its emphasis on forcing open global markets will increase as the full costs of globalization are felt amongst the West's middle classes. So could we see a return to Mercantilism which dominated European trade between 1550 and 1750? During this period protectionist measures, which included trade tariffs, were used to ensure a country maintained a trade surplus by exporting more than it imported. Only time will tell. However, the past suggests that when the political price of free trade outweighs the economic benefits powerful nations will seek to protect their markets, companies and employees from overseas competition.[73]

But is there any point in trying to protect inefficient business models? In the end they cost the nations dear because taxes have to rise or be redirected to fund the subsidies required to allow the businesses and individuals affected by commoditization to remain viable. This was clear from the recent demise of the MG Rover car company in the United Kingdom. Whereas in the past, the United Kingdom's government was more than willing to throw taxpayers' money at failing companies, often seeing them fail in any case, today's politicians do not see it as their role to protect companies who unable to survive in a changing economic environment.[74] However, this view is not a collective one, as France continues to take a more protectionist path favouring intervention, as it did with Alstom in 2005 and through its high minimum wage, generous mandatory social benefits and obstacles to eliminating redundant jobs.[75] Whether this way will ever win out against the forces of the market economy or whether there is a better approach, with a focus more on localization instead of globalization remains to be seen. But before I attempt to draw the book to its close, we should look back in history to see why protectionist behaviour is both potentially damaging and how it may, after all, spur the next new thing which will take us out of the current focus on protecting the unprotectable and into a more positive cycle of growth and possibility.

In the early 17th century, England's wool trade had virtually no competition and enjoyed huge economic success, and this in spite of the uncomfortable nature of the clothes that had to be worn by the English. However, mid century this began to change when handmade Indian cotton calicoes and muslins began to reach the ports of the country. Cotton was cheap, more colourful and most importantly a more comfortable option than wool, and it wasn't long before cotton was replacing wool as the textile of choice. Mills began to shut, wages fell and people lost their jobs and some literally starved; something had to be done. Parliament responded to the cries from its people first by restricting, by Act of Parliament, the wearing of cotton to the summer months, followed by other Acts which forced certain professions, such as law, education and the civil service to only wear woollen clothes and in 1700 to only allowing people to be buried in woollen garments and then finally in 1701 banning the wearing of imported Indian cotton. This was almost the final straw for the woollen industry because in response to such ridiculous laws, a cotton dying and printing industry emerged on English soil and this successfully circumvented the ban. The riposte from the woollen industry was predictable and after further lobbying, violence and general unrest, in 1722 Parliament made it illegal to wear or use in home furnishings any form of cotton cloth. This law remained in place for decades but in the end gave birth to the Industrial Revolution which started with the desire to manufacture cotton cloth in England and gave rise to the power loom, Spinning Jenny and the factories that could support the mass production of cotton.[76] Without the government's protectionist stance the Industrial Revolution may well have been delayed, postponed or may have emerged elsewhere.

The end game

This has been an interesting book to write if nothing else because it has brought together some broad issues which are beginning to affect an increasing number of organizations and their workers. The combination of demographic change, immigration, technological advancements, the availability of an increasing number of graduate level workers and the resurgence of China and India are forcing companies to consider the impacts of commoditization on their operations and markets and respond accordingly. The choices are not necessarily straightforward, but there are choices all the same. Whether to pursue a path focused on innovation, or one which tackles the cost issues associated with commoditization head-on or a combination of both is a decision that needs to be made in the boardrooms of every corporation. I believe that the pressure to simplify, standardize and ultimately eliminate unnecessary work from the system will increase as those organizations who manage to address the challenges will add to the competitive forces and make those companies that fail to respond increasingly unsustainable. It is also clear from writing this book that the process of commoditization will continue for some time to come and may well accelerate as the Boomer Generation finally leaves the workplace. What the end game will look like is a little more difficult to predict, but like so many changes that have affected the workplace and society in the past, there will be winners and losers, although on this occasion the losers may well outnumber the winners by a wide margin. Sitting on the sidelines and watching the commoditization juggernaut steam towards you may not be the best strategy, but I think many will have little choice but to watch and wait for the inevitable collision.

References

1 Adrianne Curry referring to the use of her body in creating a lifelike animated image of herself, quoted in Clark, D. (2006) Nvidia's powerful chip moves closer to 'reality', *Technology Journal, The Wall Street Journal*, 9 November, p. B3.
2 Lynch, D., (2006) Election pushes globalization to forefront, *The Wall Street Journal*, 14 November, pp. 1–2.
3 Betancourt, M. (2004) Labour/Commodity/Automation A response to 'The digital death rattle of the American middle class: a cautionary tale', http://ctheory.net, p. 7.
4 James, O. (2007) *Affluenza*, London: Random House, p. 17.
5 *The Economist* (2006) Meritocracy and its discontents, The battle for brainpower: A survey of talent, 7 October, p. 23.
6 Bosshart, D. (2007) *Cheap? The Real Cost of Living in a Low Price, Low Wages World*, London: Kogan Page, p. 55.
7 Hacker, J. (2006) *The Great Risk Shift*, Oxford: Oxford University Press, p. 77.
8 Clark, D. (2006) Nvidia's powerful chip moves closer to 'reality', *Technology Journal, The Wall Street Journal*, 9 November, p. B3.
9 Walsh, D. (2007) Computers ready to break speed limit in Hafnium valley, 29 January, Timesonline, www.timesonline.co.uk.
10 Ibid.
11 Betancourt, M. (2004) Labour/Commodity/Automation A response to 'The digital death rattle of the American middle class: a cautionary tale', http://ctheory.net, p. 11.
12 Hacker, J. (2006) *The Great Risk Shift*, Oxford: Oxford University Press, p. 62.
13 Betancourt, M. (2004) Labour/Commodity/Automation A response to 'The digital death rattle of the American middle class: a cautionary tale', http://ctheory.net, p. 7.
14 Hacker, J. (2006) *The Great Risk Shift*, Oxford: Oxford University Press, p. 78.
15 Sabbagh, D. (2006) Computers that digest the news to change trading, *The Times*, 11 December, p. 37.
16 Mitchell, A. (2006) P&G takes shoppers to another world in war of the brands, *Financial Times*, 18 October, p. 18.
17 Canton, J. (2006) *The Extreme Future*, New York: Dutton, pp. 97–98.
18 OECD (2007) Employment outlook, p. 117.
19 James, O. (2007) *Affluenza*, London: Random House, pp. 192–194.
20 Griffiths, S. (2007) The price of your first break, *The Sunday Times*, 8 July, pp. 4–13.
21 James, O. (2007) *Affluenza*, London: Random House, p. 7.
22 Parsons, S. (2007) Children are right to ignore their prescribed futures, *The Times*, 5 July, p. 2–7.
23 Hewlett, S. and Buck Luce, C. (2006) Extreme jobs: The dangerous allure of the 70-hour workweek, *Harvard Business Review*, December, pp. 49–60.
24 Rushe, D. (2007) Addicted to work, *The Sunday Times*, 10 June, pp. 3–7.
25 Hewlett, S. and Buck Luce, C. (2006) Extreme jobs: The dangerous allure of the 70-hour workweek, *Harvard Business Review*, December, p. 54.
26 Ibid., p. 58.
27 See www.telegraph.co.uk.
28 Parsons, S. (2007) Children are right to ignore their prescribed futures, *The Times*, 5 July, pp. 2–7.
29 Ringshaw, G. (2007) Making a bundle, *The Sunday Times*, 8 July, pp. 3–5.
30 Handy, C. (1994) *The Empty Raincoat*, London: Hutchinson, p. 9.
31 Lewis, C. (2007) Urgent call for new skills, *The Times*, Career, 28 June, p. 9.
32 Bolchover, D. (2005) *The Living Dead*, Chichester: Capstone.
33 Hutton, W. (1986) *The State We're In*, London: Vintage, p. 172.
34 Hacker, J. (2006) *The Great Risk Shift*, Oxford: Oxford University Press, p. 64.
35 Brown, P., et al. (2006) Towards a high-skilled, low-waged economy? A review of global trends in education, employment and the labour market, in Porter, S. and Campbell, M. (eds.) *Skills and Economic Performance*, London: Caspian Publishing, p. 73.
36 Hacker, J. (2006) *The Great Risk Shift*, Oxford: Oxford University Press, p.73.
37 Brown, P., et al. (2006) Towards a high-skilled, low-waged economy? A review of global trends in education, employment and the labour market, in Porter, S. and Campbell, M. (eds.) *Skills and Economic Performance*, London: Caspian Publishing, p. 83.
38 Hacker, J. (2006) *The Great Risk Shift*, Oxford: Oxford University Press, p. 7.

39 Brown, P., et al. (2006) Towards a high-skilled, low-waged economy? A review of global trends in education, employment and the labour market, in Porter, S. and Campbell, M. (eds.) *Skills and Economic Performance*, London: Caspian Publishing, p. 82.

40 Hacker, J. (2006) *The Great Risk Shift*, Oxford: Oxford University Press, p. 75.

41 Frank, R. (2007) *Falling Behind: How Rising Inequality Harms the Middle Class*, Berkley: University of California Press, p. 78.

42 Ibid., p. 113.

43 Hutton, W. (1986) *The State We're In*, London: Vintage, p. 92.

44 Hutchinson, M. (2006) How to get rid of fat cats, *MoneyWeek*, 1 December, p. 22.

45 *The Times* (2007) Overpaid bosses can cause unrest, *The Times*, Business Education, 28 June, p. 6.

46 Wilkinson, R. (2005) *The Impact of Inequality*, New York: The New Press.

47 James, O. (2007) *Affluenza*, London: Vermillion, pp. 71–74.

48 Ibid., pp. 343–346.

49 Wilkinson, R. (2005) *The Impact of Inequality*, New York: The New Press, pp. 112–118.

50 Browne, A. (2006) No school, no job for record numbers, *The Times*, 11 December, pp. 1–2.

51 Hacker, J. (2006) *The Great Risk Shift*, Oxford: Oxford University Press, p. 178.

52 Guthrie, J. (2007) We cheapskates bank on driving a hard bargain, *Financial Times*, 7 January, p. 15.

53 Ibid.

54 OECD (2007) Employment outlook, p. 120.

55 Ryan, J. (2006) Wal-Mart and China: Boon or bane for American interests, European Business School occasional & working paper series, no. 3, p. 19.

56 Bosshart, D. (2007) *Cheap? The Real Cost of Living in a Low Price, Low Wage World*, London: Kogan Page.

57 Birchall, J. (2006) Democrat leaders join fight against Wal-Mart, *Financial Times*, 15 November, p. 11.

58 Bianco, A. (2006) *The Bully of Bentonville*, New York: Currency Doubleday, p. 15.

59 Ryan, J. (2006) Wal-Mart and China: Boon or bane for American interests, European Business School occasional & working paper series, no. 3, p. 19.

60 Potocnik, J. (2005) Quoted in Gow, D., China is targeting hi-tech jobs, EU warns, *The Guardian*, 13 October.

61 Lynch, D. (2006) Election pushes globalization to forefront, *USA Today*, Money Section B, p. 1B.

62 Dyer, G. (2007) The dragon's lab – how China is rising through the innovation ranks, *Financial Times*, 5 January, p. 13.

63 Ibid.

64 Ibid.

65 Batson, A. (2007) China shifts towards higher-end production, *The Wall Street Journal*, 23–25 March, p. 4.

66 Ibid.

67 Lynch, D. (2006) Election pushes globalization to forefront, *USA Today*, Money Section B, p. B2.

68 Brown, P., et al. (2006) Towards a high-skilled, low-waged economy? A review of global trends in education, employment and the labour market, in Porter, S. and Campbell, M. (eds.) *Skills and Economic Performance*, London: Caspian Publishing, p. 86.

69 Lucas, C. and Hines, C. (2005) Europe's hi-tech future: the last colonial delusion, provided to the author through private correspondence.

70 Nixon, S. (2006) Why we must resist the coming counter-revolution, *MoneyWeek*, 15 December, p.18.

71 Wolf, M. (2006) We must act to share the gains with globalisation's losers, *Financial Times*, 6 September, p.23.

72 Nixon, S. (2006) Why we must resist the coming counter-revolution, *MoneyWeek*, 15 December, p. 18.

73 Brown, P., et al. (2006) Towards a high-skilled, low-waged economy? A review of global trends in education, employment and the labour market, in Porter, S. and Campbell, M. (eds.) *Skills and Economic Performance*, London: Caspian Publishing, p. 87.

74 Tricks, H. (2005) Bail-outs just a way of delaying the inevitable, *Financial Times*, 9/10 April, p. 5.

75 Duchesne, Y. (2000) An American lesson for France, *McKinsey Quarterly*, www.mckinseyquarterly.com.

76 Rivoli, P. (2005) *The Travels of a Tee-shirt in the Global Economy*, Hoboken New Jersey: John Wiley & Sons Inc., pp. 152–156.

Index

competition on cost 4
globalization 51, 53–8
journalism 81
mobile phones 27
price comparison 4–5, 40
price deflation 206
retailers 52
telecommunications 28
interventionist commoditization
    factors 37–40
investment capital 17
Islam 15
IT *see also* computers; technology
    artificial intelligence 33–4
    business processes 131–2
    commoditization drivers 42
    costs 36
    demand 6
    employee income 35–6
    generations
        first 32
        second 32
        third 32–3
        fourth 33
        fifth 33
    India 6
    as infrastructure 35
    investment 35
    labor arbitrage 3
    outsourcing 58, 101
    standardization 3
    standards 39
    strategic advantage 3, 35

Japan
    currency intervention 49
    demographics 70
    Fifth Generation Project 33
    immigration 74, 75
    trade deficit 49
job auctions 199
job churn 113
job security 63
job spill 66–7
jobs
    extreme 200–202
    growth in 67–8
    high-touch 191–2
    for life 63, 113
    local 191–2
    obsolete 62
    unskilled 75–6
journalism and internet 81

Kaizen 164
knowledge work 63, 114, 115, 201, 209–10

labor arbitrage 3
Lafarge 169–71
large companies 97–9
lawyers 201–2
legal training, online 82
leisure society 34
leveraged skills 187
life expectancy 69, 205
lifelong learning 51, 117, 180–81
lifestyle 19
living dead 4, 115, 202
London Stock Exchange 15
long tail products 52–3
long term business assessment 126–7
low cost commodity model 92–4
low cost competition 127–9
low cost operators 82, 129
low cost subsidiaries 127–8
luxury goods 17

mail order 26
manufacturing and offshoring 80
manufacturing sectors 63
margins
    erosion of 94–5, 102
    General Motors 98
    maintenance of 103
market-based commoditization
    factors 38, 40–42
market position 96
market research 199
markets
    change 23
    controlling 18
    dominance 19
MBAs 78
McDonalds 81
medical tourism 81–2
mercantilism 210
mergers 63, 98–9, 111–13
Mexico 75
Microsoft 40, 41
middlescence 3–4
migration 74, 75–6, 140
mindsets 179–80
mini-computers 37
mobile phones 27, 37, 66
modernization 102–4
monitoring of work 116
motivation of employees 71

If you have found this book useful you may be interested in other titles from Gower

Accelerating Business and IT Change:
Transforming Project Delivery
Alan Fowler and Dennis Lock
Hardback 978-0-566-08604-5
CD ROM 978-0-566-08742-4

Age Matters:
Employing, Motivating and Managing Older Employees
Keren Smedley and Helen Whitten
978-0-566-08680-9

Benefit Realisation Management:
A Practical Guide to Achieving Benefits Through Change
Gerald Bradley
978-0-566-08687-8

Digital Identity Management:
Building Relationships and Understanding Cultures
Edited by David Birch
978-0-566-08679-3

Estimating Risk:
A Management Approach
Andy Garlick
978-0-566-08776-9

Integrated Intellectual Asset Management:
A Guide to Exploiting and Protecting your
Organization's Intellectual Assets
Steve Manton
978-0-566-08721-9

GOWER

If you have found this book useful you may be interested in other titles from Gower

Managing the Psychological Contract:
Using the Personal Deal to Increase Business Performance
Michael Wellin
978-0-566-08726-4

The Relationship-Driven Supply Chain:
Creating a Culture of Collaboration throughout the Chain
Stuart Emmett and Barry Crocker
978-0-566-08684-7

Senior Executive Reward:
Key Models and Practices
Sandy Pepper
978-0-566-08733-2

Strategic Negotiation
Gavin Kennedy
978-0-566-08797-4

For further information on these and all our titles
visit our website – www.gowerpub.com
All online orders receive a discount

For a monthly update on new titles, join our e-mail
news update. Visit www.gowerpub.com/mail.
htm to view the latest edition and to sign up.

GOWER